Inside the
primary classroom

Inside the
primary classroom

Maurice Galton, Brian Simon
and Paul Croll
together with
Anne Jasman and John Willcocks

London and New York

First published 1980 by Routledge & Kegan Paul Ltd
Reprinted 1981 and 1987
Reprinted 1989, 1990 by Routledge
11 New Fetter Lane, London EC4P 4EE

Simultaneously published in the USA and Canada
by Routledge
a division of Routledge, Chapman and Hall, Inc.
29 West 35th Street, New York, NY 10001

© 1980 Maurice Galton, Brian Simon, Paul Croll, Anne Jasman
        and John Willcocks

Printed in Great Britain by Redwood Press Limited, Melksham, Wiltshire

British Library Cataloguing in Publication Data

Galton, Maurice

    Inside the primary classroom.
    1. Elementary school teaching – England
    I. Title II. Simon, Brian   III. Croll, Paul
    372.1'3'0942   LB1555   79–42817

    ISBN 0-415-03951-7

Library of Congress Cataloging in Publication Data
has been applied for.

ISBN 0-415-03951-7

Contents

Contents

vi

Contents

Figures

Tables

Introduction

This volume reports the findings of the first large-scale observational study of primary school classrooms to be undertaken in this country. It presents an over-all analysis of pupil and teacher activity and identifies different patterns of teacher and pupil behaviour. The findings of the study are directly relevant to the criticisms of new approaches in the primary school which received widespread publicity in the last few years. They provide a mass of objective data against which these criticisms may be evaluated.

In focusing specifically on patterns of activity and instruction within the primary classroom this volume forms part of a larger research programme, Observational Research and Classroom Learning Evaluation (ORACLE), funded by the Social Science Research Council over the period 1975 to 1980. The major objective of this programme is to study the relative 'effectiveness' of different teaching approaches across the main subject areas of primary school teaching. This forms the subject matter of the second volume of this ORACLE series. The programme also included the development of new forms of teacher-based assessment and a study of transfer to the next stage in education. Some pupils will, therefore, have been observed over a three-year period making this the first large-scale longitudinal study to use observational techniques in this country. The results of these related projects will be reported in further volumes of the series.

This volume is directed primarily at teachers, teacher educators and students, but it should prove of interest to administrators, members of education committees and indeed all who have an interest in primary education, including parents. Every effort has been made to express our

1

findings in language which is comprehensible to the layman. Whenever possible, necessary technical details have been relegated to the Appendices. However, research must also be reported in such a way that it contains sufficient details of the methodology to enable other workers in the field to criticize and evaluate the findings. Full details of the observation techniques are therefore given in Chapter 1 while the opening section of Chapter 6 describes the theoretical stance of the research programme. Those readers who are more interested in the results than in these matters could, if they so wished, omit these sections. It is hoped that in this way a successful balance has been struck between the needs of different groups of readers and that the findings will be easily understood by all.

The first chapter sets out the general objectives of the research and explicates the research methods used focusing particularly on the use of direct observational techniques within the classroom and dealing with the selection of classes (teachers and pupils) which formed the subject of the investigation. Chapters 2 and 3 place the research study in its historical setting both in terms of the evolution of the primary school as a specific stage in education and in terms of the theory and the practice of primary school teaching. There follow two chapters (4 and 5) which present an overview of teacher and pupil interactions within the primary school classroom, derived entirely from observational data obtained during the first year of our study (1976-7). Succeeding chapters (6, 7, 8) present a further analysis of this data in the search for different patterns of behaviour first by teachers and then by pupils; the relationship between these patterns is also discussed. The final chapter (9) then summarizes some of our main findings and discusses their implications for teachers and teacher educators.

The main draft of the book is the work of the two co-investigators although the views expressed have been discussed fully with the members of the full-time research team. We wish to acknowledge our debt to them, not only for these helpful discussions but for the particular contributions which they have made during the period of the field work. In particular John Willcocks, as Senior Research Fellow, has had responsibility for the day-by-day management of the project which at one time had three research students and three part-time observers besides the members of the project team observing in schools. Paul Croll has processed an immense flow of data and has been responsible for the entire data analysis for this volume. Anne Jasman, besides having responsibility for developing the teacher-based assessment procedures, which will be discussed in a later volume, also supervised the training programme in the use of the two observation instruments

Introduction

which ensured that all the observers carried out their tasks in an efficient and reliable fashion. All three members of the team have contributed important appendices to this volume.

Besides these duties, the team also carried through much classroom observation where they were assisted by Ruth Barwood, Angela Delafield, Margaret Greig, Valerie Hallam, Janice Lea and Sarah Tann. In spite of the heavy demands of the observational programme our team of observers never failed to complete their quotas. The best testimony that can be paid to their efforts is the fact that during the entire period no teacher withdrew from the project from a sense of dissatisfaction.

It is appropriate here to mention the fifty-eight teachers and their pupils who formed our sample. Many of these teachers have stayed with the project over the three years in which observations have been carried out in their schools. Although some must have felt certain reservations at the start in allowing an observer to spend considerable time in their classrooms, all have co-operated loyally throughout this period and the close links which the team have forged with the schools has been one of the important benefits of the research. We have enjoyed the fullest co-operation from the three local authorities who must remain anonymous; in particular from their advisory services who provided much help in picking the sample. We acknowledge too the support of the Social Science Research Council which funded the programme of which these findings form a part.

The project secretaries Diana Stroud and Jaya Katariya have worked consistently and cheerfully typing the various drafts and at the same time carrying out their daily secretarial duties with efficiency. In preparing the final draft of this manuscript for publication they were helped by Pat Holford. Finally we owe a special debt to Deanne Boydell, who developed the original observation instruments in earlier projects and who acted as a consultant to this one. Her detailed comments on successive drafts of the chapters of this book have been of great value, although the authors alone must be held responsible for the views expressed in the book. Throughout the text, for the sake of simplicity, the teacher has been referred to as female and the pupils as males except where a specific teacher or pupil is mentioned.

Maurice Galton
Brian Simon

3

CHAPTER I

Researching
the
primary classroom

Inside the classroom

This book has two main purposes. First to describe, using the information gathered during systematic observation, some of the richness and variety of what goes on in a modern primary classroom. Second, to search for patterns from among these events in order to help explain why certain teachers do one thing while others do something else. For much of their working lives teachers remain remarkably isolated from the direct influence of other members of the profession. Primary classrooms, in particular, are very active places, often with a constant stream of visitors, yet this very air of 'busyness' disguises the fact that a teacher rarely sees other teachers teaching or is herself seen teaching by other teachers. Even in open plan areas bookcases and cupboards often appear to be strategically placed to minimise the amount of contact between members of the team. One important outcome of this research, therefore, will be to provide a portrait of the 'typical' teacher from the descriptions in the fifty-eight classrooms where observations were carried out. This will enable primary teachers to reflect on their own practice in a way which up to now has not been possible. Similarly, it should allow those who train student teachers to bridge the gap between theory and practice by offering the means of illuminating theory with precise and detailed information about life inside the primary classroom.

In research terms, observing the behaviour of teachers and their pupils is referred to as a study of the classroom *process*.[1] In the ORACLE study some teachers and pupils were observed over a three-year period.

4

Researching the primary classroom

At certain times during the year pupils were given a variety of tests, including some which covered the basic skills of mathematics, reading and English. These were designed to assess the *products* of teaching, that is, the extent to which pupils had improved their performance in previously acquired skills or learnt new ones as a result of their classroom experiences. Process-product studies thus make it possible to comment on the effectiveness of different teaching patterns, an issue which forms the central focus of the second volume in the series. In this book, however, it is the detailed analysis of the process data acquired during the first year of this study which will be considered. Later volumes in the series will examine both the observational and test data for the subsequent years to see how far teachers and pupils are consistent over an extended period both in their behaviour and in their performance. Some pupils are also followed after they have transferred out of the primary school to the next stage of education. The inclusion of a transfer study as part of this research is important because it greatly influenced the selection of the primary school sample.

Surprisingly, until very recently, little attention was given in Britain to the systematic study of teaching by observing teacher and pupil behaviour in the classroom. The publication in America during the late 1960s of a collection of schedules under the title *Mirrors for Behaviour*, designed to collect observational data on teachers and pupils, pointed the way (Simon and Boyer, 1970). The 'Mirrors' of the title suggested the possibility of examining the extent to which teaching methods advanced by theorists and those responsible for training teachers were *reflected* in everyday classroom practice. The origin of many of these observation techniques lay in the creation of the Committee on Child Development by the American National Research Council at the beginning of the 1920s. This Committee initiated research into teaching methods at nursery and kindergarten stages and, since such children were too young to respond to interviews and surveys (the then usual method of data collection), the researchers had to observe these infants and record their behaviour 'as it happened'. At first they kept diaries or 'narrative logs' of the activities they saw but the number, range and variety of these events made such a task an arduous one. By 1929 Stevens had introduced the notion of *time-sampling* whereby certain categories of behaviour were recorded at specified fixed intervals of time. Although there were other approaches (Barr, 1935) the researchers in the Child Development movement working in the context of the rise in fascism in Europe, increasingly directed their attention towards those behaviours which they saw as essential elements of the democratic process. It was predicted that authoritarian teaching (telling pupils what

5

to do) was more likely to lead to aggressive actions by pupils than the more 'democratic' practice of asking pupils what they wished to do and then arriving at a final decision by means of discussion and consensus.

In the immediate post-war period this emphasis was still the dominant one (Withall, 1949), and culminated in the development of one of the most widely used observation schedules, the Flanders Interaction Analysis Category system (FIAC), which has ten categories and uses a three-second time-sampling unit. Certain categories are used to classify teachers either as *Direct* when, for example, a teacher lectures, questions or directs pupils, or *Indirect*, where a teacher emphasizes such techniques as using a pupil's ideas or accepting a pupil's feelings. Many subsequent American schedules have been based on FIAC which, however, has been widely criticized for its limited applicability, having been designed for relatively static classrooms where teachers stood in front of pupils who were arranged before them in rows while working on the same or similar tasks (Silberman, 1970; Hamilton and Delamont, 1974). Interestingly, very few British observation schedules, unlike American ones, resemble FIAC, although in this country during the 1970s there has been a rapid growth in the use of systematic observation in research. A recently published anthology lists over forty published schedules, of which nineteen are used to study teaching at either nursery or primary level (Galton, 1978).

Criticisms of primary teaching

The research to be described here was planned during 1974 and began a year later. The period from its inception to the present has been one which has seen primary teachers, and the methods they use, come under increasing scrutiny and in some cases hostile attack. Some of the recent strident criticism had its origins in the early 'Black Papers', the editors claiming, for instance, that traditional standards were being rapidly eroded because 'some teachers are taking to extreme the belief that children should not be told anything but must find out for themselves' (Cox and Dyson, 1969b). This theme was continued in later issues although subsequently the study on streaming carried out by the NFER indicated that only one-third of the teachers in the sample advocated mixed ability grouping and that a majority supported 'traditional practices' (Barker Lunn, 1970). The controversial study on reading standards carried out around this time by the National Foundation for Educational Research (Start and Wells, 1972; Burke and Lewis, 1975), and the later disclosures relating to the William Tyndale school in

London have been taken up by the media as an indictment of modern practice. At one time or another current methods of primary teaching have been held responsible for indiscipline, the increase in crime rate, vandalism, and also for a supposed decline in literacy and numeracy.

Government response to such pressure was to institute early in 1975 a survey of primary schools (HMI Survey, 1978), and to initiate a 'great debate' through Prime Minister Callaghan's (1976) Ruskin speech, where he voiced the unease allegedly felt by parents and others 'about the new informal methods' arguing that these appeared to work well only in 'well qualified hands'. Other 'political' views, in so far as they can be discerned through publications such as that of the Centre for Policy Research, have set their sights on deterring the 'half-hearted progressive' and 'curbing the most extreme' (Wilkinson, 1977). Thus the message to emerge from these and other writers, for example Devlin and Warnock (1977), is that progressive methods are only for the exceptional teachers and that the remainder, the average members of the profession, would do best to concentrate on using traditional approaches. They thus perpetuate an old assumption that progressive teachers spend most of their time teaching other things than English and mathematics although the evidence from surveys (Bassey, 1978), including the recent study by the inspectorate, exposes such views as false.

Those writers who are highly critical of what they take to be the widespread use of progressive methods use the research findings of the controversial Lancaster Study by Neville Bennett, published under the title *Teaching Styles and Pupil Progress* (1976), to support their case. The main conclusion of this research was that pupils taught by so called 'formal' methods (class taught, in silence, with regular testing and plenty of competition) were, on average, four months ahead of those taught by 'informal' methods on tests in the basic skills in mathematics and English. There were other groups of teachers who used so called 'mixed' styles but their characteristics were mostly too difficult to interpret from the data provided. Paradoxically, one of the findings was that the most successful teacher belonged to the 'informal' group but that her classroom was highly organized and efficient. This would appear to be one of the sources for the suggestion that informal methods are only for the 'well qualified' performer in the classroom.

Recent research findings

Thus, although a main purpose of the ORACLE study is to illuminate aspects of classroom practice for the benefit of teachers, the timing of the research has made it impossible not to treat such issues as we raise within the wider context of the debate about different educational ideologies. Here our aim overlaps somewhat with Bennett, who rightly complains that 'in all the arguments about teaching methods innovation is being urged without research' (1976, p. 9) and who sets out to provide evidence about 'the effectiveness of different teaching approaches' (p. 10). This, however, is as far as the similarity extends, in that we question the quality or usefulness of much evidence on teaching methods *when it is obtained mainly through the use of questionnaires*, the limitations of which in Bennett's case will be discussed more fully in Chapter 6 where we develop our own view of teaching.

Writers who quote Bennett tend to imply that his division between 'formal' and 'informal' teachers reflects the use of two distinct and intricate patterns of teaching behaviour which are thought to characterize differences between traditional and progressive methods. Such an assumption can only be tested using observation studies. At the time of publication much of the criticism of *Teaching Styles and Pupil Progress* concerned defects of research design and the question as to whether the results might validly be applied to other pupils besides those in schools where the research was carried out (Gray and Satterly, 1976). It was left to Wragg to point out that the descriptions of teaching which resulted from 'emotionally laden catch-all terms such as formal and informal' were of little help to teachers who wished to examine their practice in the aftermath of the Lancaster study (Wragg, 1976).

Bennett specifically argues against the use of such over-simplified categorizations to represent teaching methods. It seems strange that someone who is so critical of previous studies such as Barker Lunn's on precisely these grounds should resort to similar crude descriptions of teaching so that, in Wragg's view, he is open to criticism 'for ignoring his own advice in the early part of the book'. We would argue that this is directly attributable to the use of questionnaires which require an individual to answer each item by selecting one response from a limited number of mutually exclusive categories. For most of the items on Bennett's questionnaire only two distinct categories are used so that teachers were forced to say whether or not they smacked, tested, allowed free movement and so on. This approach inevitably leads to unreal descriptions. Teachers were asked, for instance, whether or not they gave weekly tests; those who gave tests every fortnight found themselves grouped with teachers who never tested at all.

More importantly, certain results appear illogical in that some individuals were classified both as separate subject teachers and as favouring an integrated subject approach. This came about because of the way in which the data were collected and subsequently analysed. Teachers were asked to estimate how much of a twenty-five-hour working week they devoted to 'academic subjects taught separately, integrated subjects and aesthetic subjects', the latter including PE and games. The average number of hours for single subject teaching worked out at 15¼ while for integrated subjects the corresponding figure was 4¾ hours. Because the amount of time given to aesthetics was dependent on that allocated to single subject and integrated subject teaching it was omitted from the analysis. Individuals could thus be described as single subject and integrated subject teachers if their time allocations were above the mean values on both categories. Thus a teacher who gave little attention to aesthetics (art, music and drama) could easily find herself 'above average' on these two dimensions.

Even if teachers could recognize themselves within these formal-informal labels the descriptions gave little guidance about what they might do or say to pupils during lessons. It was left to Wragg (1978), to try to identify through observation these qualities in the practice of the most successful of all Bennett's teachers (an 'informal' one), supporting the view that descriptions of teaching based on observation are likely to make better sense to teachers in that they highlight the activities by which those who differ in effectiveness differ in their treatment of pupils. The use of observation to describe the actual process of teaching, in preference to a questionnaire approach, is one of the essential differences between this study and Bennett's.

Observational research in teaching

While a limited amount of observation was carried out in the Lancaster study as part of the follow-up to the main research, Bennett is, in general, critical of the technique of systematic observation as a means obtaining data to describe and analyse teaching methods. He quotes Nuthall and Snook's (1973) concern that 'the current emphasis of observational studies has produced a proliferation of observational systems and frequency counts of the minutiae of teacher and student behaviours in their daily situations' in support of his criticism. He goes on to couple this with Rosenshine and Furst's (1973), view that increasing the number of observational systems without any attempt at validation 'has led to the current chaos which is a pretence of research'. This is taken to support the view that the present state of the art has consisted of investigators observing 'a narrow range of behaviours of a small and unrepresentative sample of teachers drawn from a population

9

of unknown parameters'. The result is that they are categorized 'according to some global, ill defined dichotomy, unrelated to any theoretical perspective' (Bennett, 1976, p. 32).

This statement is then used to justify the use of the questionnaire approach which can accommodate a larger representative sample of teachers. Both Nuthall and Rosenshine, however, in fact go on to argue, *not* for the abandonment of observational research, but for *better directed activity* where more than one observation instrument is used in the same classroom and where the categories of teaching behaviour observed are not reduced to crude descriptions such as 'indirect-direct' but are allowed to display more complex inter-relationships which are then correlated with the pupils' learning outcomes. Although random sampling of teachers will always prove to be very difficult within observational studies, careful matching of teachers on such characteristics as age and sex coupled with an element of randomization should provide samples which approximate closely to the general population. A previous national study, based in Leicester, in which over one hundred science teachers were observed provided a satisfactory representation of the total population and at the same time offered very precise descriptions of teaching methods based on classroom observation. When these process descriptions were correlated with pupil achievement it was possible to demonstrate that, rather than there being one 'best buy', each method appeared to be more effective in achieving particular objectives with certain types of pupils (Eggleston *et al.*, 1976). As a result teachers, who were failing to achieve these objectives but who wished to do so, could examine their teaching methods to see how closely they matched those of the successful teachers in the research.

The ORACLE study attempts to meet many of the criticisms levelled at the present use of systematic observation in classroom research (Rosenshine, 1970; Dunkin and Biddle, 1974). These critics argue that more attention should be given to describing the context in which observation takes place, that different systems should be checked against each other in the same classroom and that researchers should be more 'open' as to their 'beliefs' about the teaching process the observation system is being used to monitor. In the ORACLE research two observation instruments are used, the Teacher Record and the Pupil Record. Furthermore they are used within the framework of a specific model of teaching which is fully discussed in Chapter 6, and as far as possible the data from the instruments are 'filled out' by indicating the contexts within which the observations were made. For this purpose each observer was asked to collect other types of information while in the classroom, including 'descriptive accounts' of both teachers and pupils, timetables and descriptions of grouping procedures. Care was also taken to ensure that the observation in each curricular area reflected the over-all curricular pattern in that classroom since, if certain activities are associated with certain subjects, over-observation of those subjects will over-represent these activities. For example, assuming that during art and craft there will be more movement and talk than during mathematics (because pupils need to prepare materials and exchange shared implements, etc.), then if pupils are observed too often while working at art the research is likely to conclude that the particular classroom is a more mobile and noisier place than in fact it is.

   Thus although we go some way with Bennett (1978), in calling for a place within the educational system for theories of teaching based upon the results of empirical research, we would argue that the use of systematic observation rather than questionnaires should lie at the centre of any such research effort.

The observation instruments*

To obtain detailed information about teacher and pupil behaviour two separate observation instruments are required. Those used in this study were both developed during earlier funded projects on primary education at Leicester (Boydell, 1974b, 1975). The main categories of the two observation schedules are set out in Tables 1.1 and 1.2 respectively. The Pupil Record, initially modelled on PROSE (Personal Record of School Experience: Medley *et al.*, 1973) though since modified, was used to examine the nature and frequency of children's classroom activities when working alone and interacting with adults and with other pupils. One pupil at a time is the focus of observation and to distinguish him from the rest of the class he is described as the 'target pupil'. The activity and location of the teacher during the period of observation is also noted. In addition, details of curricular area, the size and the sex composition of the target's base group, together with the time of day at which the observation took place is also recorded.

---

* From this point this chapter is concerned with the techniques of the study and characteristics of the sample. Readers who do not require detailed consideration of these issues can, if they wish, move straight to Chapter 2 without losing the thread of the argument.

Table 1.1 The observation categories of the Pupil Record

Coding the pupil-adult categories

Category	Item	Brief definition of item
1 *Target's role*	INIT	Target attempts to become focus of attention (not focus at previous signal)
	STAR	Target is focus of attention
	PART	Target in audience (no child is focus)
	LSWT	Target in audience (another child is focus)
2 *Interacting adult*	TCHR	Target interacts with teacher
	OBSR	Target interacts with observer
	OTHER	Target interacts with any other adult such as the head or secretary
3 *Adult's interaction*	TK WK	Adult interacts about task work (task content or supervision)
	ROUTINE	Adult interacts about routine matter (classroom management and control)
	POS	Adult reacts positively to task work (praises)
	NEG	Adult reacts negatively to behaviour, etc. (criticizes)
	IGN	Adult ignores attempted initiation
4 *Adult's communication setting*	IND ATT	Adult gives private individual attention to target pupil
	GROUP	Adult gives private attention to target's group
	CLASS	Adult interacts with whole class
	OTHER	Adult gives private attention to another child or group or does not interact

Coding the pupil-pupil categories

Category	Item	Brief definition of item
5 *Target's role*	BGNS	Target successfully begins a new contact
	COOP	Target co-operates by responding to an initiation
	TRIES	Target unsuccessfully tries to initiate
	IGN	Target ignores attempted initiation
	SUST	Target sustains interaction
6 *Mode of interaction*	MTL	Non-verbal, mediated solely by materials
	CNTC	Non-verbal, mediated by physical contact or gesture (with or without materials)
	VRB	Verbal (with or without materials, physical contact or gesture)
7a *Task of other pupil(s)*	S TK	Same as target's task
	D TK	Different to target's task
7b *Sex and number of other pupil(s)*	SS	Target interacts privately with one pupil of same sex
	OS	Target interacts privately with one pupil of opposite sex
	SEV SS	Target interacts publicly with two or

Category	Item	Brief definition of item
		more pupils having same sex as target
	SEV OS	Target interacts publicly with two or more pupils, of whom one at least is of the opposite sex to the target
7c *Base of other pupil(s)*	OWN BS	From target's own base
	OTH BS	From another base

Coding the activity and location categories

Category	Item	Brief definition of item
8 *Target's activity*	COOP TK	Fully involved and co-operating on approved task work (e.g. reading)
	COOP R	Fully involved and co-operating on approved routine work (e.g. sharpening a pencil)
	DSTR	Non-involved and totally distracted from all work
	DSTR OBSR	Non-involved and totally distracted from all work by the observer
	DSRP	Non-involved and aggressively disrupting work of other pupil(s)
	HPLY	Non-involved and engaging in horseplay with other pupil(s)
	WAIT TCHR	Waiting to interact with the teacher
	CODS	Partially co-operating and partially distracted from approved work
	INT TCHR	Interested in teacher's activity or private interaction with other pupil(s)
	INT PUP	Interested in the work of other pupil(s)
	WOA	Working on an alternative activity which is not approved work
	RIS	Not coded because the target is responding to internal stimuli
	NOT OBS	Not coded because the target is not observed for some reason
	NOT LIST	Not coded because the target's activity is not listed
9 *Target's location*	P IN	Target in base
	P OUT	Target out of base but not mobile
	P MOB	Target out of base and mobile
	P OUT RM	Target out of room
10 *Teacher activity and location*	T PRES	Teacher present with target through interaction or physical proximity
	T ELSE	Teacher privately interacting elsewhere with other pupil(s) or visitor
	T MNTR	Teacher not interacting but monitoring classroom activities
	T HSKP	Teacher not interacting but housekeeping
	T OUT RM	Teacher out of room

The target pupil's behaviour was coded at regular twenty-five-second intervals using a method of multiple coding, the total number of codings at a given signal depending on the target's situation at that particular moment. The *target's activity* (category 8), and *location* (category 9), together with the *teacher's activity and location* (category 10) were always coded. If the target pupil was interacting with the teacher or another adult then categories 1 to 4 were used, while categories 5 to 7 covered interactions with other pupils.

Pupil activity and location

The target's activity at each time signal was recorded by ticking one of fourteen items listed under category 8 in Table 1.1. If the observer decided that the target was fully involved in what he or she was allowed or supposed to be doing then COOP TK or COOP R was used whereas for non-involvement either DSTR, DSTR OBSR, DSRP, or HPLY would be coded. In cases where the observer judged that the level of involvement was only partial then the category CODS would be ticked. When the target joined the queue at the teacher's desk or waited for the teacher to come to his table then WAIT TCHR was coded. Where the target pupil, although not concentrating on his own work, was interested in other activities in the classroom then either INT TCHR or INT PUP was used as appropriate. Another kind of involvement occurred when the pupil, although working, was not following the teacher's instructions, for example, when the teacher told a pupil to stop painting and get out his mathematics book but the pupil continued to paint. In these circumstances WOA was used.

Sometimes the observer could not code the activity either because the pupil was staring into space so that the observer could not decide whether he was thinking about work or daydreaming (RIS), or the pupil could not be seen (NOT OBS) or the pupil's activity did not fit into any of the categories (NOT LIST). In this last case a brief description of the event would be written in the 'Notes' box on the observation schedule for later discussion and classification.

The *target's location* was also always coded using one of four alternatives. The target was either in or out of his base place (P IN or P OUT), was mobile (P MOB), or had left the room (P OUT RM). In a similar manner the *teacher's activity and location* in relation to the target pupil was also always coded. T PRES was recorded if the teacher was present with the child either through interaction or physical proximity and T ELSE was used if the teacher was privately interacting somewhere else in the room. On some occasions the teacher might not have been interacting with anyone but could simply have been watching or listening to the children's activities (T MNTR) or perhaps sorting out books or resources (T HSKP). When the teacher was not present in class T OUT RM was recorded.

Pupil-pupil interaction

The Pupil Record also provides detailed information about interactions between the target and other pupils and data on the *target's role* (category 5), the *mode of interaction* (category 6) and the *task, sex, number* and *base* of other pupils (category 7). To code the *target's role* the observer had to decide whether any interaction between these pupils was taking place at the previous signal. If satisfied that it was not he had to determine the originator of the new interaction. Should this be the target pupil then the observer coded BGNS while if another pupil began the exchange COOP was used. If no pupil responded to the target's initiation then TRIES was coded while if the target pupil did not respond to another pupil's invitation IGN would be ticked. However, if the interaction was already taking place at the previous signal then the SUST category would be selected.

Such interactions might proceed either by speech (VRB), physical contact or gesture (CNTC) or through materials (MTL) as for example, when one pupil silently holds a shape for another to draw around (category 6). The task of the other pupil or pupils could either have been the same (S TK) or different (D TK) from the target's (category 7a). The interacting group could have been composed of one other pupil of the same or opposite sex (SS or OS) or alternatively it might be composed of three or more pupils (including the target) who were either the same sex or mixed (SEV OS or SEV SS) (category 7b). Lastly the observer had to decide the base area of the other pupils interacting with the target. They could be from the same base table or place as the target or come from a different part of the room (OWN BS or OTH BS) (category 7c).

Pupil-teacher interaction

The third major area covered by the Pupil Record concerns the inter-actions of the target pupil with an adult, usually the teacher. Here four headings are used to describe the *target's role* (category 1), the identity of the *interacting adult* (category 2) the nature of the *adult's interaction* (category 3) and the *communication setting* in which the interaction with the adult takes place (category 4). As with the pupil-pupil categories the observer had first to decide whether the target pupil had attempted to initiate the exchange since the previous signal and if so then INIT was coded in category 1. If the target was not predominantly responsible for securing the adult's attention or if the exchange had been going on since the previous signal then the next decision to be made concerned the amount of attention the target received in relation to other children in the class or group. If the target received most of this attention then STAR was coded but if he had an equal amount with other children then PART was ticked while if the target was listening or watching another child receive most of the teacher's attention then LSWT would be used.

The adult involved could be identified by using one of three alternatives, TCHR (teacher), OBSR (observer) or OTHER. The type of interaction was then decided, TK WK or ROUTINE, but in cases where the adult reacted positively by, for example, praising a piece of work POS was used while in the case of criticism of behaviour (or routine activity) NEG would be coded. A further situation exists where the adult sometimes ignores an attempt by a pupil to initiate an interaction and in this case IGN is coded. By definition, therefore IGN could only be used when the target attempted to initiate an interaction. Finally the setting in which the interaction took place could be thought of either as being for the sole benefit of the target (IND ATT) or directed towards a group of pupils including the target (GROUP) or concerning the whole class (CLASS). In the special case where the adult ignored the attempted interaction by the target there would be no communication setting so OTHER would be coded.

The Pupil Record thus provided a picture of the target's behaviour and his range of contacts with other members of the class. By combining (i.e. cross-tabulating) categories during the analysis it was possible to discover, for example, whether a target, interacting with another pupil, was assisting with work, causing a distraction or carrying out a minor assault!

The Teacher Record: major categories

The purpose of the Teacher Record was to record the various kinds of contact in which the teacher engaged with her pupils. The same twenty-five-second time-sampling unit was used as for the Pupil Record and at each signal the observer noted down different aspects of these interactions. Coding this instrument required the observer to determine the type of *conversation* or the nature of the *silent interaction* taking place as well as certain other features.

Table 1.2   The observation categories of the Teacher Record

Conversation		Silence
Questions		*Silent Interaction*
Task		Gesturing
Q1	recalling facts	Showing
Q2	offering ideas, solutions (closed)	Marking
Q3	offering ideas, solutions (open)	Waiting
Task supervision		Story
Q4	referring to task supervision	Reading
Routine		Not observed
Q5	referring to routine matter	Not coded
Statements		*No Interaction*
Task		Adult interaction
S1	of facts	Visiting pupil
S2	of ideas, problems	Not interacting
Task supervision		Out of room
S3	telling child what to do	
S4	praising work or effort	*Audience*
S5	feedback on work or effort	*Composition*
Routine		*Activity*
S6	providing information, directions	
S7	providing feedback	
S8	of critical control	
S9	of small talk	

The *silent interaction* categories were included to indicate when the teacher was *gesturing, showing* by writing or demonstrating on the blackboard, *marking* pupils' work in their presence, *waiting* for the class to settle, reading a *story* to the class or listening to a pupil *reading* aloud. To deal with cases where the observer had difficulty in recording the activity two further categories, *not observed* and *not coded* were available. If the latter was used the observers wrote a brief description of the event in a 'Notes' box so that a decision as to the correct classification could be made later. If *no interaction* was taking place one of the four categories under this heading was coded covering such situations as visits from teachers and parents or pupils from other classes (*adult interaction* or *visiting pupil*), *not interacting* while silently monitoring, housekeeping or going *out of room* for some purpose or other. The observer also coded the type of the teacher's *audience* (class, group or individual pupil), its *composition* in terms of the number of target pupils, if any, present, and the curricular *activity* of the child or children with whom the teacher was interacting. Mathematics was sub-divided into *number*, or *practical*, (which included the use of apparatus to weigh, measure length or capacity) and *abstract* problem, solving exercises which did not use apparatus. Language work was sub-divided into *reading*, *formal written work*, *spoken English* and *creative writing*. *Art* and *craft* and *general studies*, which included science, history, geography, topic and project work, completed the classification of curricular area.

Teacher conversation

The main part of the observation schedule, however, deals with the teacher's *conversation*. There are six major conversational categories. The observer first has to decide whether the teacher posed a *question* or made a *statement*. He then has to decide whether the teacher was talking about the pupil's *task*, providing *task supervision* or dealing with matters of class *routine*. Each of these major categories was then further sub-divided to give fourteen minor categories in all. All questions were classified in terms of the answer that the pupil gave. There were three kinds of task questions, namely those answered by *recalling facts* (Q1), those answered by *offering closed solutions* (Q2) and those which resulted in *open solutions* (Q3). The distinction between closed and open is an important one and in order to differentiate between these two categories the observer had to listen and see how the teacher handled the pupil's high level imaginative or reasoned response. This then revealed if, despite outward appearances, the teacher was only interested in one particular answer (Q2-closed), or whether she was prepared to accept a range of answers (Q3-open). The remaining two categories of questions referred to *task supervision* (Q4) and *routine matters* of classroom management (Q5).

Any utterances not coded as *questions*, including rhetorical ones, were coded as *statements*. Under *task statements* there were only two categories because it was not possible, as with questions, to differentiate between open and closed utterances in the absence of a response from a pupil. *Statements* were therefore either of *facts* (S1) or of *ideas* and *problems* (S2). *Task supervision statements* monitored and maintained task activity either by *telling the child what to do* (S3), *praising work or effort* (S4) or making neutral or critical comments by way of *feedback on work or effort* (S5). Finally *routine statements* dealt with matters of class management and *provided information or directions* (S6), *provided feedback* (S7), or exercised *critical control* (S8). Finally any statements which had little or nothing to do with classroom activities were coded under *small talk* (S9).

18

The use of the observation instruments: their reliability

Both systems used a twenty-five-second time-sampling unit. When using the Pupil Record in the ORACLE study the observer was required to observe eight previously selected target pupils in a pre-determined order. The pupils in a given class were first sub-divided into groups on the basis of pre-tests in basic skills administered at the beginning of the school year. Each class was divided into three groups, an upper quartile (the high achievers), a bottom quartile (the low achievers) and the two middle quartiles, (the medium achievers). One boy and one girl were selected at random from the high and low groups respectively and two boys and two girls from the medium group.

The twenty-five-second interval was pre-recorded on audio tape and fed to the observer by means of an earpiece attached to a small, portable cassette tape recorder. The observer visited each class for three days each term carrying out six observation sessions during each visit. During any one observation session each target pupil was observed for ten signals. At a pre-arranged time during the session the observer switched to the Teacher Record and each teacher was observed for a total of forty-five signals. The typical order of observation is presented in Figure 1.1. The eight target pupils are labelled from A to H while the teacher is labelled T. The observer's timetable over the three days was so organized that the teacher and the pupils were all seen at the beginning, middle and the end of each session. Efforts were made to carry out observation in an uninterrupted period of an hour although in some cases the observation session had to be interrupted for other activities, such as television programmes and games, which were not included in the study. Each observer attempted to fit the observation around the actual timetable to match as closely as possible the idealized scheme presented in the figure. In each session the teacher was observed for nineteen minutes and each target for four and a half minutes, allowing five minutes in every hour for the observers to move from one pupil to the next.

The teachers did not know the identity of the target pupils and the observers were not told whether they belonged to the high, medium or low achieving group. For the most part teachers preferred not to have this information and readily understood that for the purpose of research it was important to be able to refute the argument that, because the teacher knew the targets' identities, additional attention was given to these particular pupils. At the end of the year's observation those teachers who were not continuing in the project were asked to try to guess the identities of the target pupils. No teacher was able to identify

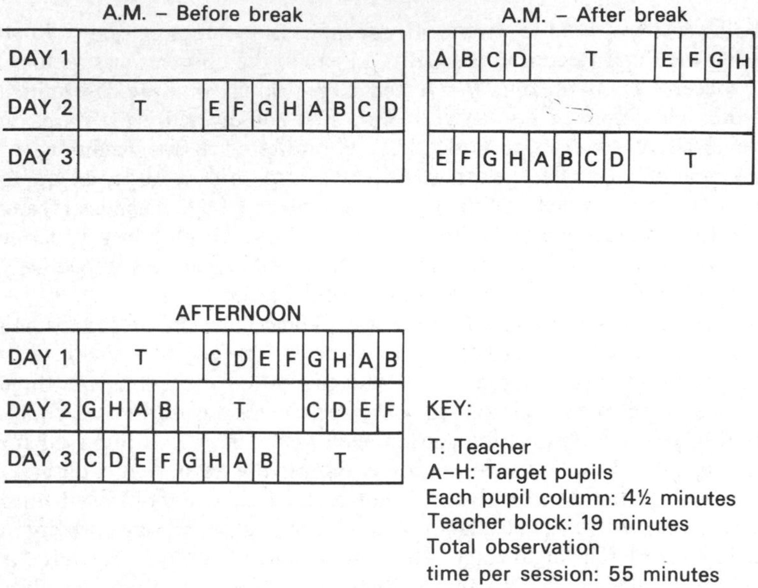

A.M. – Before break

DAY 1											
DAY 2	T		E	F	G	H	A	B	C	D	
DAY 3											

A.M. – After break

A	B	C	D	T		E	F	G	H
E	F	G	H	A	B	C	D	T	

AFTERNOON

DAY 1		T		C	D	E	F	G	H	A	B
DAY 2	G	H	A	B	T			C	D	E	F
DAY 3	C	D	E	F	G	H	A	B	T		

KEY:

T: Teacher
A–H: Target pupils
Each pupil column: 4½ minutes
Teacher block: 19 minutes
Total observation
time per session: 55 minutes

Figure 1.1   Daily observation timetable for observers[a]

a The observer using this timetable would be free before break on Day 1. After break he would start his first observation session and observe target pupils A, B, C and D (in that order) for 4½ minutes each using the Pupil Record. He would then switch to observing the teacher, using the Teacher Record for 19 minutes. He would then finally return to the Pupil Record and observe target pupils E, F, G and H (in that order) for 4½ minutes each. In the afternoon the observer would complete his second session of the day observing the teacher with the Teacher Record at the beginning of the lesson and then moving on to the Pupil Record for the remainder of the lesson. On Days 2 and 3, he would follow the timetable shown in a similar manner.

a complete list of targets and in all cases the actual naming of individuals who had undergone observation was no better than might be expected from random guessing, a tribute to the care and dedication with which the observers went about their task.

In addition to the research team, six other observers, all experienced teachers, helped with the observations in the fifty-eight classrooms. All observers received two weeks intensive training at the beginning of the study and at regular intervals throughout the year refresher training periods were held. The procedures and some problems of training observers in the use of instruments like the Pupil and Teacher Record are discussed in Appendix 1. Although the reliability of both observation instruments had been amply demonstrated in earlier studies (Boydell, 1974b, 1975), a further trial designed to check on the extent of observer agreement in live classrooms was held towards the end of the second year of the ORACLE study. Pairs of observers went into the same classroom and, using a synchronized time signal, coded the same pupils and teachers. From this it was possible to calculate the degree of inter-observer agreement by comparing the paired coding for each individual time unit. The observer agreement was calculated for each set of mutually exclusive categories (i.e. sets of categories where the coding of one does not determine the coding of the other) for both the Teacher and the Pupil Record using the Scott (1955) coefficient. The Pupil Record reliability figures were based on 300 joint observations by four pairs of observers and the Teacher Record on 180 joint observations also by four pairs of observers. Full details are given in Appendix 2A. In general reliability levels for both instruments are satisfactory with the Pupil Record appearing the more reliable of the two. The average value for the Pupil Record is about 0.90 with only one of the pupil interaction categories falling below 0.80. The reliability of the Teacher Record is slightly lower, the main categories only reaching 0.76. However, these figures were based on the individual codings of specific time units whereas in this study the total number of tallies was aggregated for each category and it is generally accepted that reliabilities of this order are satisfactory for this kind of analysis. In some cases it also proved possible to join categories together during the aggregation procedure, thus increasing the over-all reliability of the combination. Details of the reliability trial are given in Appendix 2A.

Other measures used

At the end of each observation session the observer made out a summary sheet (labelled S1) giving the order of observations, the seating

Table 1.3   Instruments used in data collection (autumn 1976 – summer 1977)

Title	When completed	Focus
Pupil Record (PR)	Each target pupil was observed once during each of the six observation sessions per term. Observations were made in the Autumn, Spring and Summer terms (1976-7).	Pupils' activities and interactions with other pupils and adults.
Teacher Record (TR)	Each teacher was observed once during each of the six observation sessions per term. Observations were made in the Autumn, Spring and Summer terms (1976-7).	Teacher questions and statements, silent interaction, no interaction and the audience, its composition and curricular activity.
Session summary sheet (S1)	This was completed at the end of each observation session. Therefore, six were collected each term (Autumn, Spring and Summer, 1976-7).	Physical layout of the classroom, seating of all pupils; outline of curricular contents and methods used; apparatus, resources, etc. and incidents. Order and time of observations.
Daily summary sheet (S2)	This was completed at the end of each day, therefore, three were collected each term (Autumn, Spring and Summer, 1976-7).	Class timetable, and outline of organization to include all activities whether observed or not.
Descriptive account (S3)	This was produced at the end of the six observation sessions (Autumn term 1976, Spring term 1977).	Prose account of the impressions of the observer as regards the teacher, classroom climate, teaching methods, etc.
Grouping instrument (GI)	This was completed for each class in the Summer term 1977.	Physical layout, grouping policy and rationale.
Teachers' questionnaire (TQ)	This was completed for each class in the Summer term 1977.	Classroom management/organization similar to Bennett's survey (1976).

22

arrangement of the class, and an outline of the curricular activities. The different forms of organization which existed during the period of observation and the use of any materials, books or apparatus were also indicated. A daily summary sheet (labelled S2), often in the form of a timetable, was also filled in. This provided an over-all view of the class activities and supplemented the details recorded for the target pupils on the S1 sheet. On it was indicated the major areas of curricular activity, details of how this work was organized and the time and manner of changeovers from one area to another during the day. Working arrangements within any groups were also noted. To ensure adequate sampling of all activities in the informal classroom, thus meeting the criticisms referred to earlier (p. 11), the S1 and S2 summary sheets, referred to throughout the text as the *observers' records*, were used to check that observations covered a range of activities which represented the actual work pattern in the particular classroom. At the end of the observation session the observer wrote a short *descriptive account* of the time spent with each teacher, covering those periods when no systematic observation was taking place. This latter record gave observers an opportunity to point out aspects of classroom life which were not covered by the observation schedule and also to indicate the few cases where ticking a category appeared to have done less than justice in capturing the 'totality' of the event or situation. In the third observation session this account was replaced by a detailed summary of the grouping procedures used by each teacher with a special note of any changes made during the year, the *grouping instrument* (GI). Finally all observers completed a short questionnaire, the *teacher questionnaire* (TQ), giving similar kinds of information as that collected during the Lancaster study. The aim here was to go beyond the argument presented earlier in the chapter and see what, if any, relationship existed between the rather general labels used by Bennett and the more precise descriptions of teaching resulting from the use of the two observation schedules. A summary of the various data-collecting instruments is given in Table 1.3.

Selection of schools and classes

This present study relates only to one aspect of a much wider programme of research. A crucial factor in the selection of classes for observation was the series of transfer studies in which pupils from primary and middle schools were to be observed following their transfer to the next stage of education. Three local authority areas were studied, all with different transfer ages. In local authority A, pupils were observed for one year prior to, and then for one year after, their transfer from junior school to 9-13 middle schools. In local authority B, pupils were observed from two years prior to, and for one year after, their transfer from junior school to 11-14 high schools. In local authority C, pupils were observed for two years prior to, and for one year after, their transfer from 8-12 middle schools to the 12-18 secondary schools.

The age of the pupils in the sample covered the range 8+ to 10+ during the first year of observation on which the analysis in this book is based. For the transfer study, data on all the appropriate schools in each local authority was examined and pairs of schools selected with contrasting curricular and organizational patterns. In each pair one transfer school utilized streaming or setting and class teaching, largely subject based, while the other kept the first year separate from the rest of the school, operated a policy of mixed ability at least for the first two years, and favoured a certain amount of integrated subject teaching. In each local authority area the pairs of schools were selected after consultation with local advisers who in some cases rated each school on the various dimensions already listed. Each pair of contrasting schools was selected so that in each local authority the catchment areas were similar, mainly suburban but extending to the fringes of the inner city or town and out towards the surrounding commuter villages.

From information collected from the observers the housing consisted largely of approximately equal proportions of semi-detached council and private estate but in the inner-city areas there were small amounts of terraced property, some of it in local authority C in such poor condition that it was gradually being knocked down and the population re-housed. There was also a limited amount of larger detached private property.

Having obtained the agreement of the two transfer schools in each area to take part in the study the sample of primary schools was then automatically selected in that it included all those which feed pupils into these transfer schools. Of these only one school in local authority C declined to take part because it was already involved in two Schools Council projects. A further number of schools in local authority B was added to the sample to include additional open plan schools and an inner-city school. The teachers selected for observation were those who happened to be taking the appropriate classes during the year.

The fifty-eight classes were drawn from nineteen schools and some details are given in Table 1.4. The suburban areas were centred on former villages which had been expanded to take up city overspill. Most of the schools were situated on these new private housing estates (estate schools) although continuing to serve nearby areas of council housing. Some, however, tended to be more closely associated with the old village identity (urban village schools), commanding strong loyalty from the local inhabitants. For example, in area C the urban village school was some two hundred yards down the road from the nearest estate school. Both were in new buildings but while the former had nearly one-third too many pupils the latter had spare capacity. Attempts by the local authority to persuade parents to change proved very unsuccessful. As might be expected the inner-city schools were housed in pre-war buildings, one with recent additions, but in area B a new school had been provided to cope with a rapid rise in the number of immigrant familes moving into the district.

Table 1.4   School characteristics

	Number of schools	Number of classes
Urban village		
New: 1965+	1	5
Post-war	–	–
Pre-war	–	–
Mixed	3	14
Total	4	19
Housing estates		
New: 1965+	8	20
Post-war	2	6
Pre-war	–	–
Mixed	–	–
Total	10	26
Urban inner city		
New: 1965+	1	3
Post-war	–	–
Pre-war	3	7
Mixed	1	3
Total	5	13
Total	19	58

Most of the estate schools were built after 1965, many of them open plan. Of the pre-war schools two were late Victorian, while in the mixed category there was one old Board school which had been imaginatively converted to provide one of the most spacious open plan areas found in the study.

The characteristics of the classes, broken down for each local authority area are shown in Table 1.5. The ratio of open plan to box type class-rooms was highest in local authority C. Only 25.8 per cent of classes were vertically grouped, schools in areas A and B having up to one-third of classes grouped in this way, while, as might be expected, in the middle schools of local authority C this form of organization was hardly ever used. Although the teachers were not a random selection they matched the characteristics of the national population of primary teachers fairly well. For example, 34.5 per cent were males and this fits quite closely with the Department of Education and Science's figure of 35.4 per cent for junior schools without infants and 36.1 per cent for middle schools deemed primary which comprise the bulk of the ORACLE sample.

Table 1.5   Characteristics of classes and their teachers by local authority area

		LEA			Total Percentage
		A	B	C	
Sex of teachers	Male	3	12	5	34.5
	Female	6	21	11	65.5
School type	Open plan	1	6	8	25.9
	Box	8	27	8	74.1
Organization	Single age	6	22	15	74.1
vertically	7+ and 8+	3	7	—	17.2
grouped	8+ and 9+	—	—	1	1.7
	9+ and 10+	—	4	—	6.9
Age of pupils	8+	8	19	—	46.6
	9+	1	12	—	22.4
	8+ and 9+	—	2	—	3.4
	10+	—	—	16	27.6

Further comparisons with the DES figures for the age of teachers and the size of the classes are shown in Table 1.6. The ORACLE sample contains slightly more teachers in their thirties and correspondingly fewer over fifty than in the national population. Part of the reason may be that older teachers generally have positions of responsibility (e.g. Deputy Heads) which take them out of the classroom for periods during the day. Some heads tended not to consider such teachers when allocating staff to the observed classes in an attempt to help the observer complete the correct number of observation sessions within the speci-fied period. The average class size in the sample was 29.9 as against the national figure of 29.2. Our classes tend to be mainly in a range of between twenty-one and thirty-five, the smallest having twenty pupils, the largest thirty-eight. Comparison with the DES data would suggest that the disproportion is a result of having no small village schools and fewer large inner-city ones. We believe, however, that the data is representative of the type of catchment areas in which the transfer schools and their feeder schools were situated.

Table 1.6   Comparison of ORACLE and DES[a] data for age of teachers and their class size

	No.	ORACLE Percentage	DES (1976) Percentage
Age of teacher			
up to 30 years	23	39.7	38.7
30-40 years	17	29.3	22.5
40-50 years	13	22.4	23.4
50 years and over	5	8.6	15.4
Class size			
up to 20	1	1.7	4.9
21-25	9	15.5	11.6
26-30	20	34.5	29.9
31-35	25	43.1	37.1
36-40	3	5.2	15.0
41 and over	–	–	1.6
Average size	29.9		29.2

a   Statistics of Education, 1976, vol. 4, *Tables*; vol. 1, *Schools*.

Conclusion

In this chapter, besides providing a description of the classes and schools where the research was carried out we have also emphasized the need to use observation rather than questionnaires to study the processes of teaching and learning. We see much of the recent debate between 'progressives' and 'traditionalists' as largely sterile because, in the absence of evidence, the protagonists have been forced to assume that the crude descriptions, provided by studies using a questionnaire approach, are associated with specific patterns of teaching. Before presenting evidence suggesting that much of this criticism is either misplaced or incorrect we shall first turn to a consideration of the wider context in which our study was carried out; that is, the development of the present system of primary schooling. Then in Chapter 3, we examine the most recent authoritative statement as to the theory and practice of primary school teaching, that presented by the Plowden Committee in its influential report, *Children and Their Primary Schools* (1967).

CHAPTER 2

Evolution of the primary school

Although several million children are now educated in separate primary schools of one kind or another, these have a comparatively recent and certainly a short history. This form of schooling was first accepted as official policy only some fifty years ago, in 1928. It then took some forty years to implement. Not until the mid-1960s were *all* children between the ages of five and eleven educated in separate 'primary' schools. No sooner was this achieved than new changes were brought about by new thinking and legislation. The Education Act of 1964 made possible the establishment of 'middle' schools covering the ages of nine to thirteen. To complicate matters further, only three years later, the Central Advisory Councils for Education for both England and Wales recommended that 'middle' schools for children aged eight to twelve should be the norm. Both these options have been taken up by a number of local authorities, with the approval of the Department of Education and Science, largely to facilitate comprehensive secondary reorganization.

'Primary' education today, therefore, in spite of its relatively recent establishment, is already again in a state of flux. What had become the norm (infant schools or departments for children aged five to seven followed by a junior school to eleven) has already been phased out in some parts of the country, to be replaced by one of two alternative systems, (i) 'first', sometimes called 'lower', schools for children aged five to nine, followed by 'middle' (nine to thirteen) and 'upper' schools (thirteen to eighteen), or (ii) first schools for children aged five to eight, followed by 'middle' (eight to twelve) and upper schools for the twelve to eighteens (or sometimes twelve to sixteen and sixteen to

29

eighteen). These three systems now exist in parallel in different parts of the country. As indicated in Chapter 1, the research project reported in this volume was carried through in each of these three systems.

It is evident, then, that primary education, the subject of our study, is in a state of transition. It is essential, if we are to place existing schools and their practices in context, to gain some understanding of their development, of the forces that have shaped their character and procedures. Only historical analysis can throw light on the changing forms of primary education, explicate the reasons for the emergence of this particular institutional form, and illuminate its evolution both in terms of practice and of theory. This chapter and the next are concerned with the evolution of the primary school itself, and with the theory and practice of teaching within it.

Origin of the junior school (1870 – 1926)

The concept that education below eleven should be defined as 'primary', and that above as 'post-primary' (or 'secondary') first appeared in an official document in the Report of the Consultative Committee to the Board of Education, known after its chairman, as the 'Hadow Report' (Hadow, 1926). The proposal was adopted as national policy in 1928. Even at that stage, however, the discussion was largely conceptual. Only with the Education Act of 1944 was a public system of education finally brought into being in England and Wales which established, in statutory terms at least, the reality of two stages of education, primary and secondary. It is in this sense that the 'primary' school in this country has a short history, and, as we have seen, the concept of 'primary' education is already somewhat confused only some thirty to forty years later.

Before 1944 the great majority of children of the present primary age range (five to eleven) were in *elementary* schools; they were educated together with older children in 'all-age' schools within the elementary system. This system was established, specifically and deliberately, for one section of society only – that is, for the working class. The original objectives of universal, compulsory education, established by 1880, were then still defined in terms of the 'standard' system brought in by 'payment by results' in 1862, though this system began to be modified after 1870. Payment by results focused the teacher's attention very specifically on the three R's; the objective was the achievement of an elementary level of literacy and numeracy by the working-class population. Clearly there were other objectives as well, though not so overtly defined; specifically those which might be described as social-disciplinary, the achievement of which was sought through what is now referred to as the 'hidden curriculum' rather than through the content of instruction (acceptance of the teacher's authority, of the need for punctuality, obedience, conformity, and so on). It is worth noting that the system of payment by results was modified in the 1880s to put greater emphasis on this latter aspect, as compared with the three R's.

The elementary system, in its origins and indeed up to the mid-1920s, did not include any special provision for younger children below the age of eleven, with the exception of infant schools and departments covering the age range five to seven in some areas. These, which constituted a unique feature of the English educational system, were connected with the early start of compulsory education. At the age of five it was, in 1870, and is still, below the compulsory age in other advanced industrial countries (in France, Germany, Sweden, the age is six, in the USSR it is seven). This early age of entry was partly a product of the establishment, from 1870 and even earlier, as an accepted and essential part of the system of infant schools and departments catering for children below the age of six or seven and including many children aged three and four.

This tradition is normally said to owe its origin to Robert Owen's famous 'infant school' at New Lanark in the early 1820s and the subsequent development of such schools by Wilderspin and others in the 1820s to 1840s. But, by the 1860s and 1870s the main objective in separating out the infants, it appears, was to ensure that the teaching of the older children should not be unduly disturbed by what Matthew Arnold (and others) referred to as the 'babies'. Originally the infant school or department passed on its children to the elementary school at six, since the first 'standard' examination (standard I), brought in in 1862 under payment by results, was designed for children aged six to seven, but the code of regulations issued in 1871 created an infant stage below standard I for the five to seven age range. Thus the age of seven became the age of transfer from the infant school (or department) to the elementary school as a whole (Whitbread, 1972, p. 41). In the evolution of the concept of the junior school, the separate existence of infant schools or departments, defining the age of entry, is clearly important. However it must not be assumed that infant schools or departments were ubiquitous; in 1930 they accounted for approximately half the children aged five to seven, the rest were still in all-age elementary schools catering for children aged five (and below) to fourteen.

If the existence of infant schools and departments cut off the

31

younger children, developments in the education system, particularly around and after the turn of the century, began to demarcate an upper limit of eleven or twelve, or at least to indicate that such a demarcation might, given the conditions, become a practical possibility. There were a number of reasons for this, all relating to the growth of new forms of 'secondary' schools following the 1902 Education Act. The scholarship and free place system, established in 1907 (but existing earlier), created a link between the elementary and secondary systems by which the latter recruited pupils from the elementary schools at around the age of ten to twelve. The same was the case with the new selective 'central' schools within the elementary system, established in London, Manchester and elsewhere from about 1910. So the age of around eleven was becoming accepted as the age of transfer to secondary and other schools already before the First World War. An impetus was given to this by the Education Act of 1918 which stated that special provision should be made for 'the older or more intelligent children' in elementary schools by means of central schools, extended courses, and the like, and by the actions taken (or proposed) by local authorities under the Act in the early 1920s. This set the scene for the proposals of the Hadow Report in 1926 for the division of the elementary school system into two stages, junior and senior, with a break at eleven for all. Here was the real origin of the junior school, or of the division between primary and post-primary education.

It is worth noting at this point that the motivation for this funda- mental change did not arise from any serious consideration of the needs and character of children aged seven to eleven (or five to eleven). It arose solely from a consideration of the needs of the older (senior) children; and indeed it is symptomatic that the crucial report on which action was taken, setting up separate junior or primary schools, was entitled *The Education of the Adolescent* (1926). The origins and significance of this report have been analysed elsewhere (Simon, 1974) so will not be gone into here; particularly since the establishment of the junior school as a separate institution was very much a by-product of the report, and little of any significance is said there on the topic. However, it is worth noting that, although in some of the large urban areas junior departments (so called) of all-age schools had already been established as a consequence of the developments mentioned above, by the mid-1920s, when the Consultative Committee reported, only some 6 per cent of children aged seven to eleven were in such departments. All the rest, the great bulk of the children in those age groups, were still organized as they had been since 1870, in all-age schools catering for children aged five or seven to fourteen. These normally were organized as separate boys' and girls' departments, usually with a mixed infants' school as the base. In large urban schools of the kind built by the School Boards following the Education Act of 1870, the infants' school was on the ground floor, the boys' and girls' departments on the floors above. In rural areas there would usually be a separate infants' class with one, two or more other classes according to the size of the school taking children up to fourteen.

Developments following the Hadow Report

This, then, marks the beginning of the separate junior school as national policy; emerging, as it were, unforeseen and as a by-product, from the womb of the elementary system, and bearing, at least in its origin, all the marks of that system in terms of cheapness, economy, large classes, obsolete, ancient and inadequate buildings, and so on. With reorganization after 1928 (when the Hadow Report's recommendations were accepted by the government) the usual practice was to provide new buildings, where possible, for the older pupils in the new senior elementary schools, since these needed facilities for specialist teaching, for the first time including laboratories, craft rooms, gymnasia, art rooms and so on. So reorganization went ahead, though very unevenly in different parts of the country. Over-all, 48 per cent of children aged seven to eleven were in separate junior schools (or departments) by 1938.

Only in 1931 was attention focused specifically for the first time on 'The Primary School' with the publication of a report by the Consultative Committee with that title. Yet even here it is interesting to note the terms of the reference to that Committee. This was simply 'to enquire and report as to the courses of study suitable for children (other than children in infants departments) up to the age of eleven *in elementary schools* with special reference to the needs of children in rural areas' (our italics).

Reference has already been made to the original, narrow objectives embodied in the elementary school tradition; the strictly instrumental approach relating to literacy and numeracy and to its social disciplinary aspects. All this is well known and is explicable in terms of the original social function of this school system. Nevertheless, what might be called peripheral, or external theoretical influences were beginning to make some impact on the system from the turn of the century, or even before. There was, first, the kindergarten movement, based on Froebel's theory and practice, which began to penetrate the schools from the

1890s, involving the concepts of 'natural development', 'spontaneity', and so on; even if contemporary analysis, for instance, an investigation carried through by a group of women HMIs in 1905 (Board of Education, 1905), indicated that Froebel's system was applied in an extremely mechanistic manner; that is, was adapted to Board school drill practice, so losing its educative significance. Nevertheless the ideas were there, and the movement institutionalized with the foundation of the Froebel Institute and other colleges for the training of teachers on Froebelian principles, often financed by wealthy philanthropists interested in transforming middle-class educational practice for young children.

This was followed, after the turn of the century, by the considerable impact made by Dr Maria Montessori, with her emphasis on structured learning, sense training and individualization. Both influences were more strongly felt in the infant schools than in other sections of the elementary system (their main impact was probably felt in middle-class private schools). Perhaps more immediately relevant to the maintained school system was the work of Margaret McMillan, with her emphasis on improving hygienic conditions, overcoming children's physical defects, and providing an 'appropriate' environment for young children. This work and that of her sister, Rachel, was certainly influential in bringing new concepts concerning activity and creativity again largely to the infant school but nevertheless affecting teachers and others in the elementary school system as a whole. Finally, given this brief survey, the year 1911 saw the publication of *What Is and What Might Be* by Edmond Holmes, ex-Chief Inspector of Elementary Schools; the first striking manifesto of the 'progressives' in its total condemnation of the arid drill methods of the contemporary elementary school, and its espousal of the enlightened, all-sided, humanist approach of the model village school-teacher Egeria (who is said actually to have existed). The publication of this book marks the start of the 'new' education; ideas to be crystallized and institutionalized with the foundation of the New Education Fellowship shortly after the First World War (Selleck, 1972).

In the immediate post-war period ideas of this kind were strongly represented in theoretical discussion on the education of young children; and partially implemented in the practice of those schools which turned towards group work and individualization. This was a central feature of the so-called Sub Dalton Plan embodying some, at least, of John Dewey's ideas which, paradoxically, although emanating from the USA, was implemented to a far greater extent in British primary schools (Kimmins and Rennie, 1932, pp. 82-4). Another potent new influence from the early 1930s was Susan Isaacs, whose two books, on

34

the intellectual and social development of young children, were published at this stage (Isaacs, 1930, 1933).

It was these aspects that were stressed in the Consultative Committee's report on *The Primary School* (1931). This emphasized the need for a completely new approach to primary education which, it was argued, was now made possible with the break at eleven. To give a sense of this report it is best to quote directly from the section on the curriculum for the primary stage of education (pp. 139-40). The report stresses the need 'to supply the pupils with what is essential to their healthy growth, physical, intellectual and moral', adding the much-quoted view that 'the curriculum of the primary school is to be thought of in terms of activity and experience, rather than of knowledge to be acquired and facts to be stored'. The importance of physical training, including training in 'good carriage and graceful movement' is emphasized, as is the fundamental importance of language training, with 'systematic training in oral expression'. Aesthetic sensibility must be cultivated through drawing, craft work and music, together with the development of manual skills. The traditional practice of dividing the matter of primary instruction into separate 'subjects', taught in distinct lessons 'should be re-considered' − central topics may be a useful alternative. Although the report emphasizes that provision should be made 'for an adequate amount of "drill" in reading, writing and arithmetic', over-all emphasis clearly reflects the new approaches; especially in the broader aims and objectives now conceived as relevant to primary education.

The 1931 report, though favourably received, made little impact at the time. Of course, very few separate 'junior' schools, as such, had by then been brought into being, while as M.L. Jacks put it, 'the conditions necessary for its implementation were almost wholly lacking' (Ross, 1960, p. 33). In 1932, for instance, well over 50 per cent of children of primary school age were in classes with over forty pupils. However this report, in general, certainly reflected the outlook of the 'new', child-centred, 'progressive' approach to education even if, as we shall see, it strongly recommended the introduction of streaming into the new junior schools. R.J.W. Selleck argues, in *English Primary Education and the Progressives, 1914 to 1939*, that the approach of the 'new' educationalists, somewhat watered down from its wilder manifestations in the early 1920s, had, by 1939, become the official orthodoxy; propagated in training colleges, Board of Education in-service courses, by local authority inspectors, and the like. How far it affected actual *practice* in the schools is, however, another matter.

The selective function of the junior school

The primary school, though now envisaged in the sense outlined above, was, however, subject to sharply contradictory influences. While the 1931 report developed the idea of universal popular education of a new, broader, child-centred, activity type, the actual emergence of the junior school on a mass scale, which only took place *after* the Second World War, coincided precisely with the crystallization of the school system as primarily a sorting, classifying, selective mechanism; a function in which the junior school played a central role and one which reached its height, in this form, as late as the mid-1950s, just at the time when 'Hadow reorganization' was rapidly being completed throughout the country. The 1931 report, basing itself on the psychology of individual differences, and fully accepting the advice of psychometrists who at that time asserted the *absolute* determination of 'intelligence' by hereditary or genetic factors (Cyril Burt and Percy Nunn were both co-opted on the drafting committee) strongly advocated the necessity of streaming as the basic form of internal school organization for all primary schools large enough to form parallel classes in each age group. New schools, where possible, were to be designed on the basis of a 'treble track' system.

With the completion of reorganization following the Second World War, and the greatly increased competition for grammar school places which the 1944 Act, in spite of providing 'secondary education for all', did nothing to alleviate, streaming spread, in Brian Jackson's words 'with barely credible rapidity throughout the country' (Jackson, 1964, p. 150). Since the selection examination consisted normally of 'objective' tests in the three R's plus 'Intelligence', this inevitably provided the main objective for primary school education *as a whole* (*all* children were now entered for this examination, whatever their stream or educational level; this was regarded as essential to allow 'equality of opportunity'). So, in spite of the call for freedom and quite new approaches in the 1931 report, and in spite of a move in this direction in the late 1940s and some modification of practice in different parts of the country, in general the old elementary school syndrome which that report had regarded as quite out-moded, inevitably persisted, if in a somewhat modernized guise. The basic class teaching approach, with the main emphasis on numeracy and literacy, continued in the new junior schools after the Second World War; in fact the tradition derived from 1870 was still dominant. The continued existence of large classes through the late 1940s and 1950s reinforced this method of school organization with its related pedagogy.

From its inception, the junior school has always had a dual role in the sense that before the Second World War a few of its pupils (about 10 per cent) were selected for the secondary school, while the majority remained in the elementary system either in the same school (where it was 'all-age') or in the senior school. This remained the case in the new dispensation following the 1944 Education Act, the senior schools being re-named 'secondary modern'. The tripartite system then established (including secondary technical schools) gave enhanced importance to the 11-plus examination, and reinforced the system of streaming which had success in this examination (in terms of gaining places in grammar schools) as one of its objectives.

It may be thought that the concepts underlying the 'child-centred' approach, and those underlying streaming are contradictory, yet both were accepted by the Consultative Committee in the report on *The Primary School* (1931) (as in other reports in the inter-war years). However this is not necessarily the case. Child-centred approaches, particularly Froebelian, were based fundamentally on the notion that the child's inborn characteristics must be allowed to flower; that the school's function is, in Froebel's words, 'to make the inner outer' (Bowen, 1903, p. 98). Hence the emphasis on natural, spontaneous development. The school's role is to provide optimum conditions for such development. This ties in closely with the views of the dominant school of psychology in the inter-war years (psychometry), whose main tenet, as mentioned above, was that the child's most important mental characteristic, defined as 'Intelligence' (seen as a measure of intellectual potential) was *wholly* fixed and inborn, and was not subject to change as a result of educational or any other experiences. What was necessary was to provide an education appropriate to the child's inborn, and measurable, intelligence level. Thus Susan Isaacs, an influential proponent of 'activity methods', as they were called, strongly insisted on the necessity for differentiation of young children through streaming based on 'Intelligence' (Isaacs, 1932). It was, therefore, possible to reconcile child-centred approaches with hierarchic organization (streaming) within the junior school. Nevertheless it is evident that a tension developed between the two approaches in the years following the Second World War, the selective function of the junior school imposing clear restraints on the teachers, whose outlook was inevitably affected by the need to get good results in the 11-plus examination, in the interests both of the pupils and of the school.

It is difficult now to reconstruct the intense pressure on schools and teachers that built up in the 1940s and 1950s relating to the selection examination; the league tables that parents drew up for local schools, the telephoning round to find out who had done well and the sense of failure that some teachers experienced when their pupils won fewer places than others, or than expected; not to speak of the effects on the children. This was the reality that teachers had to face, arising from the context of the junior school within the tripartite (or selective) system; and this clearly was a dominant influence relating both to teachers' objectives and, therefore, to the teacher's style and forms of organization within the classroom, a matter we will return to in the next chapter. Once again the fate of the junior school and its educational role depended on developments at the upper levels.

Comprehensive reorganization: the abolition of the 11-plus

But, with the transition to comprehensive secondary education, this dependence showed itself in an opposite sense. Comprehensive reorganization can be said to have got under way, in terms of entire local authority systems, from the mid-1960s, when the junior schools – or those in reorganized areas – found themselves to a large extent freed from the direct pressures and constraints just mentioned.

The abolition of the 11-plus, which was the concomitant of this reorganization (and to a large extent its motive force) now quite suddenly, and somewhat unexpectedly, created a new situation, and, in a real sense, the schools found new options open. Ironically, as we have seen, this transformation brought with it the demise of the seven to eleven junior schools as *national* policy although this system still predominates in the country as a whole alongside the new forms of age grouping defined earlier.

One striking feature of recent developments is the rapidity of change the schools have experienced. This may link with the contradiction between theory and practice which clearly developed after 1931; between the theory of the 'progressives' as crystallized in the 1931 report, and the actual practice of the junior schools as this persisted under the mounting constraints of the 11-plus. During this period, the focus of 'progressive' developments in practice was the infant school, which, although certainly affected by the increasingly competitive nature of the 11-plus (it was not uncommon to introduce streaming for six-year-olds), was relatively free to develop autonomously forms of organization and activities which were held to be educationally appropriate for five- to seven-year-olds. Practice here was certainly affected from the mid-1930s by the highly 'progressive' report of the Consultative Committee on *Infant and Nursery Schools*, published in 1933, clearly

38

influenced by the work of Susan Isaacs, as also by the ideas of Froebel, Montessori and Dewey. There is evidence that 'progressive' infant school practices spread into the lower forms (and streams) of junior schools following the Second World War, particularly during the 1950s and especially in certain specific local authority areas. It is perhaps symptomatic that when Lilien Weber came from New York to study advanced school practice in England in the mid-1960s it was to the infant school that she devoted her attention. There is very little on junior schools in her book subsequently published under the title *The English Infant School and Informal Education* (Weber, 1971).

But the ideas of 'progressive' educators, using this term in its broadest (and most positive) sense, suffered a continuous frustration as regards *practice* in the junior school both before and after the Second World War, even if pioneering books like M.V. Daniels's *Activity in the Junior School* did appear (and were influential) in the late 1940s when 'activity' methods spread quite widely and had a certain vogue. A kind of back-log of progressive ideas and practices built up almost since 1911 (Holmes) (reinforced by war-time evacuation experiences, when teachers were driven back on to their own resources and began to act both more autonomously and more flexibly than before), was liberated in those areas where the 11-plus was early abolished or profoundly modified. These were particularly Leicestershire, the West Riding of Yorkshire, Oxfordshire, Bristol and London. Here were the nests of the new breakout. It was in these areas, also, that the system of streaming, which reinforced the methodology of class teaching, was most rapidly discarded. The swing from streaming in the junior schools in these and other areas, which started very slowly in the mid-1950s, meeting strong opposition, suddenly took off with extraordinary rapidity in the mid- to late 1960s, gaining influential support from the Plowden Report of 1967.

The 1960s

Educational developments in the 1960s were so rapid, all-embracing, and, in retrospect, perhaps surprising, that it is worth spending a little time on that decade, particularly because some of the problems facing primary education today clearly have their roots in this period and the apparent subsequent reaction from ideas and practices then regarded as positive. The 1960s saw not only the swing to comprehensive secondary education — one important condition for freeing the primary schools from earlier constraints — they also saw the acceptance *in toto* of the

39

targets for a massive expansion of higher education as proposed in the Robbins Report, *Higher Education* (Robbins, 1963), and of the perspectives outlined (if somewhat ambiguously) in the Newsom Report, *Half Our Future* (Newsom, 1963). Of major importance to the subject of this book was the publication of the Plowden Report *Children and Their Primary Schools* (1967), which, if also ambiguous in parts (particularly as concerns the curriculum), clearly and definitely espoused child-centred approaches in general, the concept of 'informal' education, flexibility of internal organization and non-streaming in a general humanist approach — stressing particularly the uniqueness of each individual and the paramount need for individualization of the teaching — learning process. There is little doubt that, when it appeared, the Plowden Report effectively crystallized a growing consensus as to the ideal nature of primary education; it built on, but took further, concepts initially propagated in the Consultative Committee's reports on *The Primary School* (1931) and *Infant and Nursery Schools* (1933).

But there were other factors affecting school practice at that time. One of these was the development of what is called the 'permissive society', and particularly the tendency to place fewer restraints on children and young people by parents and those in authority generally; combined on the other hand with a new consciousness on the part of young people as to their role in society, no doubt the result of higher earning powers in conditions of full employment, relative affluence, and so increased independence and autonomy. While it is difficult to evaluate such a tendency, there is little doubt that this affected pupil behaviour and attitudes in schools — perhaps even those of young children in primary schools. But there were other factors operating as well. Over this period there was a strong tendency, not only for local authorities specifically to encourage innovation and change in primary schools, but also for the head teachers themselves to allow a high degree of autonomy in classroom practice to class teachers; a result, perhaps, not only of the increased tendency towards the questioning of authority but also of the increasing professionalization of the primary school teacher, linked to the extension of training to three years in 1963. All this enhanced the variation of practice in the classroom. Schools tended no longer to operate as a single unit with common objectives using similar methods throughout the school; instead, different approaches could be found, and were tolerated, in different classrooms within the same school (Taylor, 1974).

In addition, the 1960s saw a decline in the inspectorial role both of HMIs and, in particular perhaps, of local authority inspectors who traditionally (especially in urban areas with their School Board traditions of administration) kept the primary schools on a tight rein. The former almost entirely ceased to carry out full inspections; in the case of local inspectors the tendency was to take on an advisory rather than an inspectorial function with the diminution of authority that this implies. This does not necessarily mean a decline in influence, since an effective adviser may have very considerable impact on the schools, and, through organizing activities such as the annual Leicestershire Teachers Primary Residential Workshops, profoundly affect school practice. Nevertheless, under this system, such influence has been exerted rather through the free concurrence of heads and teachers than through reliance on the authority of inspectors.

Finally, the 1960s saw the erection of new schools on the open plan principle, or the modification of old buildings on these lines. This created a new situation which inevitably affected classroom organization and methodology.

The situation today

It is in the light of these factors, many of them generally regarded at the time as educationally positive, that contemporary attitudes to and criticisms of the schools need to be evaluated. Here it is relevant to refer to the general disenchantment with education as a palliative of society's ills, which first found expression in the USA following the supposed (and some hold premature) evaluation of the Headstart programmes as a failure. This view, embodied in the Coleman (1966) and Jencks (1972) reports coincided with the beginning of a world economic recession (late 1960s), providing a rationale for economic cutbacks in education not only in England but in most advanced western industrial countries. If schools 'make no difference', why support them? The economic climate that developed also provided the context for the views presented in the series of Black Papers referred to in Chapter 1; the first, published in 1969, specifically focused on new developments in the *primary* schools as a main cause not only of student unrest in the universities but of other unwelcome tendencies or phenomena (Cox and Dyson, 1969a). It is in this context also that, in 1975, the events surrounding the Tyndale school dispute unfolded in London (concerning the implementation of an extreme version of 'progressive' methods in a primary school), followed in May 1976 by the massive publicity given by the media to Bennett's study (1976) represented as a condemnation of so-called 'informal' methods in the primary school. All this formed the background to Prime Minister Callaghan's speech (autumn 1976) warning against certain current tendencies in education, and the events which have followed: 'The Great Debate', DES and HMI initiatives relating to the curriculum, the establishment of the Assessment of Performance Unit, the beginning of mass testing by local authorities, and so on. The climate in which schools now function has certainly changed, affecting directly their mode of operation and perhaps also their objectives. For all these reasons added importance is given to the survey reported in this volume, concerned to present an objective analysis of 'process' − of what actually goes on in primary schools today.

Summary

It appears that the history of the primary school may be divided into four phases. First, its pre-history up to 1928, when the junior school as such had no independent existence, though embryonic forms were embodied within the elementary school system including infant schools and departments. Practices, approaches, attitudes and buildings derived from this phase are still to be found. Second, the period from 1928 to 1944 when junior schools, as such, began to come into being within the system of *elementary* education, and when a specific theoretical approach to primary education began to be formulated and receive official support (for short 'progressive', or 'child-centred'). Third, from 1944 to about 1970, a period which saw the universal provision of primary schooling (in its various forms) covering the age range five to eleven; a period when the specific theoretical approach developed earlier began to be implemented on a reasonably wide scale, culminating in the Plowden Report. Fourth, the present period, from about 1970 or shortly after to today and projecting into the future; a period marked by economic difficulties, controversy over means and ends, new restraints on the teacher, and by the demise of 'primary schooling' in the sense previously established with the development of new organizational (or institutional) forms. One thing seems clear; primary education, very much the poor relation in the educational system, has been in a state of almost continuous transition throughout its short history, the result both of changes at the secondary level and of changing approaches to the education of young children. Evaluation of contemporary practice must take this into account.

CHAPTER 3

Primary school teaching: theory and practice

The brief review of the history of primary education in the last chapter focused on institutional change, though touching also on theoretical issues and their relation to practice; that is, to the actual process of teaching in the classroom. It is with this latter aspect that we are concerned in this book. The latest, and certainly the most comprehensive and authoritative statement of the principles (or theory) which should govern classroom practice is that presented by the Plowden Committee in their report *Children and Their Primary Schools* (1967). Further, the Committee set out, if only in very general terms, the implications of this theory for classroom organization and outlined their concept of the teacher's role and function. It may be useful to attempt to make explicit the Plowden prescriptions in this sense; particularly since they are nowhere systematically set out in the report. Even if much has happened since its publication, the Plowden Report has undoubtedly influenced the schools, teachers, administrators, and all concerned with primary education. It has formed, in an important sense, the backdrop against which schools and teachers have operated now for more than a decade. What, then, can be culled from this report as to the characteristics of advanced school practice?

The unique individual

The main theoretical stance of the Report is made abundantly clear in the first chapter. This stresses the uniqueness of each individual child; the 'enormously wide variability' in physical and intellectual maturity

43

of children of the same age. It is this factor which demands adaptability and flexibility on the part of the teacher. But, however wide this variation, children have one important characteristic in common, 'a strong drive' from a very early age 'towards activity in the exploration of the environment' (paragraph 45).* This behaviour is 'autonomous' and is linked to the child's 'curiosity, especially about novel and unexpected features of his experience'. Development (or learning?) is interpreted as the resultant of 'the complex and continuous interaction between the developing organism and its environment' (11). It is the nature of this interaction that, according to Plowden, enhances individual differences; even within members of the same family, it is held, such differences appear very early and lead to wide variation. Development generally is, therefore, the result of the interaction of an 'hereditary tendency and environmental factors' such as the level or degree of 'encouragement or discouragement' children experience (52). In particular, mastery of language is seen as 'central to the educational process' (55).

It is from this analysis, here very briefly summarized, that is derived the main thrust of the report as a whole — *that individualization of the educational process is the essential principle on which all educational strategy and tactics must be based.* 'Individual differences between children of the same age', it is stated, 'are so great that any class, however, homogeneous it seems, must always be treated as a body of children needing *individual* and *different* attention' (our italics). However, the matter is even more complex than this. Intellectual, emotional and physical development, it is stated, all take place at different rates. A teacher, therefore, needs to know and take account of each child's 'developmental' age in all three aspects (75).

In a sense there is nothing strikingly new about these theories; they have formed the staple of advanced thinking by educational psychologists for a long time even if they are spelt out in a more detailed way here than previously.[1] But it is in the *consistent application* of these theories to practice that the Plowden Committee take things further than before. For instance the Report, as is well known, favoured unstreaming. This is consistent with the theories just outlined concerning the enormous variability, and, in a sense, unpredictability of children's development, and with the stress on the importance of environmental factors in its determination. If the child's educational (and other) experiences are now seen as central to intellectual, and indeed over-all, development, as the Plowden Committee see them,

---

* The paragraph number is given throughout this chapter for references to the Plowden Report.

the categorization ('streaming') of children according to their *existing* level of development at any one moment cannot be justified. Instead it is necessary, so far as possible, to provide a rich environment for all children, giving scope for the realization of children's many-sided potentialities. The Plowden Committee take this reasoning (if not spelt out exactly in this form) to its logical conclusion first, in its unqualified support for unstreaming, 'We welcome unstreaming in the infant or first school and hope that it will continue to spread through the age groups of the junior or middle schools' (819), and second (and characteristically) in its insistence that 'the problem in the unstreamed class will be to translate into practice the principle of *individual learning*' (our italics) (824).

This is as clear a statement as it is possible to find of the main thrust of the Plowden philosophy towards individualization of the teaching-learning process. In the same way, and following the same line of reasoning, the Committee advocate more flexible teaching arrangements than were possible when children were confined to traditional-type box classrooms; for instance, the use of corridors and foyers where 'room for individual work' can be found; permitting pupils to visit other classrooms to use particular equipment or resources 'or consult a teacher who has the particular knowledge that they need'; two teachers working in tandem and so able 'to do more for children individually'; linked classrooms with shared facilities 'and quiet individual working spaces' (761-8). The trend of the report on the application of theory to practice is clear: structures and methodologies must be flexible to allow scope for that 'wide variability' in individual development seen as a main characteristic of young children.

Classroom organization

How, then should the classroom be organized? The Plowden Committee devote one section of their report to this question ('Developments in the Class Teacher System', Chapter 20) but before turning to this we may briefly consider certain wider, but closely related, questions concerning organization. Each teacher must decide, for instance (perhaps in consultation with the head), how the curriculum will be organized, what it should consist of, how much time will be allocated to each activity, or, where the responsibility for organizing their own learning is placed on the pupils, how this will be managed. This basically concerns timetabling matters, or whatever system takes its place (for instance, when subjects are 'integrated' or block periods allocated in place of the strict timetabling of the past). Second, the teacher is responsible for the layout and organization of the classroom itself, the physical environment; where the children will sit, whether in groups or not and, if so, how many groups of what precise size and composition, and how these will be arranged. Third, there is the complex question of the organization of materials — books, work-cards, paper, paints — where the arrangements need to be both practical and economic from the standpoint of use. Finally the teacher has to decide how she will divide her attention among the pupils in her class; whether she proposes to teach the class as a whole, as a number of groups, or as individuals; or, if she proposes to combine all these approaches, in what proportions.

All these areas of decision, of course, are closely linked, but it is arguable that the last is the most important, since this provides the setting for interaction between teacher and pupils which is commonly held to lie at the heart of the educational process, and to a large extent, to determine its pattern and character. It is on this latter aspect of classroom organization that the Plowden Committee concentrate in their chapter on the topic.

How, then, should the classroom be organized in this sense? The section starts with the uncompromising statement that 'there has always been much class instruction and we believe there is still too much' (753). Schools have provided 'far more individual work' over the last twenty years, as they have increasingly realized 'how much children of the same age differ in their powers of perception and imagery, in their interests, and in their span of concentration' (754). Thus teaching 'must often be individual though other children will look on and often learn in looking'. It seems from this and other formulations that, although the Plowden Committee never make explicit the distinction between *individual work* (whereby the child works on his own individualized task) and *individual attention* (whereby the teacher focuses her attention on individual children rather than the class as a whole) they favour the use of *both* these approaches simultaneously. Individualization is the key to effective learning — and, so, to effective teaching. This is the central message of the Plowden Report as a whole, tying in closely with its theoretical stance.

But the Committee recognize that there is a real, and practical, difficulty here. If *all* teaching were on an individual, one-to-one basis, only some seven to eight minutes a day would be available for each child. Teachers are, therefore, advised to economize 'by teaching together a small group of children who are roughly at the same stage'. Even here, the Committee add, 'ideally, they might be better taught individually', but 'they will gain more from a longer period of their

46

teacher's attention, even if it is shared with others, than they would from a few minutes of individual help' (755). This, then, is one rationale offered for organizing group work in primary school classrooms; that it is an effective expedient in default of the possibility of total individualization. Where such grouping is utilized, the Committee strongly oppose the formation of stable groups based on ability; that is, streaming within the class. Groups should be based sometimes on interest, and sometimes on achievement, 'but they should change in accordance with the children's needs' (824). In other words the class must be flexibly organized, groups forming and re-forming related to children's involvement in the topic studied or activity being carried on.

Group work is further commended for another set of reasons. Children of junior age, it is held, 'tend naturally to go about in small groups'. Such groups (of from three to fifteen pupils) 'are good for many kinds of school work'. They fulfil a socialization function: 'in this way children learn to get along together, help one another and realize their own strengths and weaknesses as well as those of others'. They fulfil a pedagogic function: children 'make their meaning clearer to themselves by having to explain it to others, and gain some opportunity to teach as well as to learn'. Timid children, it is held, need to hear others put questions they are unable to frame; apathetic children 'may be infected by the enthusiasm of a group while able children benefit from being caught up in the thrust and counter thrust of conversation in a small group of children similar to themselves' (757).

This latter point is developed in relation to the learning of science and mathematics, where small group work provides the chance of discussion, of putting forward hypotheses. A class or group interest providing a focus for activity of this kind 'depends for its value', it is said, 'on the children being absorbed in it and the teacher giving it skilful guidance' (759). Some types of group work are too ambitious: success depends on the teacher's skill in knowing 'when to drop a topic, when to intervene, to sustain or reinforce the interest of an individual, a group, or occasionally a whole class' (760).

To take up this latter point; while the Plowden Report clearly and definitely places its main stress on individualization (though recognizing the necessity, and educational advantages, of co-operative group work), and in spite of the opening sentence warning against an excess of whole class instruction, the Report is quite positive that, on specific occasions, class teaching may be desirable; for instance, when 'a topic for group or individual work is introduced to the whole class which is again brought together for discussion and instruction as the work develops'. Such procedures are 'sensible', and 'help to make the whole class a unity'.

47

There are they say, 'no infallible rules' determining when class teaching may be desirable (756).

What is proposed, then, is a combination of individual, group and class work; a highly complex, dynamic 'system' which permits, and in fact specifically encourages, differentiated treatment for individual children. This is summarized in a statement of aims (505).

> The school sets out deliberately to devise the right environment for children, to allow them to be themselves and to develop in the way and at the pace appropriate for them. It tries to equalize opportunities and to compensate for handicaps. It lays special stress on individual discovery, on first hand experience and on opportunities for creative work.

This latter point, the stress on 'individual discovery', which relates directly to the earlier emphasis on the child's inborn drive for 'exploration of the environment', is an important factor underlying the Committee's concept of the teacher's role.

The role of the teacher

The teacher's role in relation to this process of individualization is clearly stated, and is seen as a complex one. Teachers must rely both on their general knowledge of child development, 'and on detailed observation of individual children' for 'matching their demands to children's stages of development' (a precept that both Montessori and Piaget would approve) (534). Above all, the teacher must adopt 'a consultative, guiding, stimulating role rather than a purely didactic one' (540). The Committee pick out specifically for approval a statement in an HMI report that: 'the teacher has to be prepared to follow up the personal interests of the children who, either singly or in groups, follow divergent paths of discovery' (544); indeed the teacher is responsible 'for encouraging the children in enquiries which lead to discovery and for asking leading questions' (549). The curriculum, or forms of activity undertaken, should be enquiry-based. 'We endorse the trend towards individual and "active" learning and "learning by acquaintance" ', the Committee conclude, 'and should like many more schools to be more deeply influenced by it' (553).

These quotations are taken from Chapter 16 (entitled 'Children Learning in Schools') which sets out a rationale avowedly based on Piaget's theories (see paragraph 521), although also acknowledging the influence of Luria, Bruner and other psychologists. Learning is seen as taking place 'through a continuous process of interaction between the learner and his environment', resulting in 'the building up of consistent and stable patterns of behaviour, physical and mental'. Each new experience 'reorganizes, however slightly, the structure of the mind and contributes to the child's world picture' (521). The child, it is argued in a key phrase, 'is the agent of his own learning' (529). Activity and experience 'are often the best means of gaining knowledge and acquiring facts' (529). A main educational task of the primary school is 'to build on and strengthen children's intrinsic interest in learning and lead them to learn for themselves rather than from fear of disapproval or desire for praise' (532).

Hence the emphasis on the guidance, the stimulation of the child by the teacher in place of her traditional didactic role which, it is held, can inhibit children from learning (531). In a short summarizing section on 'The Role of the Teacher' (873-8) the Committee acknowledge the complexity and variety of the demands now made deriving from this theoretical outlook. This stresses the importance of diagnosing 'children's needs and potentialities', assessing individual differences, challenging and inspiring the complacent, forcing independence on the dependent. It is the teacher's responsibility 'to select an environment which will encourage curiosity', to focus the child's attention on enquiries 'which will lead to useful discovery', to 'collaborate' with children; in short, as the Committee put it, 'to lead from behind'. Generously enough the Committee acknowledge that, given their interpretation as to how children learn, the demands on teachers appear 'frighteningly high' (875).

If we attempt, then, a general sketch of the ideal Plowden-type teacher and her class, we get something like this. The children are active, engaged in exploration or discovery, interacting both with the teacher and with each other. Each child operates as an individual, though groups are formed and re-formed related to those activities which are not normally subject differentiated. The teacher moves around the classroom, consulting, guiding, stimulating individual children or occasionally, for convenience, the groups of children which are brought together for some specific activity, or are 'at the same stage'. She knows each child individually, and how best to stimulate or intervene with each. In this activity she bears in mind the child's intellectual, social and physical levels of development and monitors these. On occasions the whole class is brought together, for instance for a story or music, or to spark off or finalize a class project; otherwise class teaching is seldom used, the pupils' work and the teacher's attention being individualized or 'grouped'.

49

emphasis on Individual work in 1980.
now 'class work' 2002.

The teacher who attempted to translate these Plowden prescriptions into practice by organizing her class in this way, and who wished to monitor the extent to which her practice measured up to the criteria suggested, might be led to ask herself a number of questions about the children's activities and about her own activity as a teacher. How much individual attention, for instance, does she give to each child in her class over a period of time; in a single session, during a day, or over a full week? How is her time distributed between slow learning children with particular learning difficulties on the one hand, and 'advanced', bright or aggressive children on the other − does one of these groups gain a disproportionate amount of her time, and what, in any case, would be the correct proportions? What about the children 'in the middle' of the spectrum, those who work quietly on their own and make few demands on her; do they get a fair (or equal?) proportion of her attention?

Again, how far is she utilizing group work, and how is this activity structured? Are the topics (or tasks) which the groups undertake of a kind to encourage 'creative work' or to promote 'discovery' (i.e. are they problem focused)? Do they lead to the formulation and testing of hypotheses and the 'thrust and counter thrust' of debate? And on what basis or principle are her classroom groups formed? Do they (should they?) include both advanced and slow learning children? Do they (should they?) include both sexes? Are the groups fulfilling both a socialization and a pedagogic function; that is, are they leading to greater understanding and tolerance of each other's idiosyncracies, and providing opportunities to learn from explaining to others? Are the children gaining intellectually in the context of group activities? Are the groups too fixed and stable, in terms of the Plowden prescriptions, or do they form and reform as appropriate to the content of the central activity and pupil interests? Then as regards whole class teaching − how far is her use of it justified? Should she reduce this still further, and, if so, for what activities or subject areas is it appropriate?

These are only some of the questions a junior school teacher, concerned to implement the Plowden prescriptions, might be expected to ask herself (if she can find the time!). But of course there are many others, particularly those relating to the level of development of each individual child and the appropriateness, or otherwise, of the forms of activity on which each child in her class is engaged. With a class of thirty or more children, each having different developmental levels on three dimensions, intellectual, emotional, physical (as the report puts it), the complexity of the questioning possible arising from the Plowden prescriptions can be seen to be almost infinite; yet the effectiveness of the teacher's intervention or guidance, as discussed earlier, depends, in this view, on the teacher's deep knowledge of individual children and the dynamics of their inner development.

It is questions of this kind that arise from the Plowden perspectives. In drawing out their complexity we do not necessarily imply any criticism of the practices recommended; our aim is simply to clarify the implications of these prescriptions for the class teacher. Many other related questions of course, arise, for instance, relating to the curriculum − its balance and appropriateness − to the means of evaluating and recording children's activities and development, and so on. All these issues, concerned with the organization of teaching as well as its dynamics, relate to the teacher's management function as a class teacher, responsible for the smooth and orderly running of her class. To this complex issue, hardly referred to as such by the Plowden Committee, we may now turn.

Classroom practice: the teacher's management function in historical perspective

As the Plowden Committee themselves suggest, the stance of their report both reflected and took further what was clearly recognized as a definite, long-term, secular *trend* within primary schools themselves, both infant and junior. 'We endorse the trend towards individual and "active" learning', they state, as quoted earlier, 'and should like many more schools to be influenced by it.' This long-term movement has already been discussed, if briefly, in the last chapter, and the Committee themselves make a short analysis of it (Chapter 16) where they specifically note that Piagetian theory most closely 'fits', or 'matches' this movement (towards individualization and active learning).

Even if subject to what was earlier described as external ('peripheral' or theoretical) influences, actual classroom practice develops empirically − on the ground. This is recognized by the Committee, who themselves suggest that the 'trend' towards individualization and flexibility (as opposed to class teaching as the norm) developed at least to some extent autonomously. Even if teachers (and students) had available to them the works of Froebel, Montessori, Dewey and others, these, they claim, can hardly be regarded as directly influential since neither teachers nor students studied them (510). While this seems to underestimate the influence of college lecturers, advisers, and HMIs, all of whom clearly influenced developments in the 1950s and 1960s, the move towards what may generally be called 'informal' practices

51

probably had some other motivation. It may be important to tease this out. And this brings attention to what may be an important factor in determining contemporary educational practice; that is, the teacher's managerial function, and the constraints within which it operates.

Ever since the development of class teaching, which only became the norm in any type of school in England some 100 years ago (when it was known as the 'Prussian' system), the single class teacher has had sole responsibility for organizing and controlling the activities of a large number of (young) children within the confines of a relatively small space (the four walls of the classroom). Indeed, class teaching was and could only be adopted when at least two main conditions were met. First, when there were sufficient children in the normal school to allow them to be categorized or grouped in separate classes according to some principle of differentiation, and second, when there were sufficient trained and experienced teachers able to cope satisfactorily with up to sixty or eighty (even 100) children in the single, separated classrooms. The earlier system, from which class teaching developed, involved a single teaching space (or hall), allowing the head to supervise all activities in the school directly, including those of the pupil-teachers and uncertified (and so unqualified) teachers who then formed the bulk of the staff in elementary schools.

Class teaching, as was very clearly recognized at the time, involved specific skills relating to classroom management; indeed the success of the whole enterprise depended effectively on this; particularly, in the circumstances of the time, on the maintenance of strict teacher control over all movements of the pupils (whose role, for their part, was that of immediate obedience to the teacher's commands). Manuals for students training as teachers in the 1880s and 1890s, and later, specifically and understandably stress these control aspects of the teacher's function,[2] as did earlier books, for instance David Stow's famous *The Training System* (1836) where the theory of 'simultaneous' teaching through the 'gallery' system was originally expounded. Apart from concentration on such matters as entering and leaving the classroom, the start and finish of written work, and indeed all points at which disorder or confusion might break out, the whole methodology of teaching originally advocated by Stow, and certainly implemented in elementary school classrooms in the nineteenth century, was worked out with an eye to the disciplinary, or control function, of the teacher (specifically the techniques of questioning and answering elaborated with the intention of ensuring that *all* pupils focused their attention on the teacher and his or her activity).

It is suggested that any interpretation of what happens in the primary

school classroom today must take account of its own empirical development over time; and that, in interpreting this development, particular
attention should be paid to the teacher's management function in the
sense described above. The average size of a primary class today is still
over thirty; some are less, but as many as 45 per cent are above thirty
and some still exceed forty (DES, 1977). Although more space per
child is now provided than was the case in the past the fact remains
that, as Philip Jackson has pointed out (Jackson, 1968) primary (or
'elementary') school classrooms contain a higher concentration of
human beings in a small space over long periods of time than is the case
with any other social activity. To ensure the smooth and orderly
functioning of a dynamic group of young children is a highly skilled
task. Understanding of the nature of the activities, interactions and
relationships in such classrooms must take the teacher's managerial
function into account.

Put in another way, the primary classroom (as the school itself)
can be seen as a social institution, one which, though certainly subject
to external influences, has also its own specific and continuous 'inner'
historical development. Further, in spite of the considerable resources
devoted to building new schools in the period following the Second
World War, nearly a quarter of all primary schools have operated in
the same buildings for seventy-five years or more (DES, 1978). Some
of their staff (particularly heads) may have held their posts over a long
period. It should not be surprising, therefore, to find in some such
schools vestiges of practices relating more closely to the techniques and
outlook of say fifty years ago, than to those of the Plowden ideal-type
teacher of today. Indeed, as with every educational institution, contemporary practice embodies an amalgam of procedures brought in, or
modified, as a result of changing circumstances at different historical
periods, practices which tend to be tenacious. Concern with the management function of the class teacher has necessarily been a common
factor through all changes the schools have experienced, even if it has
expressed itself differently at different times, and in different
circumstances.

Classroom practice: the teacher's management function today

How, then, do we interpret, or account for, those new developments in
primary school practice with which the Plowden Committee so closely
associated itself; given that these developments were partially, at least,
'autonomous' as we saw earlier? Clearly the factors already mentioned

(in the last chapter) have some importance (progressive education as the 'orthodoxy' by 1939, evacuation experiences, the upward movement of infant school procedures, etc.). However, it may do no harm to examine this development in terms of the evolution of appropriate managerial techniques in the new conditions following comprehensive secondary education, and the concomitant move in the junior schools to unstreaming.

This was very much a teachers' movement, in its inception, at least. It was not promoted by any authority, whether the DES, HMIs, or even local authorities (although some did begin to give official support and encouragement once the movement had got under way in their schools). If this transition was legitimized, in the eyes of some teachers, on strictly educational grounds, it also had the function of easing the teacher's (and the school's) management function, since, as was well understood at the time, it tended to obviate centres of disaffection and alienation with attendant disciplinary problems associated with the C and D streams in large urban and suburban primary schools (by the same token it was also seen as tending to equalize disciplinary problems among the school's staff as a whole).

Where the head, or school staff, took the decision deliberately to unstream a junior school, a variety of options were open as to the new forms of class organization and procedures to be adopted. One possible solution was the retention of class teaching as the norm in the non-streamed situation, a solution certainly found in the Soviet Union and eastern Europe (and, to a large extent, in western Europe and the USA). This is a complex issue, but it seems that, in spite of some exceptions, this option was not open to teachers in any real sense in this country, and this both for theoretical and practical reasons: theoretical, since the concept of the overriding importance of *individual* differences had been hammered home insistently from the 1920s (the rationale even for streaming was, paradoxically, precisely this), and practical, because teachers, habituated to the class teaching of homogeneous groups under streaming, had not developed the specific expertise required to teach unstreamed classes as a unit. Hence, although some schools did try this option (Freeland, 1957), the mass of primary school teachers never really considered it.

The second option was that of complete individualization; a system based primarily on the work-card and 'assignment' technique already widely utilized in primary schools, particularly for the basic subjects, number and reading. This appeared to allow a systematic approach while also solving management problems provided that the system was understood by the children, and continuity assured. Here 'peripheral' or external influences may also have been important in that indivi-dualization matched 'progressive' ideas of the kind the Plowden Committee itself espoused (but also given expression in the two Consultative Committee reports of 1931 and 1933) in that it seemed to permit each child 'to go at his own pace'. It is probable that this option was widely implemented.

The third, and clearly the most popular, option as unstreaming spread comprised individualization together with the use of grouping within the class. This solution, that of grouping, was already embodied in primary school practice, in particular as' a technique for teaching reading, but also for other more informal activities; indeed the use of grouping had been a specific feature of the Sub Dalton Plan referred to earlier, widely utilized in elementary schools in the late 1920s and early 1930s. But a further, perhaps more long-lived and more important use of grouping, had been the use made of it in rural schools where, of necessity, one or more age groups, each at different stages, had to be taught by one teacher (the origin, also of vertical grouping, another managerial ploy developed first as a means of solving a practical prob-lem before legitimization in theory).

This option, individualization together with grouping plus some class teaching, provided a rational means of controlling (or managing) the independent activities of some thirty plus children. If the pupils are seated in five or six groups each comprising from four to eight pupils, the teacher is able to build a clear geographical (and social) structure into a class whose activities, if allowed at least a degree of autonomy (or choice), would otherwise be too complex to grasp, let alone control (with the educative aim expected of the teacher).

It is suggested that this may be one reason why the Plowden Committee found that the highest proportion of the sample of primary teachers surveyed (by questionnaire) approved of giving more time to 'group' teaching than to either class instruction or individual work, though the latter was also strongly supported (Plowden, II, p. 27). From this (and other information) the Committee concluded that Piaget's theory (and outlook) seemed most closely to 'match' what they saw as empirical developments in the English primary school classroom. Although group teaching was favoured, observational studies (though on a small scale) have since shown that, although *seated* in groups, most children work on their own, diverse, individual tasks. It is this which matches so closely (even if only in a formal sense) Piaget's emphasis on the uniqueness of development of each individual child; at least, as interpreted by the Plowden Committee.

The fact that the only systematic surveys of teachers' classroom practice carried through in the early 1970s have clearly shown that, with the move to so-called 'informal' methods of organization, teachers in general keep a tight control of children's activities in the junior school classroom, appears to lend weight to the view here presented. Thus Bealing found, in a survey of classrooms in the Midlands, that despite the 'relatively informal classroom layouts adopted by the vast majority of teachers' there was 'so much evidence of tight teacher control over such matters as where children sit and move' that it seems 'highly doubtful that there is much opportunity for children to choose or organize their own activities in most classrooms'. This, she held, questions 'widely held beliefs about the "primary school revolution" ' (Bealing, 1972). Moran, who studied teachers implementing the 'integrated day' techniques, generally regarded as highly permissive, found much the same thing (Moran, 1971).

The contemporary critique of primary education

It is, of course, the case that the Plowden analysis and prescriptions have been subjected to criticism and are now regarded as controversial. In 1969 *Perspectives on Plowden*, edited by Richard Peters, and containing a set of critical articles by Professors Bernstein, Foss, Peters and others, challenged the theoretical analysis made by the Committee and subjected it to a stringent criticism. This critique, in particular, focused on the interpretation of the inborn 'nature' of the child as essentially enquiring, the grounds on which the Plowden Committee recommended enquiry-based discovery learning as the main mode of teaching. Further, as is well known, the whole 'trend' with which the Plowden Committee so overtly associated itself, towards giving increased responsibility to pupils and generally towards 'informal' and 'flexible' approaches, came in for sharp attack, as we have already seen, in the first Black Paper (1969), which saw this movement as underlying, and therefore to an extent responsible for, the student unrest which characterized that period. Further 'cause for concern' resulted from developments in the notorious Tyndale school affair, where a group of teachers (who claimed ideological support from Plowden) seemed to many to carry the cry for flexibility and lack of structure to extremes; an issue taken up in a very big way by the mass media, leading to enhanced criticism of teachers, and of primary school teachers in particular. The movement of criticism of what may be called the Plowden 'trend' (which took little account of the Report itself) reached a climax with the mass media presentation of the 'Bennett report', which claimed that 'formal' teachers obtained better results, in terms of traditional tests, than 'informal'; though the most successful teacher turned out to be one who organized her class on so-called 'informal' lines. Succeeding Black Papers fuelled this movement, which reached the proportions of a national political issue by the autumn of 1976 with Prime Minister Callaghan's speech in which he referred specifically to the dangers of carrying 'informal' techniques too far in the primary schools, issuing a call for concentration on literacy and numeracy. It was in this context that the present research project was, in fact, launched in October 1975, though planned in the year before. Since then the HMI survey, *Primary Education in England*, has been published (October 1978) which, in general, allayed many of these fears and indeed criticized teachers from the opposite angle; that the real danger was too exclusive a concentration on 'the basics'.

The HMI survey contains much interesting material. It was not, however, based on systematic classroom observation — rather on material and impressions derived from visits to sample schools and on questionnaire material gained from a random sample of all primary schools in the country. The survey set out to make a general assessment of the state of primary education as a whole, dealing with the curriculum, the ethos and organization of the schools, and like matters. The study reported in this volume, however, has a different and more specific focus. For one thing it does not (and in the circumstances could not) set out to be representative of primary classrooms as a whole. Because of the restraints of research design, it focuses only on the fifty-eight classrooms which form part of the study, located in three local authority areas. But, so far as this volume is concerned, it sets out to describe and analyse the inner dynamics of these classrooms. Utilizing the procedure of systematic observation, its aim is to discover precisely what is happening in these classrooms, without reference to the rhetoric either of 'progressive' or 'traditional' prescriptions as to what should happen; and certainly avoiding the impressionistic and highly subjective accounts of 'advanced' practice produced, and widely publicized, by educationists and journalists from the USA, for whom the 'English primary school' is part of the American history of education rather than the English. Nevertheless it certainly is the case that the structural and organizational developments within English primary schools over the last fifty years or so remain unique. In no other country has the 'trend' with which Plowden associated itself been so marked. It remains a fact that many educationists both from the USA and European countries regard this movement with respect and, to some extent, envy (Gruber, 1977). It is certainly worthy of serious study and research, however controversial it may be. As regards its practice, the Plowden Report still remains the most authoritative prescriptive document to hand. In the next two chapters, giving the results of our investigations concerning 'process' (or the dynamics of the primary classroom), we examine how far the Plowden prescriptions are actually carried out in the classrooms observed.

CHAPTER 4

Teachers and pupils in the junior school classroom (1)

The junior school classroom: an overview

If we open the door into a junior school classroom, what do we see? At first glance the chief impression may be of 'busyness', or activity. The children, typically about thirty, are seated in groups around flat-topped tables or desks drawn together to form working surfaces; some are talking intermittently to each other as they get on with their work, whatever its nature. One or two of them will be mobile; that is, moving round the classroom to use the pencil sharpener, collect some paper for drawing or writing, talk to a child in another group, and so on. This movement, together with the slight hubbub made by the children in the different groups will give the visitor the general idea of an active, perhaps fairly noisy classroom (compared with those of the past) with a good deal of movement by individual pupils.

If the visitor then focuses his attention on the teacher, she will normally be seen moving about the room, talking first to one then another group of children, or to an individual child within one of these groups. She may stop to help a child with a problem, ask another how it is getting on, tell another how to spell a word, possibly check another for disruptive (antisocial) behaviour; all the time unobtrusively monitoring the activity of the class as a whole, perhaps keeping her eye on the clock, and occasionally making a 'routine' announcement, for instance, warning the class to finish what they are doing and put their work away as break time is approaching. On other occasions the teacher may be seated at her desk or table where a queue has formed with work to be marked or evaluated. In either case she is fully involved in the

59

situation. If we take the 'typical' teacher from our study (that is, the mean, or average, of all observations of all teachers), we find she spends most of her time in a teaching session interacting with her pupils. Most of this interaction is with individual pupils, some with groups of pupils, the rest with the class as a whole. Hers is a life, while teaching, of considerable activity, and direct involvement with her pupils.

This is the immediate or surface impression that may be given; but if the visitor stays a little longer, with the aim of penetrating more deeply into what is happening, and if, to do this, he focuses his attention on a number of individual pupils in succession (as our observers did), a rather different picture begins to emerge. To provide an 'overview' a description will be given of the 'typical' child's behaviour as derived from all observations of individual children over the year covered in this study.*

In spite of the general air of talk and movement, the visitor would now find that the 'typical' pupil spends nearly two-thirds of his time working on his own, individualized task, in isolation, interacting neither with his teacher, nor with other pupils. For the rest of the time he is either talking with one or other members of his group (or possibly with pupils based in another group) or he is in some sort of contact with his teacher. Thus so far as individual children are concerned, the general impression of 'activity' needs to be modified. Because a classroom contains a large number of children in a relatively small space, the fact that *some* of them are 'active' or 'mobile' at any one time contributes to a general impression which is, to some extent, illusory. On the whole, in a normal lesson session, the children are sitting in their places for most of the time getting on with the task in hand.

(i) Teacher-pupil interaction

This points to one striking feature of the junior school classroom which emerges very clearly from analysis of our data. This is the 'asymmetry' of teacher-pupil interaction; the fact that, while the 'typical' teacher spends most of the lesson time interacting with pupils (either individually, as a member of a group, or of the class), each *individual* pupil, by contrast, interacts with the teacher for only a small proportion of his time. And most of that interaction is experienced by the pupil when the teacher is addressing the whole class. The key facts here are set out in Table 4.1, derived from both the Pupil and the Teacher Records.

This table confirms the point already made; while the teacher is

---

* The aggregated figures for both the Pupil and the Teacher Records are given in Appendix 3, pp. 181-2.

interacting with pupils for most of a teaching session, the individual pupil interacts with the teacher for only a small proportion of this time. In a one-hour session, this latter figure (15.8 per cent) amounts to a total of nine minutes, twenty-nine seconds. Table 4.1 also confirms the supposition that the bulk of this interaction is experienced by the child when the teacher is addressing the class as a whole, even though she does this relatively seldom as the Teacher Record shows.[1]

Table 4.1   Forms of pupil-teacher interaction[a] (Pupil and Teacher Records), 1 (percentage of total observations)[b]

Teacher interacts with	Pupil Record	Teacher Record
Individuals	2.3	55.8
Groups	1.5	7.5
Whole class	12.0	15.1
Total interaction	15.8	78.4
No interaction	84.2	21.6
	100.0	100.0

a The Pupil Record data in Table 4.1 is derived from analysis of the pupil-adult categories. The great bulk of pupil-adult interactions are with the class teacher (see Table 1.2, p. 17).

b In tables giving percentages of observations, Ns are not given. See Appendix 2B for an important note concerning the interpretation of the tables and the use of tests of statistical significance. In all tables percentages have been rounded and do not necessarily total to 100, but by convention they are recorded as such.

What is striking is the very small amount of *individual attention* of what might be called the Plowden-type the teacher can give to pupils in a 'typical' teaching session. The 2.3 per cent recorded in Table 4.1 amounts to only one minute and twenty-three seconds in a one-hour session. This is clearly very small, even with the addition of the fifty-four seconds attention each hour (1.5 per cent) which the pupil receives as a member of a group; an approach specifically recommended, it will be remembered in the Plowden Report as a substitute for the more favoured total individualization of the teaching-learning process.

The 'asymmetry' of the interaction process is brought out more sharply if, instead of presenting the data as percentages of *total observations*, it is presented as percentages of *total teacher-pupil interaction*. To do this we exclude from the analysis of both records the time when no such interaction is taking place (most of the time as far as individual pupils are concerned).

Table 4.2   Forms of pupil-teacher interaction (Pupil and Teacher Records), 2 (percentage of total pupil-teacher interaction)

Teacher interacts with	Pupil Record	Teacher Record
Individuals	14.6	71.6
Groups	9.4	9.4
Whole class	75.9	19.3
	100.0	100.0

The distinction between the teacher's and the pupil's interaction patterns are now clearly apparent. The great bulk of the teacher's contacts are with *individual* pupils. By contrast, the bulk of the pupil's interaction with the teacher is as a member of the whole class. Only a small proportion of such interactions are experienced by the pupil *as an individual*. This is the first striking finding of our study.

(ii) Time on task

If our visitor, having taken in the general scene, was interested in the amount of actual 'task work' that was being done in the classroom, and was able to observe the pupils closely enough to pick this up (as we were), what would he find?

Although he would see a good deal of talk and movement, as already indicated, close observation of individual pupils would show that, on average, pupils concentrate on the job in hand for about three-fifths of the whole teaching session. For most of this time the 'typical' pupil is working on his own, but for some of it he is listening to, or (much less often) talking with the teacher. For a smaller proportion of time he is talking with other pupils. Table 4.3 sets out this general pattern, breaking down the interaction patterns under two headings, (i) when the pupil is fully involved in working on his task ('task related'), and (ii) when he is engaged in some other activity ('non-task related').

Table 4.3   Interaction and task activity (Pupil Record) (percentage of total observations)

	Task related	Non-task related	Total
No interaction	40.5	25.1	65.6
Interaction with teacher	12.4	3.4	15.8
Interaction with other pupils	5.2	13.4	18.6
Total	58.1	41.9	100.0

It would be wrong to jump to the conclusion, from the data in Table 4.3, that the proportion of time the 'typical' pupil spends not actually working on his task is 'wasted' time in the ordinary sense of the word. The sub-category 'co-operating on task' (i.e. 'task related') was only coded when the target pupil was 'fully involved' in what he was 'allowed' or 'supposed' to be doing, whether theoretical or practical (for instance, reading, writing, drawing, modelling, and so on). If interacting with another pupil, this category was coded only if that interaction was specifically on the given task, for instance, a discussion about the best way to assemble apparatus for a joint activity. In the same way, as regards interaction with the teacher, co-operating on task was coded only when the pupil initiated, contributed to or fully attended to any conversation (or silent interaction) about his task, for instance, listened when the teacher explained to his group how to start work on the next topic. Such activities comprised 58.1 per cent of the 'typical' pupil's time (Table 4.3). But the pupil may also be engaged on 'routine' activities under the teacher's direction; that is, on matters involving the maintenance of suitable physical conditions in the classroom, preparations for task work, discussions about materials, and so on — activities auxiliary to carrying out the task work effectively. Again, he may be waiting for the teacher to check over or mark his work. If the time spent in these ways is added to the time spent fully involved in the task in hand, the proportion of time the 'typical' pupil spends actively engaged rises from 58.1 per cent to 74.3 per cent.*

Hence the general air of 'busyness' or 'involvement' the visitor notices on entering the normal junior school classroom. The children *are* talking to each other for some of the time (about one-fifth in the case of the 'typical' child in our study, see Table 4.3); and it is the case that, while some of this talk is about the individual pupil's task work, most is not. On the other hand, as might be expected, most of the pupil's interaction with *the teacher* is about the task in hand, though some is not. For most of the time the pupil is on his own; and for most of this time he is fully involved in his task.

So far we have focused on giving an overview of the typical junior school classroom in our study, inevitably drawing attention to certain features rather than others. Such classrooms, or rather the relationships between pupils and between pupils and teachers within them, are both dynamic and complex. In the rest of this chapter we will explore

---

* The Pupil Record codes summed here include (i) Coop Task (58.1 per cent) (ii) Coop Routine (11.9 per cent) (iii) wait teacher (4.3 per cent). A detailed analysis of the 'typical' pupil's behaviour on these lines is given in Chapter 5.

certain features of the processes of interaction within these classrooms in a systematic manner, starting with a key issue, the distribution of the teacher's attention between members of her class.

Individual attention

Our visitor, sitting in a junior school classroom, watching the teacher moving from group to group, individual to individual, would certainly get the impression that the teacher has individual contact with many members of the class in a normal teaching session; but are there any groups of children who miss out on this? Does the teacher, for instance, focus, perhaps unwittingly, on the more backward pupils who are likely to have learning difficulties, and therefore specifically to need assistance in organizing their own learning? Or on the more advanced who, pressing ahead, may make extra demands on her compared with the rest of the class? Or does she, again perhaps unwittingly, focus more on the girls than the boys, or vice versa, or on older children compared to younger? Some studies of classrooms have suggested that this is so; for example Garner and Bing, in their study of first year junior classes (1973), found that teachers gave more attention to active hardworkers and active miscreants than others, who received less of the teachers' attention. What, then, is the position in the classrooms observed in our study?

Analysis in terms of groups of pupils differentiated by achievement may be made from our data. As explained in Chapter 1, when the sample of eight children in each class was initially selected, the sampling procedure involved dividing children in each class into high, medium and low achievers on the basis of standardized tests. This ensured that the achievement range *in each class* was represented in the sample. High achievers were those in the top quarter of the class on the achievement tests, low achievers were those in the bottom quarter and medium achievers the rest. Two high, two low and four medium achievers were chosen from each class randomly selected from the relevant groups, the sexes being equally split at each level.[2]

The amount and character of teacher attention devoted to each of these three main groups of pupils is given in Table 4.4.

This shows (in row 1) that there is, in fact, very little difference in the distribution of teacher-pupil interaction between the three groups of pupils; over-all, it is almost identical. There is no evidence here that there is any discrimination either in favour or against any particular group of pupils according to their achievement level.

Table 4.4   Achievement and teacher-pupil interaction (Pupil Record)
(percentage of total observations)

	High achievers	Medium achievers	Low achievers
1 All teacher-pupil interactions	15.9	16.0	15.6[a]
1a Individual interaction	2.1	2.1	2.7
1b Interaction as member of a group	1.9	1.5	1.3
1c Interaction as class member	11.6	12.0	11.5
1d 'Other'[b]	0.3	0.4	0.1
2a Interaction on task work	13.1	13.4	12.8
2b Interaction other than on task	2.8	2.6	2.8
N =	118	254	117

a $p < 0.05$.
b   This sub-category was used when the teacher ignored a pupil's attempt to initiate interaction.

Some minor differences are, however, apparent, and they are worth drawing attention to. For instance, the group of low achievers do receive rather more *individual* attention than the other two groups (row 1a); the high achievers rather more attention as members of a group (row 1b), while the medium achievers receive rather more attention than the others as members of the class as a whole. The differences are small, and, with one exception, do not reach statistical significance; nevertheless they may point to slight differentiations in the form of teacher-pupil interaction. We see also (row 2a) that, in general, the same proportion of teacher-pupil interaction is concerned with task work for all three groups, although in the case of low achievers this is marginally less.

Generally speaking, then, the main conclusion from this analysis is that, while the weaker pupils are more likely to be helped individually than the other two groups, the teacher's attention is equally divided between all three achievement groups. No single group is either favoured or discriminated against.[3]

The second area of interest is that of sex; do teachers tend to have more contact with one sex rather than the other? The data are presented in Table 4.5.

Here again over-all interaction is shown to be very similar, with a slight (but statistically non-significant, $p > 0.05$) tendency for boys to receive more attention than girls both in total, and at each of the different levels (individual, group, class). Analysis as to whether the sex of the teacher affects interaction patterns across the sexes indicates that no such differences are shown.

Table 4.5   Sex differences and teacher-pupil interaction (Pupil Record) (percentage of total observations)

		Boys	Girls
1	All teacher-pupil interactions	16.5	15.3
	1a Individual interaction	2.4	2.1
	1b Interaction as member of a group	1.6	1.4
	1c Interaction as class member	12.0	11.7
	1d 'Other'	0.5	0.1
2a	Interaction on task work	13.6	12.8
2b	Interaction other than on task	2.9	2.5
	N =	245	244

Generally, then, there is little difference in the distribution of teacher attention across the class either according to achievement levels or to sex differences, with the proviso that there does appear to be a slight tendency for low achievers to receive more individual attention and for boys to receive more contact than girls. A third possibility is that a child's age within the class may have an effect on the amount of attention he receives. Even in a class containing a single year group children may differ in ages by up to twelve months, a substantial amount at this age. Here, for purposes of economy of presentation, the conclusions from the data analysis are given in terms of correlation coefficients. The correlation between age within the class and the amount of teacher attention received is 0.02, that between age within the class and the number of teacher interactions initiated by the pupil is 0.04, and between age and the number of interactions initiated by the teacher, 0.05. These correlations, all well below 0.1, mean that older children within the age groups are no more likely to receive the teacher's attention than the younger children in the class. Furthermore the older children are no more likely to seek out the teacher's attention or be sought out by the teacher than the younger ones. The obverse, of course, also applies.

In all three areas of analysis, then, we find that, on average, teachers distribute their attention across the class roughly equally. This is an important finding.

One factor which does appear to influence how much individual attention the individual child receives is, not surprisingly, the size of the class he is in. Here the average figures presented earlier (Tables 4.1, 4.2 and 4.3) conceal important variations. We would expect children in smaller classes to receive more individual attention than children in larger classes, and the data show this is so. There is a negative correlation between the size of the class and the average amount of pupil interaction with the teacher, amounting to -0.27. In plain words, the larger the class, the less teacher attention each individual child receives. We find also that, in larger classes there are more times when the teacher is not available to individual pupils needing help; there is a positive correlation between class size and the amount of time the pupils spend waiting for the teacher (+0.25).

Nevertheless, considering the wide range of class sizes found in this study (from twenty to thirty-eight), these correlations are not particularly high. In fact teachers with larger classes compensate as far as possible by spending *more* of their time in interaction with pupils than teachers with smaller classes. The correlation between size of class and the proportion of the teacher's time spent in interaction with pupils is 0.16. A further analysis of this throws up some points of interest in relation to the correlations between class size and the proportion of time the teacher spends on different types of interaction. Paradoxically we find that, the larger the class, the *greater* the proportion of time spent in interaction with individuals (correlation of 0.12), and with groups (0.24); and the *less* the time spent in interaction with the whole class (-0.13). This means that what might seem to be the easiest strategy for increasing teacher-pupil contact in large classes, that is, teaching the class as a whole, is *not* adopted by teachers. Instead they concentrate on spending time with individual pupils and particularly with groups of pupils; the proportion of time available for class teaching is consequently lower than for teachers with smaller classes. This generally seems to bear out the Plowden prescripts.[4]

What conclusions, if any, can we draw from all this? Basically, that the teachers in our study do in fact distribute their attention roughly equally across the class as a whole in terms of achievement groups, sex and age, though, as already mentioned, there is a tendency for low achieving pupils to receive more *individual* attention, and for boys to receive slightly more contact over-all (and at each level) than girls. When faced with large classes, teachers compensate by spending even more time in interaction with their pupils, specifically devoting this extra time to interacting with pupils as individuals or in groups rather than in the class teaching situation. These are all important findings which cast a good deal of light on the inner dynamics of the primary classroom. Nevertheless, in spite of all this, the actual *amount* of individual attention accorded to pupils remains small at all levels. This remains a main finding of this study.

Grouping and group organization

We may now turn to the system of group organization which we find strongly represented in our sample. It will be remembered that the Plowden Report advocated grouping within the class for a number of reasons. What precisely was the situation in the classrooms in our study?

Excluding six classes in open plan areas (where special conditions applied) and four others which will be referred to shortly, all classes for which we have detailed information (forty-eight) were organized as a number of separate groups, normally six or seven, each typically consisting of from three to seven pupils (average size 4.6). Thus seating the pupils in groups round tables (or grouped desks) is one mark of the junior school classroom today. In the four other 'box' classrooms just mentioned the pupils were seated in rows of desks or in pairs, as in the traditional teaching system derived from the past. In many classrooms using the grouping system, one or two children were seated on their own, often close to the teacher.

Each individual child normally has his classroom 'base' within such a group; in some classes he will carry on the bulk of his activities there, sometimes *all* classroom activities except art and craft. But the situation in many classrooms is more complex than this. In addition to membership of what we may call a 'base' group, the individual pupil may be a member of one or more other groups brought together for work in specific areas of the curriculum, usually mathematics or language. This second type of group, which may be called 'curriculum' groups, normally has a semi-permanent membership, and, unlike the 'base' groups, is sometimes based on 'ability'. But there is also a third type of grouping used in many classrooms; these are more evanescent (or ephemeral) groupings brought together for particular, specific, and sometimes temporary purposes, often related to 'topic' or 'project' work (for instance, to complete a piece of co-operative painting, construct a map or model, and so on). Thus many junior school classrooms develop a complex internal structure, the dynamics of which are difficult to comprehend by a visitor, the class teacher having, in her mind, ideally at least, a clear picture as to what each child and group is doing.

How are these groups composed, and what goes on in them? These are clearly important questions since these groupings play a key part in the life of the junior school child. As already indicated, they provide the context in which the child works for most of his time – and this raises an issue right at the start. The Plowden prescription, it will be remembered, was that stable groupings were not desirable, especially if these were so-called 'ability' groups (that is, streaming within the class). From the information at our disposal it is evident that, in the forty-eight classrooms studied, the 'base' groups (the first category above) were not normally ability groups in this sense. In most cases teachers allowed pupils in the first instance to form their own 'base' groups; that is, the criterion used is 'friendship' grouping. This procedure is often justified on the grounds that children may work best when with their friends; though the probability is that, if this criterion only is used, groups will be formed that are homogeneous both as regards sex and achievement (or 'ability'). However it is clear that most teachers using this method reserve to themselves the right to 'guide' children into specific groups, to move pupils around from group to group and occasionally to isolate individual children; probably either to ensure a better working atmosphere by such changes, or for disciplinary reasons (grouping makes it possible to break up centres of disaffection by this method). As many as 70 per cent of our teachers in fact used seating for disciplinary purposes (observers' records, S1, S2, GI).

If these initial classroom 'base' groups were the only form of grouping found in junior classrooms, the policy would not appear to follow the Plowden prescription about the need for flexibility in group work. Groups, according to Plowden, should form and reform for different activities and in relation to the different interests of the pupils (see p. 47). Nor, for that matter, does the second type of group mentioned above, those brought together for work in specific areas of the curriculum, appear to meet the Plowden criterion, since these were found to have a 'semi-permanent' membership in particular curriculum areas (for instance, 'red' group for mathematics). Here we found a difference with the HMI survey *Primary Education in England* (1978). While this reports that over 70 per cent of teachers claimed (in a questionnaire reply) to organize their pupils in homogeneous ability groups for mathematics, and well over 50 per cent for language, in the forty-eight classrooms where practice was actually observed in our study, only about one-fifth organized these as homogeneous groups. In the rest of the classes such groups were of 'mixed ability' or heterogeneous, often deliberately so organized by the teachers.

Only the third type of grouping, what we have called 'evanescent', grouping used for specific purposes, usually in the area of 'topic' or 'project' work, seems to tally directly with the Plowden prescript.

However, as we will see later, the amount of time devoted to such work is relatively small in the average classroom, and in any case this type of grouping was not used in all classrooms.

But the most striking thing we found about these forms of grouping concerns neither their composition nor their degree of stability. It concerns their activity. One thing that emerges quite clearly from our data is that, though the children are typically seated in groups, for the great majority of their time they work as *individuals*, concentrating on their own, individual tasks. It is exceptional, in other words, to find a 'base' group (of the first type) functioning as a group on a group task; on an activity, whatever it may be, on which the whole group co-operates, for instance, to investigate a particular scientific problem, construct a model, write a play, or engage on some other joint activity or enterprise. It is also exceptional (though this may seem more surprising) to find a group of the second type, that is, one specifically organized for work in mathematics or language, working together as a group on a joint task. Here again the work is normally individualized. Where this does happen, it is likely to take place as a result of the formation of an evanescent (or ephemeral) grouping of the third type, though here also it by no means follows that *all* such activity is of a co-operative group character.

Some of the evidence for these assertions has already been presented. For instance Table 4.3 (p. 62) showed that the 'typical' pupil is operating independently (in isolation) for 65.6 per cent of lesson time whether he is working directly on his task or not. Further relevant data is that presented in Table 4.1 (p. 61), where it is shown that the 'typical' teacher spends only 7.5 per cent of her time interacting with pupils in the *group* situation, while the 'typical' pupil receives such interaction for only 1.5 per cent of his time. These figures are consonant with our finding that, on average, there were about six groups in each class where grouping was used. If the teacher divides such time she gives to groups equally between these, she will, of course, interact with the groups as a whole about six times longer than she will with the pupils in any specific, single group. The relatively small proportion of time that the 'typical' teacher gives to interacting with pupils working as members of a *group* implies that this is not accorded a high priority by the teachers in our sample. As we stressed earlier, this priority is given to interacting with pupils as *individuals* (see Table 4.1), which accords with the individualization of the teaching-learning process as the overriding consideration.

Pursuing this further we may refer to data provided by our observers as to the incidence of co-operative (or joint) group work in our classrooms. The essential data here, derived from the observers' records (S1, S2) where co-operative group work was distinguished from individual work, is set out in Table 4.6.

Table 4.6   Percentage of teachers using co-operative group work

Subject	All the time	Sometimes	Never	Total
Art and craft	10.3	20.7	69.0	100
Topic work	12.1	19.0	69.0	100
Single subjects[a]	5.2	5.2	89.5	100
N = 58				

Source: Observer records (S1, S2).

a   Single subjects are the first seven subjects listed in Table 4.10 (p. 77). The percentage in the first column (5.2 per cent) refers to teachers using co-operative group work all the time for at least one of these subjects.

This indicates that almost 90 per cent of our teachers never use co-operative group work when teaching single subjects (which include, of course, language and mathematics, on which a high proportion of time is spent); more surprisingly, perhaps, 69 per cent never use group work either for art and craft, or for 'topic' work, both of which lend themselves to this approach. In fact, according to observers' records, only 10 per cent of all the work actually observed during the year was *co-operative* group work, but some children never experienced it at all.

How, then, do the 'base' groups and the other two types of groups ('curriculum' groups and the more temporary groupings) operate, and what is their function? We have already seen that the 'typical' pupil is seated with a group for the bulk of his time (during observed teaching sessions), but, for most of this time he is engaged individually, on his own specific task.[5] This may be some task in the same subject area as the other members of the group, or it may not. Thus some teachers maintain 'base' groups of the first type for most activities, circulating these activities (or curricular areas) round the groups in some kind of order (or in turn). In this case the composition of the group remains the same, whether the group is working on language, mathematics, general studies or whatever. Other teachers move the children into groups of the second type (curriculum groups), having a different composition to the 'base' groups, but keep the whole class on the same activity (or curricular area), all such groups working, for instance, on maths or language at the same time. In both cases the children will be working on *the same* curricular areas as the other members of the

71

group. Some teachers, however, allow individual pupils to some extent to choose their own activities, if not for all, at least for part of the time. In this case the individual pupil often works on a *different* curricular area from the rest of his group. However, whether the pupil is working on the same activity as other members of his group or not, he will rarely be working co-operatively, even if the group organization so widely favoured enhances the opportunity for such joint or co-operative working. Normally the pupil will be working alone on his own, individual task.

In effect, it seems that the extent of co-operative working depends primarily on the degree of individualization favoured by the teacher. If it is highly favoured, as it is with many of our teachers, there is likely to be a low degree of co-operative working (as we in fact found in practice). To put this another way: if the teacher's aim is specifically to 'match' the child's level of task with his 'needs' (or developmental level as perceived by the teacher), then total individualization will be favoured, as in fact is prescribed on these theoretical grounds by Plowden. Such individualization clearly limits the possibility of introducing co-operative group work in the classroom.

The general picture, then, as reconstructed from our data, is of the pupils each working independently for the bulk of their time, though seated in groups. This 'fits', in a sense, with the Plowden prescript of individualization. Very occasionally the group in which our 'typical' pupil is sitting is given, or choose themselves, a group task of some kind, to be worked on by the group as a whole; or, more likely, individual pupils will be called out by the teacher to function in such a group with other selected children. But this seldom happens; though we must remember here we are dealing with *average* figures. Over half our teachers (53 per cent) according to observers' records (S1, S2, GI), made *no* use of co-operative work whatever.

While seated with his group (of whatever kind) and engaged on his task the 'typical' pupil, as we have already seen (Table 4.3, p. 62) spends most of his time on his own, interacting with no one (65.6 per cent), and most of this time is spent working on his task. But nearly a fifth of his time is spent interacting with other pupils (18.6 per cent). Some of this is 'task related' interaction though, as Table 4.3 indicates, most is not. Where it is task related, it is specifically concerned with the curricular task in hand. In this sense, then, a certain amount of co-operation between pupils does take place spontaneously, as it were, facilitated by the grouping structure.

A closer analysis of this form of interaction may be made from our data. The data in Table 4.3 show that task-related interaction forms

28 per cent of total pupil-pupil interaction on average; and conversely that 72 per cent of pupil-pupil interaction is not related to task. Table 4.7, which gives an age and sex breakdown on this topic, indicates that girls have a slightly higher proportion of task-related pupil-pupil inter-actions than boys, and that the proportion of task-related interaction declines with age; that is, older children are less likely to talk with each other about their work than younger children.

Table 4.7   Percentage of pupil-pupil task-related interactions, by sex and age (Pupil Record)

	Percentages	Numbers
All pupils	28.0	489
1 *By sex*		
Boys	26.8	245
Girls	29.4	244
2 *By age*[a]		
8- 9 years	31.1	225
9-10 years	28.7	124
10-11 years	22.4	140

a $p < 0.01$.

With whom, on the whole, does our 'typical' pupil interact? This depends, to some extent, on the nature of the group of which he forms part. Table 4.8 gives the average distribution of the composition of groups to which our sample pupils belonged when observed during teaching sessions. It tells us nothing about which of the three types of groupings defined earlier these are; it simply presents the *average* of all such grouping structures in the classrooms when under observation. The groups of two include the four classrooms mentioned earlier, where the pupils were seated in pairs (in rows). But seating in pairs was also quite widely used in informally organized classrooms; in fact two-thirds of the observations made of pairs were in classrooms of this kind. The heading 'alone' refers to pupils based on their own, a fairly common occurrence, as mentioned earlier (p. 69), or occasionally to children alone at a table where the other seats had been temporarily vacated.

Table 4.8 indicates that, although the highest proportion of groups of three pupils and over in the classrooms observed consisted of child-ren of both sexes (43.5 per cent), a substantial minority (30.8 per cent) were single sex (perhaps a result of pupil choice in group formation). As we have seen from the Plowden prescriptions, pupil grouping should serve a socialization function. But here we have another striking finding. The 'typical' pupil interacts very largely only with pupils of the same sex.

Table 4.8   Composition of base of pupil during observation sessions (Pupil Record)

	Percentages
Alone	5.1
2 same sex	15.3
2 opposite sex	2.0
Several same sex	30.8
Several opposite sex	43.5
Not coded	3.3
	100.0

So marked is this tendency that it is worth pursuing it in greater detail. Table 4.9 sets out the relevant data across each of the grouping types already discussed (Table 4.8). For each type of group it gives the proportion of time when the 'typical' pupil is not interacting with other pupils and the proportion of time when he is interacting with other pupils either of the same sex, or of the opposite sex. (Perhaps it should be made clear that a child based 'alone' can, of course, quite easily interact with others at a table nearby.)

Table 4.9   Pupil-pupil: base and interactions (Pupil Record)
(percentage of all pupil-pupil interactions)

Base group	*Percentage not interacting*	*Percentage interacting with same sex*	*Percentage interacting with opposite sex*	*Total*
Alone	89.6	6.8	3.6	100.0
Pair − same sex	81.9	16.1	2.0	100.0
Pair − opposite sex	89.1	3.6	7.2	100.0
Several same sex	79.9	19.4	0.7	100.0
Several opposite sex	83.3	10.9	5.7	100.0

Table 4.9 indicates that, if we exclude pupils working alone, pupil-pupil interaction reaches its highest point in groups consisting of several pupils of the same sex, and conversely its lowest point in the case of pairs of pupils of opposite sex. The table brings out what appears to be a general pattern: that pupils are much more likely to interact with

other pupils of the same sex than of the opposite sex. A pair of pupils of the same sex are, of course, likely to interact with each other, and, as indicated in the table, do so; in this case there is very little interaction with a pupil of opposite sex who, in any case, would be located in a different group; but pupils located in a pair of opposite sex interact together about half as frequently (7.2 per cent) as same sex pairs (16.1 per cent), and almost twice as much with pupils of the *same* sex (seated elsewhere, 3.6 per cent) as same sex pairs contrive to do with pupils of the opposite sex (2.0 per cent). Where groups consist of several pupils of the same sex the proportion of time spent interacting together is not only highest, but interaction with pupils of the opposite sex is almost entirely excluded. Where the group contains several pupils of both sexes not only is the amount of interaction reduced, but interaction between pupils of opposite sex within these groups is only half that between pupils of the same sex.

Over-all the pupil record indicates that 82.6 per cent of pupil-pupil interactions were between members of the same sex rather than between pupils of opposite sex. Table 4.9 makes it clear that this difference arises from choice and is not just a consequence of seating patterns in the classroom. It shows that, over-all, when given an equal chance of interacting with their own or the opposite sex (for example in a mixed sex group), pupils are approximately twice as likely to choose someone of the same sex. The data also show that same sex interactions are more likely to be task related than opposite sex interactions. While 29.7 per cent of same sex interactions are task related, only 20.2 per cent of opposite sex interactions are of this kind.

From the data presented in this section we can, perhaps, conclude that our 'typical' pupil, although he talks with other members of his group (and other groups) both on matters concerning his own task and sometimes on those concerning his partner's (and sometimes on neither!), generally experiences little, if any, co-operative or joint group work of any kind, whether exploratory, problem-solving, constructive, or creative. For most of his time in lesson sessions his 'group', however composed, defines the area where he sits and the other pupils he sits with rather than a team to whose joint work he contributes. While some time is spent in talk, and some of this talk is related to his task, it does not seem that generally, pupils experience 'the thrust and counter thrust' of debate as Plowden puts it; nor does it appear that there is much opportunity to use pedagogic skills (explaining), though there may be some. As we have seen in the last few paragraphs, the socialization function of grouping, to which Plowden also pointed, may be fulfilled to some extent through interaction with others, but even here the scope of that interaction is somewhat limited, particularly across the sexes.

The curriculum

So far we have discussed, and analysed, some important aspects of junior classroom activity, particularly individual attention and its distribution, and group organization and its character. We turn now to the content of the pupils' activities, the curriculum. What, in fact, were the pupils engaged on during the lesson periods we observed?

It should be made clear at the start that our observations were concentrated on normal lesson periods, both during the morning and afternoon. The observation instruments were designed to record those activities which take place in the classroom, and which involve interaction between the teacher and her pupils as well as between the pupils themselves. It was never our intention to observe activities taking place outside the classroom; curricular activities such as organized games, physical education, dancing, singing, and so on; these are excluded. So too are classroom activities in which the teacher plays no active part, such as watching a television programme (though preparation and follow-up lessons are included under whichever curricular heading they fall). Our focus was strictly on sessions comprising normal teaching and learning activities in the classroom.

Every effort was made to distribute observation sessions across the day in such a way as to give a representative sample of classroom activities, of the type we wished to concentrate on, as they in fact occurred during the day. A full analysis of the actual times of observation during the year is given in Appendix 2D, to which the reader is referred for a detailed breakdown of this matter. Here it is enough to say that, in general, observations were concentrated between 9.30 and 10.30 and 11.00 and 12.00 in the mornings, and between 1.00 and 2.00 in the afternoons. These proved to cover the main teaching sessions, though some observations were also made between 2.00 and 3.00 p.m., and at other times. Just over half the observations (55.8 per cent) covered the morning sessions (to 12.00); just under half (44.2 per cent) the afternoon. This pattern seems accurately to reflect the balance of activities in the schools.

The main curricular areas studied fall generally under the headings of mathematics, language, arts and crafts, and 'general studies'. Mathematics and language can be further broken down; the first into number work, practical mathematics, abstract mathematics; language into reading, writing, spoken English and creative writing. 'General Studies' is more complex. It includes specialized subjects, such as history, geography, science and religious knowledge, that are taught as separate subjects in some schools. It also includes 'topic' or 'project' work as often organized, as also 'integrated studies', the form in which historical, geographical or scientific approaches are sometimes brought together in primary schools. These areas were categorized together under 'general studies' because of the very real problems of differentiating the content of the curriculum; some teachers use a thematic approach while others organize their teaching in terms of distinct bodies of knowledge (a more detailed analysis of this particular curricular area is given in the notes to this chapter[6]).

During observation sessions, the curricular area each sample pupil was engaged in was noted while the observations were being made of that pupil; when the teacher was being observed, the curricular area of the pupil with whom the teacher was interacting was noted. It is possible, therefore, to make a precise analysis, from observational data, of the proportion of time spent on average on each subject area by all observed pupils (the pupil sample); so giving us the breakdown for our 'typical' pupil. In just the same way a curricular profile of our 'typical' teacher may be presented (from the Teacher Record). Table 4.10 presents the results of this dual analysis.

Table 4.10   Curricular areas (Pupil and Teacher Records)
(percentage of curricular area codings[a])

Curricular area	Pupil Record		Teacher Record	
Mathematics				
Number work	14.0 ⎫		16.0 ⎫	
Practical mathematics	4.3 ⎬	28.5	4.9 ⎬	33.1
Abstract mathematics	10.2 ⎭		12.4 ⎭	
Language				
Reading	4.4 ⎫		7.9 ⎫	
Writing	21.2 ⎪		20.6 ⎪	
Spoken English	2.0 ⎬	36.1	3.3 ⎬	37.8
Creative writing	8.5 ⎭		6.0 ⎭	
Art and craft	10.9 ⎫		10.3 ⎫	
General studies	24.4 ⎬	35.1	18.7 ⎬	29.0
		100.0		100.0

a   The curricular area was not coded when the teacher was not interacting (Teacher Record).

The two sets of figures do not coincide precisely, as would be the case if class teaching were the rule in primary schools, in which case both teachers and pupils would spend the same amount of time on each curricular area. However individualization and group work, together with the practice of allowing pupils a measure of responsibility in choosing the particular activity they will engage on at any particular time, naturally leads to some differentiation in the time allocated to different curricular areas by teachers and pupils respectively. These differences will be discussed shortly.

If we focus first on the data derived from the Pupil Record, the main pattern emerging from Table 4.10 is clear enough. This indicates that the bulk of our observations covered what some refer to as the 'basic' subjects (or skills), the 'typical' pupil spending just under a third of his time on mathematics and number work (28.5 per cent), rather more than a third (36.1 per cent) on language (of which writing forms the bulk[7]) and the remaining third on arts and crafts (10.9 per cent) and general studies (24.4 per cent).

This finding generally bears out the conclusions of the HMI survey, *Primary Education in England*, in that it shows that the distribution of the pupil's time is fairly traditional; language and mathematics (or number) have formed the staple of the curriculum from the days of payment by results (1862), though then, of course, in the form of the 'rudiments': reading, writing and arithmetic. Certainly the content of these subject areas has changed over time, while presentation is more attractive than in the past. But the main focus of actual lesson time remains much as before. There is little in our data to suggest that teachers have in any sense moved seriously away from what has always been regarded as the main function of the junior (or elementary) school: the inculcation of basic skills, or the grasp of elementary concepts relating to numeracy and literacy.

Given the emphasis (in some quarters) on the need for choice on the part of pupils in determining their own activities, it may be worth comparing the distribution of pupil time with that of teacher time across the same subject areas. It is sometimes argued that, if such choice is available to pupils, the resulting distribution of pupil time may be unbalanced; the pupil will 'choose' to work on, say, arts and crafts or 'topic' and therefore ignore number and language. Our data do not support this contention. Although our 'typical' pupil worked on 'tasks of his own choice' for one third of his time (32 per cent —observers' records, S1, S2), he distributes his time over-all roughly equally between the three main subject areas (if we lump art and craft with general subjects). Our 'typical' teacher does precisely the same. Though there are slight variations between the allocation of time to different subject areas by pupils and teachers, as Table 4.10 shows, in general the correspondence is extremely close. It seems likely (from our general observations) that when teachers allow a 'free choice' of activities, what is meant is that the pupils have a 'free choice' of the *order* in which they will do the work, the general character of which (at least in terms of subject areas) is determined by the teacher.

Examining over-all the distribution of time by teachers and pupils respectively, we may tackle each of the three main subject areas in turn. First, then, mathematics (the first three categories). Here we find that, although the teacher spends more time on this area than the 'typical' pupil, the differences are relatively small. In the second main category, language, although over-all the discrepancy in time allocation is small, there are interesting differences in the individual subject areas within the category as a whole.

The chief of these occurs with reading. Here we may note the relatively small amount of time our 'typical' teacher spent on this area (7.9 per cent). As we suspected, this masks a variation in time allocation by age of pupils; Table 4.11 gives the breakdown by age on this item in terms both of the time spent by teachers on reading, and of the time spent by pupils. Both sets of figures show that the amount of time devoted to reading by teachers diminishes with the pupil's age, as might be expected.

Table 4.11 Pupils' and teachers' involvement in reading activities (percentage of observations)

Age of children	Teachers[a] (Teacher Record)	Pupils[a] (Pupil Record)	No. of pupils
8+	9.8	6.8	225
9+	6.3	2.7	124
10+	2.3	1.9	140

a $p < 0.01$.

This bears out the supposition that the junior school teachers in our sample do not see their function as including the teaching of reading to all pupils; traditionally this has been regarded as the major role of the infant school. Their concentration may be on pupils having reading difficulties, and mainly working on this individually. This seems to be borne out by the larger proportion of *teacher* time devoted to reading than that of individual pupils (7.9 per cent compared with 4.4 per cent, Table 4.10).

We may note also (Table 4.10) the very small amount of time pupils give to 'Spoken English': 2.0 per cent. This amounts to just over one minute per hour (on average) by the pupils. That this is deliberate policy seems to be supported by the fact that the typical teacher also spends only 3.3 per cent of her time on this. In other words, in spite of all the official exhortations (perhaps rather muted) about the importance of this dating back to the 1931 Hadow Report, it seems to be given little priority.[8] It may be that, in the normal forms of group work, the pupil will use speech a good deal, and of course the pupil does interact verbally with fellow members of his group as we have seen, and occasionally with the teacher. But this does not alter the fact that the time given in our observed lessons to the deliberate development of oracy is small.

There is, here, a discrepancy between the ORACLE data on this issue, and that presented in the Bullock Report (1975), derived from their survey based on teachers' self-reports. Teachers who took part in this survey estimated that, on average, nine-year-old pupils spent about one hour a week on oral English (though the range of estimated time spent varied enormously). The ORACLE figures, derived from classroom observation, of 2.0 per cent of curriculum time (pupils) and 3.3 per cent (teachers) amount to 21.6 minutes (pupils) and 35.6 minutes (teachers) per week, compared with the Bullock survey's mean estimate of 61.8 minutes (pupils). There is, therefore, a considerable discrepancy between the ORACLE and the Bullock data as regards time spent on oral English, as is also the case with the time given to other aspects of language teaching, especially writing (where the ORACLE data show a much higher proportion of curriculum time than Bullock) and reading (where the opposite is the case). In view of the interest and importance of this issue (and also the rather complex analysis involved) the matter is dealt with at greater length in Appendix 4.

Returning to Table 4.10, one further point may be made concerning creative writing and general studies. It will be noticed that in these cases the proportion of pupil and teacher time differs markedly; when summed together the pupils spend 32.9 per cent of their time on these areas, the teachers only 24.7 per cent. The probable reason for this discrepancy is that, in these areas, teachers generally allow the pupil to direct the bulk of his work; by the nature of these activities (which include 'topic' and 'project') the teacher cannot and probably does not wish to maintain a constant control. Thus in these areas the pupils are generally working on their own but approaching the teacher for assistance in, for instance, setting up a piece of work, or for feedback or help on specific aspects of the work. The teacher will not be involved in its ongoing character. For this reason the teacher spends proportionately less time on these activities than the pupils.

How far were our observations relating to curriculum representative of the 'real' or actual curriculum realized by pupils and teachers in the classrooms observed? It was necessary to make a detailed check on this both because sampling errors may have arisen through the technique used, and because it might be that our observers picked up a distorted picture of teacher and pupil activities by concentrating observation, as they did, on two main sessions each day (sometimes three). The normal day, on the other hand, is often divided into four sessions, two in the morning and two in the afternoon.

In order to monitor this effectively, observers recorded each day the curriculum areas worked on at each point throughout the day as a whole. Here, then (Table 4.12) is a summary of the time spent on the 'real curriculum', presented alongside the data from the Pupil and Teacher Record from Table 4.10 (some of the subject categories have been collapsed).

Table 4.12   Curricular areas

	Pupil Record	Teacher Record	'Real' curriculum
Maths	28.5	33.1	30.0
Reading	4.4	7.9	8.2
Writing (including creative)	29.7	26.6	24.2
Spoken English	2.0	3.3	3.0
Art and craft	10.9	10.3	10.2
General studies	24.4	18.7	24.3
Total	100.0	100.0	100.0

The data in Table 4.12 suggest that the Pupil and Teacher Records are closely representative of the 'real' curriculum.

Conclusion

What are the main points deriving from our analysis so far? In Chapter 3 we examined the Plowden prescriptions for classroom practice, derived from their theoretical stance which focused particularly on the 'nature' of the child as a questing, exploratory animal who required opportunities both for learning about the world and for developing his own abilities and skills in a free, flexibly organized, environment. This should be richly endowed with relevant resources including the teacher who plays (ideally) a guiding, stimulating and supportive role, responding to initiatives from the pupils, knowing when to intervene and when to stand aside, and contriving where possible to 'match' the pupil's activity to his developmental stage.

It cannot be said that the picture derived from our data of the classrooms observed match at all closely these prescriptions. This, it should be added, is no criticism of these classrooms, but merely a statement of the position as emerging from analysis of intensive classroom observation. There is certainly some freedom of choice, for instance, about seating, and, in some cases, the order in which activities are undertaken; but, as previous research has found, teacher control is all-pervasive (Bealing, 1972). On the other hand classrooms are mostly 'informally' organized, if by this is meant the use of grouping and individualization. There is in fact no contradiction here, since such forms of organization do not necessarily involve a slackening of teacher control. This is a matter that we refer to again in Chapter 9.

To revert to the Plowden prescriptions, while we find that these are borne out in the sense that work is largely individualized, and, related to this, the teacher devotes her attention mainly to individuals (though there is a good deal of variation here, as we shall see in Chapter 6), the content of the work itself is seldom of the questing, exploratory character prescribed by Plowden. This is for two reasons. First, such an approach demands co-operative, joint enterprise in the solution of problems or in joint activities of various kinds. This we find rarely used; many pupils do not experience it at all. Second, the Plowden approach demands a change in the balance of the curriculum; from a concentration on individualized work in the restricted fields of number and language to a greater focus on topic or project work, where integrated approaches may be utilized. We find, on the contrary, that primary schools concentrate very heavily on basic number and language work, with a particularly strong focus on writing (normally copying from books, work-cards, or from the blackboard). General studies and creative writing are not substantially represented in the curriculum, and in any case the content of these studies scarcely reflects the Plowden ideal.

Of particular significance are our findings on group work, already mentioned. As we have stressed, Plowden placed great emphasis on the importance of such an approach, though the reasons for this were never clearly set out and developed. In essence, it seems, most teachers concentrate on *individualization* both of work and of attention, as Plowden prescribed. While grouping exists, both spatially (geographically) and to some extent notionally, in reality the pupil works on his own. Grouping is utilized, as Plowden suggested it should be, in default of the practicability of total individualization of the teaching-learning process. No convincing (or effective) theory of group work in primary schools was either adumbrated by Plowden, or is realized in practice in the schools. This is a main conclusion.

It is, however, too early as yet to make any firm statements about primary classroom 'process'. In Chapter 5 we explore this matter further.

CHAPTER 5

Teachers and pupils in the junior school classroom (2)

There are two important aspects of life in junior school classrooms that deserve looking at in more detail than was possible in Chapter 4; first, the quality (or level) of teacher-pupil interaction, and second, the degree of 'involvement' by pupils in their work. Our data permits analysis of both these issues. In the second part of this chapter we turn to two related matters. As mentioned earlier, some of the classes in the study were taught in open plan situations; others differed from the normal primary class in that they covered more than one year group (known as 'vertical grouping'). An analysis will be made of the differences in the interaction patterns between normal, single year classes taught in 'box' classrooms and those taught in open plan areas and between the former and those organized as 'vertically grouped' classes. In the last part of this chapter we turn again to an issue already discussed earlier; management and control in the primary classroom.

Teacher-pupil interaction: an over-all analysis

Most interaction between teachers and pupils in lesson time relates to the pupil's task or work. We have already analysed the distribution of the teacher's attention to different groups of pupils categorized by achievement, sex and age, and found that, generally speaking, the teacher interacts evenly across the class as a whole. What can be said about the nature of that interaction?

The Plowden prescript here was referred to at the end of Chapter 4; this emphasized discovery learning, the teacher having a guiding,

84

probing, questioning role, generally (tactfully) intervening, but only when appropriate with individuals and groups engaged on this querying, discovery process. Such was their image of the ideal-type primary teacher.

What do we find? First, as already indicated, the bulk of teacher-pupil interactions are concerned directly with the pupil's task (84.5 per cent); 15 per cent are concerned with 'routine' matters (for instance, the distribution and collection of materials and equipment, running messages, shutting doors, and so on). Thus most of the 'typical' inter-action between teacher and pupil is focused on the pupil's actual work or task.

What is the nature of this interaction, which clearly plays a central role in the child's classroom experience? We may start by giving an over-all breakdown of the different modes by which the 'typical' teacher interacts with her pupils. Table 5.1 indicates the proportion of the teacher's time devoted to (i) questioning pupils, (ii) making state-ments, (iii) 'silent' interaction and (iv) no interaction (only coded when the teacher is not interacting in any way with pupils in the class).

Table 5.1 Teacher activity in the classroom (Teacher Record)
(percentage of total observations)

		Percentage
1	Questioning	12.0
2	Making statements	44.7
3	Silent interaction	22.3
4	No interaction	21.0 [a]
		100.0

a This figure differs by 0.6 per cent from the figure for 'no interaction' given in Table 4.1 (p. 61); the reason for this discrepancy is that in Table 4.1 'No interaction' includes instances of 'Not observed' and 'Not coded' which are included in 'Silent interaction' in Table 5.1. But there were occasions when the observers were able to code the audience category but not the interaction category. These two factors together account for the differences in the two tables.

(i) Teachers' questions

We may focus first on questioning by the teachers, bearing in mind that the time spent in questioning amounted to 12.0 per cent of teacher activity in observed lesson sessions. A question is defined as any utterance which seeks an answer. Thus rhetorical questions classify as statements, and commands which evoke a spoken response as questions. All such questions were categorized under three groups; first, task questions, second, task supervision questions, and third, questions concerning 'routine' matters.

Task questions are questions about the theoretical, practical or observational content of a child's work. These are divided into three sub-categories, the first of which covers questions resulting in factual answers rather than imaginative or reasoned responses or problem solving. The following examples illustrate the kinds of questions categorized in this way: Teacher. 'Which city is the capital of Scotland?' Pupil. 'Edinburgh'; or, T. 'Does anyone know what this is?' P. 'A fossil.' The second sub-category consists of questions resulting in the child giving imaginative or reasoned ideas or solving problems on the spot. However, the teacher is only prepared to accept one answer (or one of a very restricted range) and the questions are therefore termed 'closed' questions. Often 'closed' questioning of this kind will cause the child to pause and reflect before replying as he works out the answer. A simple example will be given although such questioning can cover a wide area. In this case the teacher poses a 'Why?' question to the child: T. 'Why did you multiply by six?' P. 'Because the price is given for one.' T. 'Yes, that's right.' The third sub-category covers questions which again result in the child giving imaginative or reasoned ideas or solutions to problems. However this time they are 'open', in the sense that the teacher is prepared to accept more than one answer. Two examples from many that might be given run as follows: T. 'Can you work out the witch's age in the story?' P. 'I think she's a thousand years old.' T. 'Yes, she might be if you believe her — any other ideas?'; or again: T. 'Why do you think London was built on the Thames?' P. 'So that people could get water.' T. 'Good, any other reason?'

Task supervision questions form the second main category. They monitor or maintain task activity and are not sub-divided. They cover questions which result in the child intimating whether he has finished his work, recalling the teacher's instructions about his task, and so on. Sometimes the questions result in one word or yes/no replies: for instance: T. 'Have you finished your story yet?' P. 'Almost.' Sometimes the response is longer: T. 'Can you remember how to use this plumb line?' P. 'Yes, you told us to hold it up like this.'

The third and final category covers questions concerned with 'routine' matters of classroom management and control, for instance: T. 'Who would like to give out the paper?' P. 'I would.' Or again, concerning behaviour: T. 'Do you really think that was sensible?' P. 'No, I'm sorry.'

Table 5.2 gives the breakdown, under these headings, of all teacher questions in the observed classrooms, both as a percentage of all teacher questions and as a percentage of all observations.

Table 5.2 Nature of teacher questions (Teacher Record)

Questions	Percentage of all teacher questions	Percentage of all observations
Task		
Q 1 Of fact	29.2	3.5
Q 2 Closed questions	18.3	2.2
Q 3 Open questions	5.0	0.6
Task supervision		
Q 4 Referring to task supervision	32.5	3.9
Routine		
Q 5 Referring to 'routine' matters	15.0	1.8
	100.0	12.0

We have gone into this matter in some detail because of its importance, the observational instrument having being carefully designed to allow differentiation in questioning to be analysed in detail. While questioning by the teacher represented a relatively small proportion of teacher activity in the classroom (12 per cent), its significance, in terms of type of questioning, may prove of importance for analysis of the effectiveness of different teaching styles.

As Table 5.2 indicates, 'open questions', the form of questioning most closely related to encouraging enquiry and discovery learning (promoting thought and imagination), represent an extremely small proportion of all questioning (5.0 per cent) (and, of course, an even smaller proportion of all teacher-pupil interaction). 'Closed' questions do, of course, also promote the pupil's thinking in relation to his task; if the two are summed, the percentage they represent of all questioning rises to 23.3 per cent (nearly 3 per cent of all observations). Nevertheless a higher proportion are questions of fact and a still higher proportion are concerned with supervising the child's work; that is, generally making sure that the pupil has a clear grasp of his materials and knows how to set about completing his task.

(ii) Teachers' statements

A similar analysis can be made of teachers' statements which were defined as all teacher utterances which do not seek an answer. These, as

87

we have seen (Table 5.1) comprise a much higher proportion of all observations than questioning by the teacher (44.7 per cent compared to 12 per cent). The analysis of teachers' statements parallels the analysis of teachers' questions which was outlined in the previous section. Thus statements are differentiated into three main groups, first, those relating to the pupil's task; second, those concerning supervision of this task; and third, those concerning 'routine' or management matters.

Task statements are themselves divided into two sub-categories. The first of these includes all kinds of task statements which provide factual information as distinct from imaginative or reasoned ideas or problems. For example: T. 'Edinburgh is the capital of Scotland'; or again, T. 'This is called a fossil.' The second sub-category consists of statements which are of a higher cognitive order in terms of content. Included here are all types of task statements which provide imaginative or reasoned ideas or which pose problems not resulting in the child working out a solution aloud on-the-spot. A statement offering imaginative suggestions related, perhaps, to an activity like creative writing, might run as follows: T. 'Perhaps the story could end with something sad happening, like the kitten disappearing'; or again, T. 'The house might be old and creepy with cobwebs and dust and a musty smell.' Other higher order statements might offer reasons in the form of hypotheses, speculations, interpretations, and so on; for instance, T. 'To find the price of the set you have to multiply by six because the price is only given for one.' Others might pose problems: T. 'Say we used this hollow nail instead of this solid one, what do you think would happen? Do you think it would float ..?' (Teacher continues talking — there is no overt response.)

At this stage we will deal briefly with the other two categories of teacher statements, task supervision statements, and routine statements. The former, like task supervision questions, monitor and maintain task activity. These are split into three sub-categories. First, those which tell the child what to do, for instance: T. 'Draw a picture to go with your story.' Second, those praising a child's work or effort, for example: T. 'That's a very good way to show your findings' (science). Third, those which provide neutral or critical feedback on a child's work or effort, for example: T. 'Yes, that's the right answer to the first question.' Routine statements, dealing with matters of classroom management, are also divided into four sub-categories. First, those which provide information or directions, for example: T. 'Go and join John's group'; second, those which praise or provide neutral feedback on a routine matter, for example: T. 'You've made a nice job of clearing up!' (smiling); third, those concerning 'critical control'; that is, statements which give firm evidence that the teacher greatly disapproves of the child's behaviour or 'routine' activity or task work or effort when he is not work-oriented, for example: T. 'Stop this playing around at once!'; finally, statements concerning 'small talk'; that is, routine statements which have little or nothing to do with the classroom or school activities, for example: T. 'Our neighbours have a new kitten.' Or again 'My car wouldn't start this morning.'

Table 5.3 gives the breakdown of these different forms of statements, both as percentages of all teacher statements and as percentages of all observations.

Table 5.3 Nature of teacher statements (Teacher Record)

Statements	Percentage of all teacher statements	Percentage of all observations	
Task			
S 1 Of facts	15.4	6.9	⎫ 9.4
S 2 Of ideas, problems	5.6	2.5	⎬
Task supervision			
S 3 Telling child what to do	28.1	12.6	⎫
S 4 Praising work or effort	2.5	1.0	⎬ 23.2
S 5 Feedback on work or effort	21.4	9.6	⎭
Routine			
S 6 Routine information	14.5	6.5	⎫
S 7 Routine feedback	4.5	2.0	⎬ 12.1
S 8 Critical control	5.1	2.3	⎬
S 9 Of small talk	2.9	1.3	⎭
	100.0	44.7	

Here again we find that the thought-provoking, stimulating, or enquiry-based type of statements (of ideas) forms only a small proportion of all teachers' statements (and only 2.5 per cent of all observations). The highest proportion are those concerned with telling the child what to do. It is worth drawing attention to the relatively high proportion concerned with giving feedback to the pupil on his work; both these, and praising (2.5 per cent) are, of course, means of reinforcement. Worth noting here also is the very small amount of 'small talk'; it seems that the junior classroom is normally a fairly serious place (in that it is primarily work or task centred and focused). 'Critical control', resorted to when a teacher greatly disapproves of a child's behaviour when he is not work-oriented occurs relatively rarely — a matter we refer to at the close of this chapter.

If we sum 'higher order' questioning, as defined in the previous section, with 'higher order statements' (those of ideas), we find that these form 5.3 per cent of all observations; these are all questions and statements having a substantial cognitive content. This figure is perhaps the most important finding of this analysis, clearly having considerable implications. We also find that, the larger the class, the fewer higher level cognitive interactions take place (correlation -0.22, significant at $p < 0.05$ level). It seems evident that the general pattern of teachers' questions and statements are directed mainly towards ensuring that the pupils understand the work on which they are engaged, that they receive feedback on it, and in general, that the activity of the class proceeds smoothly and uninterruptedly.

(iii) Silent interaction

To obtain an overview of teacher-pupil interaction, and complete the analysis, the two further categories in Table 5.1 may be examined. The third category, defined as 'silent interaction' (or, better, interaction 'other than by questions and statements') covers 22.3 per cent of all observations from the Teacher Record. This category was used when, at the signal, interaction was taking place, but (with two exceptions) was not of an oral nature. Thus the teacher might be (i) gesturing (smiling, frowning, nodding, pointing, etc.), (ii) showing (demonstrating with apparatus, writing on the blackboard), (iii) marking, checking or looking at a child's work in front of her — that is, seriously monitoring on a one-to-one basis, (iv) waiting (for instance, for the children to raise their hands, show that they are ready, etc.). However, for convenience, this general category includes other forms of teacher activity of a rather different kind: 'Story', when a teacher tells or reads a story, and 'reading', used when the teacher listens to a child reading. It also includes, again for convenience, two other sub-categories, 'not observed', coded when the teacher cannot be heard (if talking) or seen (if silently interacting), and (ii) 'not coded', used when the observer was unable to define precisely which category, in the whole instrument, should be used, or, again, when a pupil is talking at the time of the signal and at the time of the succeeding signal (a rare occurrence). As is evident from Table 5.4, observers seldom had recourse to this sub-category.

Several points might be made about these figures. At this stage, however, attention will be drawn only to one aspect; the fact that the 'typical' teacher spent a relatively high proportion of her time checking over or 'marking' work in the presence of the pupil. This kind of close monitoring of the pupils' actual work is, of course, essential, particularly where work is individualized. As we shall see in Chapter 6 the variation here between teachers is considerable.

Table 5.4 Interaction other than by questions or statements (Teacher Record)

Interaction	Percentage of such interaction	Percentage of all observations
Gesturing	8.5	1.9
Showing	11.7	2.6
Marking	45.3	10.1
Waiting	8.5	1.9
Story	4.0	0.9
Reading	15.2	3.4
Not observed	4.5	1.0
Not coded	2.2	0.5
	100.0	22.3

(iv) No interaction

Finally there is the category of 'no interaction', comprising again about one-fifth of the teacher's time during lesson sessions observed. A small proportion of this, as Table 5.5 indicates, is spent talking with another adult (usually a teacher) who has come into the room; for a still smaller proportion of time the teacher herself is out of the room, and in a few cases the teacher is interrupted by a visiting pupil from another class. All these together, however, do not amount to more than a small proportion of the teacher's time. The main cause of lack of pupil-teacher interaction, it seems from our data, is that the teacher herself decides to do something else, for instance, monitoring the class, housekeeping, or even deliberately shutting off interaction between herself and the pupils for a time (perhaps mostly when the whole class is busily

Table 5.5 No pupil-teacher interaction (Teacher Record)

Activity	Percentage of no interaction	Percentage of all observations
Adult interaction	8.1	1.7
Visiting pupil	1.9	0.4
Not interacting	83.8	17.6
Out of room	6.2	1.3
	100.0	21.0

engaged). Once again, this is a matter where considerable variation exists among teachers; we have already seen, for instance, that, as the size of the class increases, non-interaction time by the teacher is correspondingly reduced.

(v) Audience and content of teacher interaction

We may conclude this section with an over-all analysis of the nature of teacher-pupil interactions. This is provided in Table 5.6 which analyses these in terms of the teacher's audience, whether with individuals, groups, or the class as a whole. The type of interaction is divided into interactions (i) directly on the pupils' task, (ii) on task supervision and (iii) on routine. In addition, task interactions are differentiated into (i) higher level and (ii) lower level interactions, and these again differentiated according to audience for special consideration.

Table 5.6 Audience and content of teacher interaction (Teacher Record) (percentage of all questions and statements)

Type of interaction	(1) Percentage of all interactions	(2) Percentage of individual interactions	(3) Percentage of group interactions	(4) Percentage of class interactions
1 Task	27.8	22.4	30.2	43.0
2 Task supervision	47.6	54.5	39.2	30.8
3 Total (1 and 2)	75.4	76.9	69.4	73.8
4 Routine	24.6	23.0	30.6	26.2
5 Total (1, 2 and 4)	100.0	100.0	100.0	100.0
Task interactions				
6 Higher level	9.3	6.9	8.9	16.8
7 Lower level	18.5	15.5	21.3	26.2

Several points of interest are illuminated by this table. Column 1 gives the over-all picture, showing that task supervision interactions, that is, all teacher utterances concerned with 'monitoring and maintaining task activity' comprise the highest proportion of all interactions. The next highest proportion comprises task interactions, that is, all teacher utterances referring to 'the substantive content of the topic under study or investigation'. Task interactions contain a definite cognitive content (for instance, when the teacher asks a question or makes a statement relating to the child's task) while task supervision interactions do not contain a substantial cognitive content in themselves. These two forms of interaction together comprise just over

92

75 per cent of all interactions (column 1); the third main category, 'Routine', covering the rest. Interactions on routine, as we have seen, deal generally with the *management* of classroom activities.

Examining the data in Table 5.6 in more detail, we find some important differences in the proportions of the three main types of interaction according to the teacher's audience. The most striking of these is the substantial reversal in the proportions of task and task supervision interactions in the case of whole class interactions (column 4). Here, task interactions (those with a definite cognitive content) form a substantially higher proportion of all interactions than task supervision interactions, and a considerably higher proportion of all interactions than is the case with individual or group interactions. Indeed task interactions are nearly doubled in the whole class situation as compared with the individual, one-to-one situation. Conversely, Table 5.6 shows that task supervision interactions reach their highest point in the individual situation, while interactions specifically on task content are actually minimized in individual interactions. In the group situation the proportions of these two types of interaction fall between those found for individual and whole class interactions, though it may be worth noting that the total amount of both task and task supervision interactions is marginally less in this situation than in the case of both individual and whole class interactions. These differences may prove to have significance in terms of learning.

If we now include 'Routine' in the analysis we can gain an over-all picture of differences in the interaction patterns according to the three main organizational approaches, individualized, grouped, or whole class. Table 5.6 shows that task related interaction (taken as a whole) is maximized (and, conversely, 'Routine' minimized) in the individual, one-to-one situation, (though, as we have seen, the bulk of this interaction has no specific cognitive content). Interaction on 'Routine' matters is maximized in the *group* situation. Interaction with a specific cognitive content is maximized in the whole class situation. It should be remembered at this stage that by far the highest proportion of all teacher-pupil interactions take place in the individualized, one-to-one situations (see Tables 4.1 and 4.2, pp. 61 and 62).

Turning now to 'higher level' task interactions, included in Table 5.6, we again find some striking, and perhaps unexpected, differences. The data presented in row 6 is the sum of both open and closed questioning and of statements of ideas by the teacher (Q2, Q3, S2). That in row 7 is the sum of questions and of statements of fact (Q1, S1). 'Higher level' cognitive interactions, which average out at 9.3 per cent of all teacher-pupil interactions, are *most* likely to occur when the

93

teacher is interacting with the class as a whole, and (paradoxically, perhaps), *least* likely to occur when she is interacting with a particular, individual child. The figure for groups fall between the two extremes, but is very substantially less than for the whole class situation (about half). In so far as this type of interaction, charged with a higher level of cognitive content than other types, is important in terms of learning, these differences may have significance. It may be noted, however, that 'lower level' task interactions, mainly factual in nature, are also maximized in the whole class situation.

Aspects of pupil activity and 'involvement'

We have now analysed some important aspects of the teacher's interaction with her pupils in the classroom, drawing attention, in particular, to the quality of that interaction, and to differences in this according to the teacher's audience. We turn now to a more detailed analysis of certain aspects of pupil behaviour during the lessons observed, focusing specifically on the degree, or level, of 'involvement' of the 'typical' pupil in his work.

The data on which this analysis is based is derived from category 8 of the Pupil Record, coded at *every* signal, whether the pupil was working on his own, interacting with other pupils or with an adult. Table 5.7, which lists the sum of all observations across fourteen sub-categories, provides material from which a measure of the level of pupil involvement may be derived.

Before discussing Table 5.7 in detail, reference should be made to the two sub-categories 'not observed' and 'not listed'. The former was coded when, for one reason or another, the target pupil's behaviour could not be seen, perhaps because the teacher or some other pupil interposed herself between the observer and the target pupil at the moment of the signal. The fact that 0.6 per cent of all observations fell into this category is evidence that observers were normally able to position themselves in the classroom effectively from the standpoint of carrying through their work; not always an easy task in, for instance, a highly mobile classroom. The sub-category 'not listed' was coded only when the target pupil's activity could not be coded in any other sub-category. The fact that codings here were so small (0.3 per cent) implies that the category system used proved, to all intents and purposes, to be inclusive.

Table 5.7 brings out clearly the high level of involvement of the 'typical' pupil. As already indicated in Chapter 4, he is 'fully involved and co-operating on his task' (as the observers' manual puts it) for well over half his time. If to this is added the time he spends 'fully involved and co-operating on approved routine' activities — for instance, sharpening a pencil, asking to borrow a rubber, or taking part in a conversation about routine work, over-all involvement rises to 70 per cent of the time. However the 'typical' pupil also spends a proportion of his time waiting to interact with his teacher (4.3 per cent), an activity which is (normally) work or task oriented — for instance, he may be queueing at the teacher's desk waiting for his work to be seen or unsuccessfully trying to attract the attention of the teacher by putting up his hand. If this is included, as it legitimately may be, the amount of time spent in 'involved' activity rises to almost three-quarters of the lesson (74.3 per cent).

Table 5.7 Pupil activity (Pupil Record)

	Percentage of total observations	
Co-operating on task	58.1	} 70.0
Co-operating on routine	11.9	
Distracted	15.9	
Distracted observer	0.3	
Disruptive	0.1	} 16.5
Horseplay	0.2	
Waiting for teacher	4.3	4.3
Co-operating/distracted	1.9	
Interested in teacher	1.7	
Interested in pupil	3.4	} 8.2
Working on other activity	0.4	
Responding internal stimuli	0.8	
Not observed	0.6	} 0.9
Not listed	0.3	
	100.0	

If we tackle this issue from the opposite angle, we see that the typical pupil is by contrast *distracted* from work activity for about 16 per cent of the time. This sub-category was coded when for instance, at the moment of the signal, the target pupil, if working on his own, 'looks out of the window, turns to see who coughed, plays with his rubber, watches horseplay by other pupils, and so on'; or when the pupil is gossiping with another pupil on any matter not related to either his own or his partner's task; or again when, for instance, he ignores the teacher's question to his group and goes on playing with a piece of paper, rubber, or whatnot. Coding under this sub-category, then, meant distraction from the task in hand, even if only very short-lived and temporary. It is worth noting here that distraction caused by the presence of the observer covered only a very small proportion of the time (0.3 per cent). But two further sub-categories also imply total distraction from work or task, 'disruptive' and 'horseplay'. Disruptive behaviour is defined as 'physical or verbal aggressive interaction', and is, therefore, never applicable when the pupil is working on his own, and normally involves such incidents as, for instance, fighting another pupil for possession of some apparatus. Horseplay was coded only when the target pupil was engaged in 'playful interaction' involving physical contact or materials. What is striking about the data in Table 5.7 is the very small extent to which such behaviours figured in the classrooms observed (a total of 0.3 per cent). If we add these four sub-categories together, we reach a total of 16.5 per cent of lesson time when the pupil is clearly not involved in his work, compared to 74.3 per cent when he is. If we remember that, for most of normal lesson time, the pupil is working individually on his own task, it can be concluded that the level of over-all involvement is high (few people, even adults, concentrate on the given task, however 'involved' and motivated, for 100 per cent of the time — some relaxation is normally necessary).

There remains, however, about 9 per cent of lesson time to be accounted for. This is split between five categories, reflecting pupils' actual behaviour, whose implications, in terms of work (or learning) are somewhat ambiguous. It may be best, therefore, to take these in turn. 'Co-operating/distracted' means that the target pupil is 'partially co-operating and partially distracted' from what he is 'allowed' or 'supposed' to be doing. For instance, when alone, he works in a desultory manner, perhaps with one eye on the teacher, other pupils, or alternative work; or, while continuing to work on his task, he takes part in a discussion with another pupil about something unrelated to what he is 'supposed' to be doing; or, finally, when he only partially attends to an adult who has included him in her audience; for instance, doodles while the teacher tells the class a story. The time spent in this way is relatively small (1.9 per cent).

'Interested in the teacher' means that the target pupil is not actually engaged on his task, but is interested in what the teacher is doing; for instance moving apparatus about the room, marking, talking to other children, and so on. It also covers talk about the teacher with a fellow pupil, for instance, about her clothes, or other matters (1.7 per cent). The next sub-category, 'Interested in a pupil', is used when the target pupil, if working on his own, focuses on another pupil's activity which he either observes from afar or with which he becomes actively involved; or when the target pupil talks with another pupil about that pupil's work (for instance, spells a word for another child at his table), and similar situations (3.4 per cent). These two sub-categories together amount to just over 5 per cent of the 'typical' pupil's time. Given the amount of both teacher and pupil activity going on in the normal classroom this may seem a surprisingly small proportion of time.

'Working on another activity' was coded when the target pupil was specifically focusing on an 'alternative activity to the one he is "allowed" or "supposed" to be doing' — something selected from outside the permitted range and unrelated to another pupil's work; for instance, if the pupil ignores the teacher's task directive and starts to read a library book to himself, or ignores the teacher's question about the television programme and continues with his story writing. Such activity accounted for only a small proportion of the pupil's time (0.4 per cent). For a slightly higher proportion the 'typical' pupil is staring into space, or, as put in the Pupil Record, 'responding to internal stimuli'; for instance gazing out of the window with a glazed expression as if 'totally cut off from the external environment' (0.8 per cent).

It cannot be said that the behaviour depicted in this group of sub-categories (which amount to 8 per cent of the pupil's time)* is the equivalent to that coded under 'distracted', 'disruptive' or 'horseplay'. It is not possible to penetrate into what the pupil is thinking about when staring into space, for instance; nor is it possible to make any assessment of the educational value or otherwise of the pupil's working on another activity, while the sub-category 'co-operating/distracted' clearly includes an element of task related activity. If an assessment is made of the level of involvement from category 8 as a whole, then, the most definite data are those analysed above relating to co-operation and distraction, and giving a ratio for the *typical* pupil of 75:16.

Perhaps we can make use again of our visitor, who first penetrated into a junior school classroom at the start of Chapter 4. Let us suppose that he has now become a relatively sophisticated observer as to what is going on, and is able to penetrate below surface appearances. What, then, will he see?

As before, he cannot fail to be impressed with the high level of teacher activity, the almost continuous play of talk and interaction generally between the teacher and the pupils in the class. He will note that, even when the teacher is not actually talking, she is often monitoring

---

* The remaining 1 per cent is covered by the two categories 'not observed' and 'not listed'.

or checking pupils' work, and that generally her whole activity is directed to helping or encouraging the children to make progress with whatever it is they are doing. He will also note that, while the bulk of her activities take this form, a fair amount of her time is spent on routine or management issues whether they concern an individual child, a group, or the class as a whole. He may also note that few of the teacher's questions and statements make serious or challenging demands on the imaginative or reasoning power of the child.

On this occasion, our visitor will be less impressed by the degree of 'activity' of the pupils. The amount of talk and movement by groups or individuals will now fall into place and he will be more likely to be struck by the degree to which, within this context, individual pupils are in fact concentrating on their work on their own. He will notice that, although the pupils are seated in groups, individualization is overwhelmingly the major form of work activity in the classroom; and he will be impressed by the high level of involvement of most of the children in their work. While he will observe some horseplay or disruptive behaviour, this does not usually predominate. Generally he will see that the teacher's techniques of classroom management, which pervade many of her interactions, are such as to ensure orderly behaviour and maintain a positive working atmosphere.

If he focuses attention on the content of the pupil's activities, he may perceive the extent to which they are concentrated on mathematics and language – in other words on the skills involved in numeracy and literacy, and within that, perhaps, on the relatively large amount of time given to formal written English work. Within a general atmosphere that is informal, friendly and probably 'caring', he may be impressed by the extent to which most classroom activities are in the firm control of the teacher and that, while there is a fair amount of movement and talk, this goes on within what appears to be clearly understood limits.

Open plan areas and vertically grouped classes

At the start of Chapter 4 attention was drawn to the fact that the sample of classrooms observed, though mainly of the single ('box') type, included some (15) situated in open plan teaching areas; also to the fact that, though most of the classrooms observed comprised a single year age group, some (again 15) were 'vertically grouped', that is, comprised children from two age groups, e.g. eight- and nine-year-olds, or nines and tens. The pattern of activities in all three types (box, open plan, vertically grouped) was, it was suggested, roughly similar, a

98

conclusion derived from our observations. However, we did find variations in the pattern of activities according to type, and these will now be explored.

(i) Open plan areas

An open plan area is one where space is provided for two or more classes to be taught in a single general area without dividing walls; although in some such areas withdrawal spaces are provided where a class, or part of a class, may to some extent be separated from the rest. Such areas vary in their design; where an old building has been converted by demolishing walls, the open area may be irregular in shape, these irregularities providing withdrawal areas as described above. Where the school is new, the open area is more likely to be of the single space type, although also provided in some cases with withdrawal areas.

Open planning facilitates team teaching, where two, three or more teachers work together, grouping the children in different ways for different areas of the curriculum; some teachers, on the other hand, prefer to keep their own classes together under their own aegis for most of the time. Examples of both approaches will be given, but first we may examine our over-all data to determine the main differences in interaction patterns between open plan and box classrooms. Table 5.8 provides comparative data on some key features of pupil activity.

Table 5.8 Pupil activity in open plan and box classrooms (Pupil Record) (percentage of observations)

	Open plan	Box
Co-operating on task	55.8	58.8 [b]
Co-operating on routine	13.0	11.5 [a]
Waiting for teacher	3.9	4.5
Pupil-teacher initiates		
Pupil initiates	1.1	1.3
Teacher initiates	1.3	1.7
Audience		
Individual	2.1	2.3
Group	0.9	1.7 [b]
Class	6.6	13.5 [a]
All pupil-teacher interaction	11.2	17.4 [a]
All pupil-pupil interaction	17.3	18.8
N =	15	43

a $p < 0.05$.   b $p < 0.01$.

99

The differences here, though comparatively slight, are surprising because, with one exception, they are all one way. Thus the 'typical' pupil co-operates on his task less in the open plan situation than in box classrooms; further, both he and his teacher *initiate* less interaction together and, indeed, the table shows that the total amount of pupil-teacher interaction is very considerably *less* in open plan classes. There is marginally less one-to-one (individual) interaction with the teacher, but interaction as a member of a group is, in open plan areas, less than half what it is in box classrooms, an indication that group work is seldom used. Interaction as a member of a class also scarcely reaches half that obtaining in box classrooms; a reflection, perhaps, that teacher talk to a whole class is difficult in open plan areas, since it interferes with the work of other children and teachers sharing the same area. It is worth noting also that there is a slight reduction, in open plan classes, of the amount of talk *between* pupils. The only activity where there is an actual increase in open plan areas is in co-operating on 'routine'; a reflection, perhaps, of the increased complexity of the situation requiring more attention to management on the part of the teacher.

The general impression, then, is of reduced activity in open plan areas as far as pupil-teacher and pupil-pupil interaction is concerned. However, full analysis of the pupil record data indicates that, in the open plan situation (as might be expected) the pupil spends more time interested in what the teacher is doing (2.2 per cent compared to 1.6 per cent in box classrooms) and in other pupils' work or activities (4.6 per cent compared with 3.0 per cent). Both differences are highly statistically significant at the 0.01 per cent and 0.001 per cent levels respectively, and may reflect a team teaching situation and enhanced pupil co-operative activity in some schools.

Further light on these differences is thrown by the data presented in Table 5.9, derived from the Teacher Record. The full data are presented here to facilitate comparative analysis.

The reduction in the extent of teacher-pupil interaction in open plan areas as compared to box classrooms is here made abundantly clear. It must be remembered that these data are derived from observation of the teachers, whereas that previously presented was derived from pupil observation. The two sets of data reinforce one another. The 'typical' pupil participates less in open plan areas, while the 'typical' teacher also interacts less; in box classrooms all such interactions comprised nearly 82 per cent of the time, in open plan areas it is down to 73 per cent. Again, just as the pupil interacts less with the teacher whether individually, as member of a group or a whole class, so the teacher interacts less with pupils at each level, particularly with groups of pupils, but

*Table 5.9 Teacher interaction in open plan and box classrooms
(Teacher Record) (percentage of total observations)*

			(1)	(2)	(3) Difference open plan vs box (col 1 - col 2)
			Open plan	Box	
Questions	Q1	Fact	3.8	3.5	+0.3
	Q2	Closed solution	1.5	2.5	−1.0
	Q3	Open solution	0.3	0.7	−0.4
	Q4	Task supervision	4.4	3.8	+0.6
	Q5	Routine	1.8	1.8	−
		Total	11.8	12.3	−0.5
Statements	S1	Fact	5.3	7.5	−2.2
	S2	Ideas	2.1	2.7	−0.6
	S3	Telling	12.1	12.7	−0.6
	S4	Praising	1.1	1.0	+0.1
	S5	Feedback (task S)	7.6	10.3	−2.7
	S6	Information	6.2	6.6	−0.4
	S7	Feedback (routine)	1.7	2.1	−0.4
	S8	Critical control	1.9	2.4	−0.5
	S9	Small talk	1.3	1.3	−
		Total	39.3	46.6	−7.3
Silent interaction		Gesturing	1.4	2.1	−0.7
		Showing	2.0	2.9	−0.9
		Marking	12.5	9.3	+3.2
		Waiting	1.7	1.9	−0.2
		Story	0.5	1.1	−0.6
		Reading	2.6	3.7	−1.1
		Not observed	0.9	1.0	−0.1
		Not listed	0.3	0.6	−0.3
		Total	21.9	22.6	−0.7
No interaction		Visiting adult	3.2	1.2	+2.0
		Visiting pupil	0.1	0.5	−0.4
		No interaction	22.6	15.1	+7.5
		Out of room	1.2	1.3	−0.1
		Total	27.1	18.1	+9.0
Audience		Individual	56.0	55.7	+0.3
		Group	5.5	9.8	−4.3
		Class	11.4	16.4	−5.0
All interaction			72.9	81.9	−9.0
		N =	15	43	

also with the class as a whole.

Examining Table 5.9 in more detail, we see (starting from the top) that teachers in open plan areas ask fewer questions (and particularly fewer 'higher cognitive level' questions, those with closed and open solutions); and that they make fewer statements (including higher order statements, of ideas). They spend more time in checking over and monitoring ('marking') pupils' work but give less feedback apart from this. Most striking, however, is the increase in the time spent not inter-acting with the pupils at all which equates precisely, of course, with the reduced over-all interaction figure. Some of this is probably accounted for by the extra time spent talking with other teachers in the open plan area, but most of it cannot be explained in this way. It may be due to the tendency, reported by our observers, to organize pupils' work in open plan area largely on an individualized basis with a high degree of self-direction by pupils, with the accompanying need for more 'moni-toring' of pupil activity by the teacher (reflected by the increase in time spent in marking).

To help the reader to understand how teaching and learning was organized in open plan areas in the study, we will draw on two accounts by observers, each relating to different systems. No claim is made that either of these is in any way typical of open plan teaching as a whole, or even of those in our study. However both cast light on approaches which some teachers have found appropriate in the circumstances.

The first area is in an old building converted to provide open plan areas, in one of which one hundred children are taught by three teachers using individual work programmes for all areas of the curriculum observed in our study. The pupils are divided into three 'register groups' which only function as 'classes' for set subject work in, for instance, French, physical education, drama and music taught in classrooms outside the open plan area. For the bulk of the curriculum (language, mathematics, general studies, art and craft) the team teachers prepare *individual* work programmes which are ready at the beginning of the week. These are divided into blocks covering each curriculum area, and pupils have to complete each block and have it checked and signed by Friday lunch-time. The open area contains all the resource materials (much of it compiled by the teachers) necessary for the completion of all assignments. Input sessions are provided in creative writing and practical maths, but again, not in register groups.

Our observer writes:

> The philosophy is based on 'self-discipline', and the pupils have total freedom as to the order in which they attempt the assignments (if a pupil

wishes, he could do all his maths on Monday), they may sit where they choose, in whatever group formation they choose, and have freedom of movement within the base area. When an assignment is completed it is taken to the nearest teacher where it is checked. A child who misbehaves has his base area privileges withdrawn and has to sit by the teacher and work silently. No child is smacked or forced to stay in to complete extra work. No marks or grades are given. The general atmosphere is one of great industry, organization and quietness. There is little evidence of wasted time.

This description is given at some length, since it sets out the 'system' clearly, and throws some light on the reasons for the findings discussed earlier. The approach requires very careful and meticulous preparation by the team of teachers, who hold frequent team meetings in the base, compiling worksheets and discussing children's progress. The observer continues, 'The three teachers tend to be very static during most lessons. Each sits at a desk and stays there for purposes of marking; very little interaction between teacher and pupil seems to occur.'

The second area is a newly built open plan area with built-in partitions, housing 180 children or six classes. Our observer writes:

Although this class is in an open plan setting, it is conducted as if it were a standard classroom. Only one side of the class area is open to other classes, and bookshelves, room-dividers, etc. are erected so that no children in any other area are visible to the children in this class from where they are sitting. There is no movement beyond the class area except for art (which takes place in an adjacent area), and very little movement within it. The children have their own places where they *always* sit. They are not grouped by ability except for one table of four particularly slow children by the teacher's desk.

In this situation the teacher conducted the lessons as in the box classroom situation; the supposed potentialities of open area teaching or organization were here being successfully evaded.

These two examples offer what are probably two extremes of organization relating to open plan teaching. In the first the teachers operate as a team and have together devised a 'systems' approach to learning which appears to function smoothly whatever other criticisms may be made of it. In the second example the teacher has found it possible to continue an approach appropriate to the box classroom within an open area. Other organizational forms may lie between these extremes, or differ on other dimensions.

(ii) Vertically grouped classes

A comparative analysis of vertically grouped and single age classes can be made in just the same way. The former are classes whose pupils comprise more than one year group. This system, as mentioned earlier, is quite widely used in infant schools (where it is sometimes known as 'family grouping'), and in small junior schools with insufficient teachers to form one class for each year. Some larger junior schools have adopted the system either for administrative reasons or on educational grounds.

The HMI survey *Primary Education in England* (1978), which found that quite a high proportion of junior school classes were organized in this way, pointed to certain educational difficulties facing the teachers (relating to 'matching' tasks with developmental level). There were fifteen such classes in our study. How did their interaction patterns compare with those in single age classes? The data concerning pupil activity are presented in Table 5.10.

Table 5.10 Pupil activity in vertically grouped and single age classes (Pupil Record) (percentage of observations)

	Vertical	Single age
Co-operating on task	56.5	58.6
Co-operating on routine	12.7	11.6
Waiting for teacher	5.3	4.0[a]
Pupil-teacher initiates		
Pupil initiates	1.1	1.3
Teacher initiates	2.0	1.5
Audience		
Individual	2.6	2.1
Group	1.7	1.5
Class	10.6	12.2
All pupil-teacher interaction	15.0	16.2
All pupil-pupil interaction	19.1	18.2

a $p < 0.01$.

In this case the differences are slight across the board. There is a small reduction in the degree to which the 'typical' pupil in vertically grouped classes concentrates on his work, together with an increase in the time spent on 'routine' interaction and in waiting for the teacher. Both these increases may reflect the enhanced complexity of organization required in such classes. The increase in teacher initiated interaction may also be a product of this situation, as also the decrease in whole class interaction experienced by the pupil, which is only partially balanced by an increase in individual and group interaction. All this points to enhanced organizational complexity due to the presence of two or more age groups with the resulting wider developmental levels than in single age classes.

Table 5.11 Teacher interaction in vertically grouped and single age classes
(Teacher Record) (percentage of total observations)

			(1) Vertically grouped	(2) Single age	(3) Difference v/grouped vs single age
Questions	Q1	Fact	4.1	3.4	+0.7
	Q2	Closed solutions	2.8	2.0	+0.8
	Q3	Open solutions	0.7	0.6	+0.1
	Q4	Task supervision	5.3	3.5	+1.8
	Q5	Routine	2.0	1.7	+0.3
		Total	14.9	11.2	+3.7
Statements	S1	Fact	6.4	7.1	−0.7
	S2	Ideas	2.7	2.5	+0.2
	S3	Telling	11.8	12.8	−1.0
	S4	Praising	1.4	0.9	+0.5
	S5	Feedback (Task S)	7.9	10.2	−2.3
	S6	Information	6.8	6.4	+0.4
	S7	Feedback (routine)	1.5	2.2	−0.7
	S8	Critical control	3.5	1.8	+1.7
	S9	Small talk	1.2	1.4	−0.2
		Total	43.2	45.3	−2.1
Silent interaction		Gesturing	1.1	2.2	−1.1
		Showing	3.2	2.4	+0.8
		Marking	9.9	10.2	−0.3
		Waiting	1.6	2.0	−0.4
		Story	1.2	0.8	+0.4
		Reading	4.4	3.0	+1.4
		Not observed	1.8	0.7	+1.1
		Not listed	0.5	0.5	−
		Total	23.7	21.8	+1.9
No interaction		Visiting adult	2.0	1.6	+0.4
		Visiting pupil	0.6	0.4	+0.2
		No interaction	14.7	17.9	−3.2
		Out of room	0.8	1.5	−0.7
		Total	18.1	21.4	−3.3
Audience		Individual	56.1	55.6	+0.5
		Group	10.8	7.8	+3.0
		Class	15.0	15.2	−0.2
All interaction			81.9	78.6	+3.3
		N =	15	43	

The same general picture emerges from analysis of the teacher's activity in vertically grouped classes. This is set out in Table 5.11.

Although here again the differences are slight, they tend to reinforce the analysis already made of pupil activities. Thus the teachers spend more time interacting with pupils than in single age classes, perhaps a reflection of the increased demands made on the teacher in vertically grouped classes. Most of this extra time is devoted to interaction with groups which again may reflect increased organizational complexity. The difficulties related to this may also be reflected in the doubling of 'critical control' (coded only when the teacher expresses thorough disapproval of a child's behaviour), and, perhaps, the increase in 'praising' (reinforcement of good work).

There are indications here, then, of enhanced class control or management problems in vertically grouped classes. But generally the interaction patterns are similar and the differences are slight. It may be worth noting that 'higher order' questions and statements are greater in vertically grouped classes, 6.2 per cent compared to 5.1 per cent in single age classes.

Classroom management

We have suggested in Chapter 3 that management and control is and always has been a primary concern for teachers — as it must be, given the situation. Primary class sizes have always been relatively large in this country, much larger than secondary, with classes up to forty and fifty not unusual until quite recently. Even in the year that the Plowden Report was being drafted recommending total individualization (1966) more than 650,000 children were in classes with over forty pupils per class (DES, 1966, p. 44). In such conditions, even the grouping solution was hardly, in any realistic sense, available to many teachers.

With the gradual reduction in class sizes to more manageable numbers, grouping and individualization becomes a possibility, and there is evidence that it has been implemented by the majority of teachers, as also by the bulk of those in our sample (Bealing, 1972; HMI survey, 1978). Even so the variation in class size is still great: from twenty to thirty-eight in our sample (with 29.9 as the mean).

One of the teacher's first concerns must be to create in the classroom an atmosphere conducive to work. For one thing, too much 'activity', noise and mobility is extremely wearing for both teachers and children alike. No doubt there are variations in the amount of movement and talk that different teachers regard as optimal, but even where

106

a good deal of noise and movement prevail, the teacher needs to feel that she is in over-all control, and can bring the class back to a normal work-oriented atmosphere whenever she feels it is necessary.

Grouping, as we have already suggested, is one means by which the teacher controls the activities of her class. But there are others. When Resnick observed infant classes she interpreted the teacher's extremely frequent short interactions with pupils one after the other as primarily managerial in function (Resnick, 1972). Here pupils were constantly breaking into the teacher's longer interactions with individuals with a question, something to show, seeking reassurance or feedback from the teacher. Such interactions were interpreted as having a management function (and so being acceptable to the teacher) in that they kept things moving happily and allowed the children to feel that they and their work were being appreciated.

How far do our data give the grounds for a similar interpretation in the junior school classroom? We also find that the tendency is for teacher-pupil interactions to be short-lived – although some teachers did engage in long interactions with individual pupils. Unfortunately we cannot provide empirical evidence from the observational instruments on this; it remains an over-all assessment based on the observers' accounts of classroom practice. In general it seems that, by interacting in this way with many children over a short period, the teacher keeps things humming, as it were, so that the class moves along smoothly. It is the necessity for these constant but short interactions to do just this that keeps the teacher so busy, so 'involved', during a typical lesson period. She is interacting, not all the time, but most of it (for 79 per cent of the time according to the Teacher Record – see Table 5.1). When she is not interacting in this way, as we have seen, she has either been interrupted by someone coming into the room (pupil or adult), or is marking pupils' work without the pupils present, monitoring or 'housekeeping' – that is, normally, preparing materials for future work, tidying up, and so on – all activities which are needed to keep things moving in the longer run than the immediate lesson in hand.

Even so, and in spite of the fact that the great bulk of the lessons observed proceeded in a smooth and orderly way, there will be disruptive behaviour occasionally on the part of pupils. The teacher may then feel that some action is needed to restore equilibrium (or to prevent it being upset). Before going into her actions in this situation, we may briefly examine how far our 'typical' pupil in fact engages in disruptive or other behaviour that might be regarded as anti-social by the teacher. The main point to make here is that such behaviour occurs infrequently. Activities characterized as 'disruptive' accounted for only 0.1 per cent of all observations; those as 'horseplay' for 0.2 per cent (see Table 3A2, p. 182). In a class of average size (30) this means that such behaviour takes place for 9 per cent of the time. What action does the teacher take?

One solution which teachers use to cope with a disruptive or difficult child has already been hinted at; it is to isolate the child at a table of his own, often positioned close to the teacher's desk. The pupil record showed 5.1 per cent of children positioned in this way, though not necessarily for this reason; this works out at about one child in each class. Pupils may also be moved between groups (70 per cent of teachers used this method). Another approach is a general demand for quiet in the classroom (62 per cent), and restriction of movement (48 per cent). Some teachers administer what is often described as 'a good talking to'. This was used surprisingly little in our experience. Only 2.9 per cent of teacher-pupil interactions were coded under 'critical control', although there was a good deal of informal good-natured giving of instructions and directions about routine and behavioural matters as well as about tasks and work activities. Finally it seems that many teachers sometimes resort to smacking. Bennett found this to be the case; more than 50 per cent of teachers in his survey reported doing so on a self-report questionnaire (Bennett, 1976). We found that 38 per cent of our teachers used smacking as a disciplinary measure — conversely 62 per cent did not (the source for the data in this paragraph is observers' records, TQ).

Teachers also, of course, have other sanctions at their disposal, for instance, a quarter of our teachers (26 per cent) occasionally sent a child out of the room. But the main impression which comes across very clearly from our data is how little disruptive behaviour goes on in the 'typical' classroom. This speaks very highly of the teachers' management skills, and of the relative effectiveness of the system of teaching that has evolved in junior school classrooms (grouping and individualization); but, as we have seen, this raises educational issues of various kinds which we revert to in the final chapter.

Over-all, then, we find that the 'typical' classroom is orderly, the teacher very definitely in control, and, though some degree of choice is often given to children, generally all pupils are covering what are now regarded as the main subject areas in a balanced way, though with a concentration on language and mathematics. As we shall see later, there is evidence from the observers' descriptions that some of this work tends to be repetitive and not very stimulating. In spite of this, behaviour on the part of the children is in general exemplary; for the great majority of their time they are working on their tasks, and conform to the situation in which they find themselves — one set up by the teacher. With few exceptions, their socialization to the school situation appears complete.

CHAPTER 6

Teaching styles in junior school classrooms

The preceding two chapters have attempted to provide a portrait of the 'typical' junior school pupil and teacher. In the latter case each category on the Teacher Record schedule was considered in turn and the data for all the teachers added together. These category totals were then expressed as a percentage of the total sum of all recorded observations. This gave an estimate of the average amount of time spent on each of these activities in a typical classroom.

However, most of the teachers differed in some respects from this typical profile. Some asked more questions, others made less routine statements while yet others gave pupils a higher percentage of feedback. If, despite these differences, it can be shown that certain teachers had similar patterns of variation then a basis exists for sorting them into groups whose characteristics, as described by the relative frequency with which they made use of the categories on the Teacher Record, define in a very precise way their *teaching style*. This definition of teaching style differs in important respects from that used by other authors, notably in the report of the findings of the Lancaster study (Bennett, 1976). It is therefore necessary to examine the term in more detail before identifying and then describing the characteristics of the different styles used by teachers in junior school classrooms.

The Teacher Record used in this study clearly bears certain similarities to the Science Teaching Observation Schedule (STOS) which was developed at about the same time at Leicester to identify the range of teaching styles used in the new secondary science curricula (Eggleston *et al.*, 1975). In developing their notion of teaching style these researchers laid stress on the idea of a *teaching strategy*, as first put forward by Taba and Elzey (1964) and the subsequent elaboration of this concept by Strasser (1967). For Taba a strategy consists of a teacher's attempts to translate her aims into practice. Strasser separates the strategic decisions about teaching which are made before the lesson begins from the 'minute by minute exchanges' between the teacher and the pupils through which such strategies are implemented. These exchanges he calls *teaching tactics* and the use of observation schedules with their precisely defined categories of teacher-pupil interaction provides an ideal means of examining these tactical exchanges. If we apply Taba's notion of strategy to the discussion in the earlier chapters (see Chapter 3, p. 50) then a primary teacher who wished to evaluate her teaching would be concerned with three over-all strategic decisions: first, how to manage the learning environment (organizational); second, what to teach (curriculum) and third, how to teach it (instructional). In the classroom she would then try to use tactics designed to implement these strategies.

Teaching strategies

The *organizational strategy* will seek to ensure that both the teacher's and pupils' time is used as efficiently as possible so that the latter take the maximum advantage of their opportunities for learning. It seeks to avoid prolonged waiting by pupils in need of help, undue hold-ups for books or materials and extended transition periods from one curricular activity to another. It concerns decisions such as the balance to be struck between individualized instruction, class teaching and group work. If groups are used then further decisions will be needed about their composition, for instance, whether such groups should be homogeneous or heterogeneous in terms of ability, whether they should be of single or mixed sex, what size they should be and so on. In Chapter 3 it was argued that the main function of such managerial arrangements is to facilitate teacher control although here it should be noted that certain aspects of these decisions may be determined at school rather than at class level. In some of our sample schools with open plan buildings the problems of overcrowding were such that the area was too small for the whole of the register group to be taught as a single unit. Thus class teaching was difficult if not impossible. Nevertheless, even within these base areas, the teacher's own preferences largely determined the strategies for organizing groups and their working arrangements, for instance whether pupils worked individually on their own tasks in their own base or whether groups of pupils rotated round

111

different activity (or curricular) areas.

Information about organizational strategy in the ORACLE project was obtained from the teaching questionnaire and the grouping instrument completed by the observers. However the audience categories on both observation schedules provided additional and detailed information concerning the proportion of time when the teacher's attention was given to the class, to a group or to an individual pupil.

The *curriculum strategy* is concerned with the content and balance of the curriculum. Decisions about the over-all content in different curricular areas are often taken by the staff as a whole but this still leaves considerable freedom for individual teachers to emphasize certain aspects of specific subjects. For example, a study by Ashton showed that many teachers wished to give equal emphasis to applying basic mathematical skills to everyday practical situations as to mastering the four rules (Ashton *et al.*, 1975). Such teachers would presumably give as much time to activities such as measuring and shopping games as to learning tables and doing formal sums. Again, in the field of language, some teachers may give a higher priority to formal written work than to reading or oral work. Others may prefer an 'integrated' rather than a 'single' subject approach. In the ORACLE study, information about curricular strategy was collected both by means of the S1 and S2 summary sheets (see pp. 21-3) and, as we have already seen (Chapter 4) by coding the curricular activity on both observation schedules at every time signal.

The instructional strategy corresponds to what is loosely called 'teaching method' and may include lecturing, demonstrating, class or group discussion, the use of work sheets or project work. Taba, who was primarily concerned in her work to develop in pupils the capacity for what she terms 'productive thinking', regards the assumption that such thinking cannot take place until a considerable body of factual information has first been accumulated as questionable. Instead she emphasizes that pupils must acquire 'sets to learn', ways of thinking which they can then use to solve problems as and when these arise during a learning task. By way of illustration Taba cites an example of what she would consider an incorrect learning set in a child of primary school age who obtained good marks in arithmetic but, when asked how she decided which method to use to obtain the correct answer, replied as follows:

> I know what to do by looking at the examples. If there are only two numbers I subtract. If there are lots of numbers I add. If there are just two numbers and one is smaller than the other then it is a hard problem. I divide to see if it comes out even and if it doesn't I multiply.

112

In this admittedly extreme example, the pupil has acquired what Taba defines as an 'unproductive' model of thought. Instead of using appropriate procedures to think through the problem, this pupil's learning set provides her with rules which can solve a problem only when it is presented within a certain format.

Taba devotes most of her attention to instructional, rather than organizational strategy, although she appears to support an individualized learning approach. She favours a strategy of carefully guided discussion arguing that pupils cannot simply be told how to think productively, nor left to find out by themselves. The teacher must use a questioning rather than a telling approach (although the types of question asked would, in Strasser's view, concern tactics). A decision to engage in a strategy based on questioning clearly raises the issue as to what are the most appropriate organizational and curricular arrangements to facilitate this activity. It would appear from the analysis in Chapter 4, for example, that there may be special problems in promoting discussion among mixed sex groups.

Teaching tactics and teaching style

Once the teaching session has begun these strategies have to be implemented by means of transactions which take place between the teacher and her pupils, the *teaching tactics*. We would argue that, although most tactics will have more than one function, they will tend to emphasize either aspects of class *control*, the development of *social and personal* skills or the pupil's *cognitive* development. Thus when a teacher asks a pupil the question, 'two times two?' and receives the reply 'four' she is mainly concerned with a cognitive outcome (category Q2). If she tells the pupils, in a normal tone of voice, to 'carry on working and wait until I come to you' (S6) she is primarily exercising control. The third type of tactic which relates to social and personal development is not directly monitored by the Teacher Record although it is reflected in some exchanges which give rise to teacher praise or criticism (S4, S5, S7, S8). However, because the teachers who responded to the Ashton (1975) survey rated this a very important area it is being examined as part of the ORACLE programme in a separate study the findings of which will be reported in a separate volume.

The researchers using STOS (Eggleston *et al*, 1976) found that, after a settling down period, during which the teacher and the class got to know each other, 'equilibrium' was established. The teacher began to use a consistent *set of teaching tactics* which in their study was

113

defined as a *teaching style*. The same definition is used in this research. Initially, according to Strasser, the use of a consistent set of tactics, related, as they must be, to the teacher's strategy, evolves mainly as a result of careful observation of pupil behaviour rather than from previous knowledge of test performance. Typically, however, researchers interested in teacher 'effectiveness' have sought to define 'good' and 'bad' teaching mainly in terms of test results and to ignore pupil activity in the classroom.

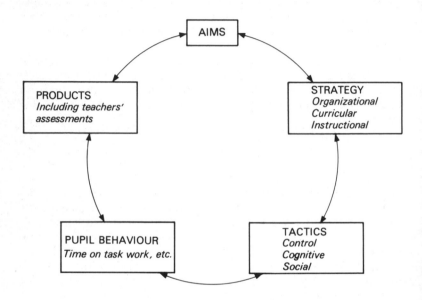

Figure 6.1   A description of the teaching process

We would argue that any notion of 'good teaching' which is defined mainly in terms of pupil test scores is too limited. A complete evaluation must concern itself with all five elements in the teaching process listed in Figure 6.1. For simplicity only the outer links are joined although some elements of teaching strategy may have a direct effect on pupil behaviour so that inner links may be appropriate in some cases. The arrows are double headed because there is, as yet, little research evidence clarifying in which direction these links operate. ORACLE is one of the few studies even to investigate whether there is a relationship between certain kinds of teaching tactics and different types of pupil behaviour, the issue dealt with in Chapter 8.

Although, at present, this descriptive model is presented mainly for the benefit of researchers we believe it has important implications for teachers. Clearly some of the decisions which the teacher makes in the classroom are taken on the spur of the moment, without conscious thought. Others, however, are the result of rational planning. Until the time when studies, such as ORACLE, provide evidence about which combination of teaching strategy and tactics relate to particular features of pupil behaviour, a teacher could use the model independently to act as his own researcher. Those who share Taba's aim relating to productive thinking, for example, should initially be more interested in the process by which children tackle problems than with their obtaining correct solutions. To ignore process is to risk producing pupils like the one in the example earlier who applied the four rules in such an original way. This approach requires very careful monitoring by the teacher to discover, for example, which types of question (cognitive tactics) and what kinds of topics (curriculum strategies) encourage pupils to think in 'productive' ways. Techniques of systematic observation are of little help for this particular purpose, but other techniques are available, for instance, those developed by the Ford Teaching Project (Elliott, 1976a). Teachers in the project made tape recordings of lessons in which they attempted to use an approach similar to that advocated by Taba; it is interesting that the styles of teaching emerging from the Ford Project make use of similar ideas to those defined in the model described here.

The earlier criticisms made in the first chapter concerning the use of questionnaires in the study of teaching should now become even more pointed. Only observational studies can supply information about a teacher's style. At their best questionnaires tell us about a teacher's aims and offer global descriptions of teaching in terms of strategies. The characteristics of the groups derived from the analysis of Bennett's questionnaire data reflect the ways his teachers operated in the classroom at this strategic level and his definition of 'style' is based largely on descriptions of organizational and curricular strategies. In placing such emphasis on these strategic functions Bennett would appear to reject the model of teaching proposed here and to support the views advanced by Harnischfeger and Wiley (1975) who dispute the notion that teaching behaviour directly influences pupils' achievement. They argue instead that 'active learning time' is the most satisfactory indicator of a pupil's progress. The importance of teaching tactics is played down. Instead, according to this theory, the success of Bennett's 'formal' teachers is to be attributed to the organizational strategies they adopted (working in silence, class teaching, giving rewards, etc.) since these result in their pupils spending more time on work-related activity (Bennett, 1978).

Teaching styles and other variables

In this study the use of the Teacher and Pupil Records within the same classroom enables the relationship between *teaching styles* and pupil behaviour to be investigated; the relationship between the classroom process and *pupil products* forms the subject matter of the next volume in the series. In the remainder of this book we shall examine the links between *teaching strategy*, *teaching style* (the tactics) and *pupil behaviour*. When the links between these four elements in the model (including pupil products) are complete it will be possible to evaluate the two contrasting theories of teaching here described. We shall be able to see, for example, whether a particular combination of strategy, style and type of pupil behaviour gives a better prediction of pupils' test performance than is obtained when information about style is excluded. If style is shown to have a marked effect, then Harnischfeger and Wiley's theory is called into question.

We begin the analysis, in this chapter, with a description of the various teaching styles used by primary teachers in the study. The data from the Teacher Record will be analysed and groups of teachers who differ in the relative frequency with which they use certain categories on the schedule will be identified. The different patterns of behaviour of each group define the different teaching styles. In the final section, the characteristics of the teachers who used each style will be discussed and, in the following chapter, the relationship between organizational and curricular strategies and teaching style will be examined. In particular, the prescriptions advanced by Plowden and the assumptions about current practice made by the critics of 'progressive' methods will again be considered. In the light of the evidence presented here, it will be shown that much of the criticism appears to be misdirected.

In Chapter 8 the data concerning the pupils will be considered in more detail. Using the same techniques of analysis as for teachers, groups of pupils ('pupil types') will be identified in terms of differences in behaviour reflected in categories of the Pupil Record. The results of the analysis of both sets of observational data will then be brought together in the search for relationships between particular teaching styles and the particular kinds of pupil behaviour which constitute the main features of each pupil 'type'. Thus, in earlier observation studies, as we saw in Chapter 4, questions have been raised about the different amounts of individual attention teachers give to some pupils at the expense of others (Garner and Bing, 1973), although we found no significant differences in the case of the 'typical' teacher across sex, achievement and age-differences within the class. Detailed analysis, however, indicates that the amount of attention individual pupils receive is a distinctive feature of a particular 'type' of pupil in this study. By comparing the proportion of such pupils taught by teachers utilizing each of the differentiated styles, it will be possible to assess whether some teachers distribute their attention more evenly among the whole class than others.

Thus whereas, in the earlier chapters, we provided a portrait of a 'typical' classroom from our study on the basis of which a teacher could reflect on her own practice we now wish to take the process a stage further. We would like to direct the teacher's attention to how different sets of tactics (the teaching style) appear to be related to specific types of pupil behaviour which it is the object of a teacher's strategy to evoke. This might, we hope, provide partial guidance for teachers if, to take one example, they wished to encourage pupils to engage in enquiry-based learning. By the end of this book they will know which combinations of strategies and teaching styles seem most likely to achieve this aim, given existing conditions. First, however, it is necessary to engage in a brief account of the statistical techniques required for carrying out this kind of analysis. For those interested, a fuller account of the methodology is given in Appendix 2C.

Analysis of teacher data: clustering techniques

As we have seen the Teacher Record and other data gathering procedures have provided a large amount of information about the fifty-eight teachers who were observed during the first year of field work. This information must be summarized if it is to be usefully interpreted. One way of doing this is to present average values on each of these variables, such as the categories on the Pupil and Teacher Records as was done in Chapters 4 and 5. This provides us with descriptions of typical classroom practice. It is also important, however, to see how far individual teachers (or groups of teachers) depart from these norms. For this purpose some kind of 'multi-variate analysis', involving the use of correlational techniques, is required. When the emphasis is placed on the relationships between people rather than between the variables themselves a particular technique known as *cluster analysis* is generally used. This study is concerned to determine the teaching styles of different groups of teachers; it is, therefore, this technique which is the most appropriate in this case.

Cluster analysis is a statistical technique which attempts to sort people, for instance teachers or pupils, into groups (or clusters) whereby each individual in a group has more characteristics in common with other members of that group than with people belonging to other groups. Once the clusters have been identified the data is then re-examined to see which of the variables, on which the clustering was based, shows the greatest contrasts between the different groups. These variables are then used to provide a description of each cluster.

Cluster analysis was developed in biology in order to identify and classify different organisms (Sokal and Sneath, 1963). There are now many different methods for carrying out this type of analysis but early workers used a technique where a 'similarity co-efficient' between each pair of people was obtained which indicated how alike each member of the sample was with another. The two individuals who were most closely related were then merged to form the first cluster. The similarity co-efficients were then re-calculated, most often using the average scores of the first pair on each variable to represent their joint value. Thus at this second stage the number of groups or individuals has been reduced by one. The analysis is then repeated and each time two of the remaining individuals or existing groups are merged until eventually only two clusters remain. Thus if we had chosen to use physical features as the variables for the clustering we might in the early stages of classification have obtained groups which differed from each other by the colour of their hair, the colour of their eyes, their height, weight and so on. We might obtain, for example a group of short fat people with blue eyes and red hair. Eventually as the groups merged we should end up with two clusters which might only be separated by a simple characteristic such as 'short' or 'tall', each group containing individuals with different coloured eyes and hair. In other words the fewer the groups the less detailed the classification becomes.

Applying this principle to the Teacher Record data, if clustering is allowed to proceed too far then the distinguishing characteristics of each group are likely to be very general, for instance, one group of teachers who ask more questions than the other. In this case we would lose the details of the types of questions which different teachers ask, possibly an important variable in the definition of teaching style as well as other, also possibly important, differences. On the other hand, to stop the clustering too early might provide so many groups that, for example, in any subsequent analysis of the relationship between teaching style on the one hand and the behaviour of high, medium and low pupil achievers, there would be too few individual pupils within each of these defined categories to allow useful inferences to be made from the data. This problem was encountered by both Barker Lunn (1970) and Bennett (1976). In the latter case merging the twelve clusters of teachers obtained into three broader categories (defined as 'formal', 'informal' and 'mixed') still left Bennett basing important conclusions on tiny samples (in one case of only four pupils, see Bennett, 1976, p. 146). If the original clusters defining 'informal' teaching had not been merged then these four pupils would have had to be further sub-divided. The decision as to the actual number of clusters finally chosen rests on the need to balance these opposing tendencies.

In educational research it is becoming more common to use a technique known as 'relocation' rather than the simpler procedure described above. Here groups are chosen so that the variation within a group (the spread of its member's scores about the group mean) on the variables used for the analysis is a minimum while the variation between the groups (the spread of the group's mean scores about the over-all mean) is maximized. At each stage of the analysis the two most similar groups are combined and the relocation process between the merged and the remaining groups repeated. This procedure differs from that described earlier in that, when a new merger takes place, the members of previously merged groups can be moved to any of the remaining groups instead of staying together. To begin the analysis it is necessary only to decide on the number of starting groups and then allocate individuals at random to one of these. The technical details associated with the use of this technique are dealt with in Appendix 2C.

In this study the object of the cluster analysis was to group teachers according to variations in their interactions with pupils, as recorded in the Teacher Record. Consequently the variables used in the analysis were the twenty interaction variables (excluding the categories 'not observed' and 'not listed') and the two audience categories 'class interaction' and 'group interaction'. The third audience category 'individual interaction' was not included because of the problem of its lack of independence from the other two categories.

This difficulty always arises when a category system, such as the Teacher Record, is utilized for cluster analysis. The more observations that are made in one category the fewer the tallies that can be recorded in others. If a teacher spends almost all of her time making factual statements (S1) there will be correspondingly less time available for the remaining categories. This was not a particularly serious problem with the interaction categories of the Teacher Record since there are a large number of these and no more than ten per cent of observations did, in fact, fall into any single category. However, in the case of the audience categories in the Record, where there are only three possibilities (class, group and individual), what are apparently discrete variables are not in fact measuring completely separate things. The most frequently utilized audience category, 'individual attention' was therefore excluded. Low values for 'class' and 'group' necessarily mean high values for 'individual' interaction and vice versa.

The details of the relocation procedure used are given in Appendix 2C. The procedure yielded a four cluster solution which was replicated on two further occasions, first, to check that using a different initial random allocation would make no difference to the result, and second, to test the effect of excluding the audience categories. This latter procedure was carried through because the audience variables are concerned more with organizational strategy than with teaching style and it was possible that the former might exert a disproportionate influence in determining the clusters and mask variations in the use of tactics by different teachers. However, when the audience categories were omitted, the solution remained unchanged, an important finding as will emerge in the course of discussion.

Characteristics of the teaching styles

The main characteristics of the 'four cluster' solution of the Teacher Record data are given in Table 6.1. The most obvious feature relates to the different use made of the audience categories which, as has already been pointed out, is an element in the organizational strategy. In terms of the total amount of teacher-pupil interaction taking place, all groups showed similar patterns in that the teachers in all four groups were actively involved on more than three-quarters of the occasions when observations were made. The manner in which this attention was distributed, however, varied considerably. Style 1 teaching has the lowest amount of either class or group interaction and the highest level of individual contact. Style 2 teachers combine class teaching with an individualized approach. Style 3 shows the highest amount of teacher contact with groups of pupils although individual attention is still common and some class teaching does occur. Style 4, containing the largest proportion of teachers, shows the second highest amounts of contact under each of the three audience categories. It appears to represent the most balanced mixture of the three organizational strategies.

In spite of the degree of variation between these organizational strategies, it is in fact not these differences but those between the teacher-pupil *interaction categories* which determine which teacher falls into which cluster. This is the case because the distribution of the teachers between the four styles remained the same when the

120

Table 6.1 Cluster characteristics as a percentage of total observations

			(1) Individual monitors	(2) Class enquirers	(3) Group instructors	(4) Style changers
Questions	Q1	recalling facts	3.9	4.1	2.4	3.4
	Q2	solution (closed)	1.1	3.3	2.0	2.4
	Q3	solution (open)	0.3	1.0	0.9	0.6
	All task questions		5.3	8.4	5.3	6.4
	Q4	task supervision	2.9	4.1	3.2	4.5
	Q5	routine	1.3	2.2	1.5	2.0
	All other questions		4.2	6.3	4.7	6.5
Statements	S1	of facts	5.6	8.0	11.9	6.0
	S2	of ideas	2.1	4.2	1.0	2.6
	All task statements		7.7	12.2	12.9	8.6
Task supervision	S3	telling	15.8	11.2	11.6	11.8
	S4	praising	1.0	1.3	0.6	1.1
	S5	feedback	8.7	10.9	15.9	8.7
Routine	S6	information	5.6	7.0	6.7	6.8
	S7	feedback	1.8	2.3	2.3	2.0
	S8	critical control	2.0	1.5	2.4	2.6
	S9	small talk	1.3	1.7	0.6	1.4
	All other statements		36.2	35.9	40.1	34.4
Silent interaction	Gesturing		1.8	0.9	3.7	1.8
	Showing		2.4	3.3	2.0	2.6
	Marking		16.4	5.7	7.4	9.4
	Waiting		1.7	1.6	2.1	2.0
	Story		0.6	1.8	1.0	0.7
	Reading		3.0	3.4	2.2	3.8
	All other interactions		25.9	16.7	18.4	20.3
Audience	Individual		66.9	42.5	52.3	55.3
	Group		5.5	5.8	17.7	6.3
	Class		6.9	31.2	11.4	14.6
	Total interaction		79.3	79.5	81.4	76.2
	N =		13	9	7	29
	% of sample		22.4	15.5	12.1	50.0

121

audience categories were omitted from the analysis. This suggests, however, that use of a certain set of teaching tactics may be linked to a particular organizational strategy. We shall examine the implications of this finding in the next chapter.

The descriptions of each teaching style that follow are based on the variation in the use of the twenty categories of teacher-pupil interaction (reflecting the teachers' use of teaching tactics), since these are the major source of differentiation between the clusters.

Style 1: individual monitors

This group accounts for 22.4 per cent of the sample and is characterized by the low level of questioning and the high level of non-verbal interaction consisting largely of monitoring individual pupil's work (marking). The teacher engages in the highest number of interactions concerned with telling pupils what to do (task supervision S3). The general impression gained from a variety of accounts provided by the observers is of pupils working mainly on individual tasks with teachers under a considerable amount of pressure. They move rapidly from table to table but sometimes sit at their desks with pupils queueing up either for information or for clarification of the instructions in the text book or work-sheet. The observers' descriptions indicate that most of these interactions are brief. Some pupils want to know how to spell a word, others whether they should go on to the next exercise. Any attempt by the teacher at prolonged interaction with a pupil is usually prevented by the pressure that results from the demands of the other pupils and from her concern to keep waiting time to a minimum.

Within such a complex organization the task of monitoring the pupils' work takes on a high priority. It is important not only to correct books but also to record progress so that where pupils are involved in planning their own timetables regular checks can be carried out to see if each pupil has fulfilled his quota. There is thus a very high level of interaction concerned with marking. Under the ground rules of the observation schedule marking consists of the teacher giving feedback by writing corrections on work in the presence of the pupil rather than by making oral comment. It is this particular characteristic which suggests that Style 1 teachers could be labelled as *individual monitors*.

Style 2: class enquirers

This group comprises 15.5 per cent of the sample and they appear to place the emphasis on questioning, particularly questions relating to task work (Q1–Q3). The level of statements made is also relatively high which suggests, in keeping with the amount of time devoted to class teaching, that much of the learning is 'teacher managed'. However, when examining the sub-categories of teacher talk it can be seen that, although the level of cognitive discourse in junior school classrooms appears, for the most part, to be concerned with the transmission of factual information, Style 2 teachers use a higher proportion of both closed and open questions (Q2, Q3) and in particular, make more statements of ideas and problems (S2) than do the remaining groups.

The pattern to emerge from the observers' descriptive accounts is of teachers who introduce new topics to the whole class and engage in question and answer exchanges concerning ideas and problems. When not talking to the class they move among pupils questioning and giving feedback on work. Because of this emphasis on problem solving and ideas, coupled with teacher control of these activities by means of class teaching, it seems appropriate to describe this group of teachers as *class enquirers*.

Style 3: group instructors

This cluster consists of 12.1 per cent of the teachers and is in many ways the most interesting. The amount of group interaction, although accounting for less than one-fifth of the observations is, on average, three times that for the rest of the sample. The lower amount of individual attention allows the teacher time to engage in more question-ing and to make more statements than Style 1 teachers. The main distinguishing features are the relatively high level of factual statements (S1) as compared with the presentation of ideas (S2). This is coupled with a high level of verbal feedback (S5) and demonstrating by showing or gesture. Presumably, and the observers' descriptions tend to confirm this, these teachers prefer to structure the work of the group carefully before allowing them to engage in discussion among themselves. Hence the emphasis on giving information (S1) and, once the group begin to interact, on returning to re-join the discussion and provide verbal feedback on the pupils' ideas and solutions to problems. Set against the general low level of cognitive questioning these teachers do never-theless engage in above average amounts of open questioning (Q3). This suggests that they allow the groups of pupils to offer alternative answers to problems and do not always insist on theirs being the one correct answer. Such teachers appear to come closest in adopting the grouping strategy suggested by Plowden for coping with large sized classes (Chapter 3, p. 46). Although there is some evidence of problem solving the main emphasis is placed on the informational aspects of their teaching. Consequently these teachers may be thought of as *group instructors*.

Style 4: style changers

Fifty per cent of the sample come within this cluster. It appears to be a mixture of the other three since, in the audience categories for example, these teachers have the second highest levels of individual, group and class interaction even though some of these differences are slight. They ask the highest number of questions relating to task supervision (Q4), make more statements of critical control (S8) and spend more time hearing pupils read than do teachers using the other styles. All of these features are, however, also associated with one or other of the remaining clusters. Style 2, the *class enquirers*, also engage in task supervision questions and spend time on reading while Style 1 and Style 3 teachers show a similar need for an element of critical control.

Taking this analysis further we note that the instructional characteristics of Styles 1 to 3 appear to be closely linked to particular organizational strategies. The fact that Style 4 teachers use a mixture of the other styles, and also have the second highest levels in each of the three audience categories, suggests that these teachers should be called *style changers* in that it appears that they will tend to adopt the characteristics of a particular style whenever they change to its pattern of organization. To explore this possibility the descriptive accounts of the observers together with the information given on the grouping instrument and the S1 and S2 forms were carefully examined. This confirmed that all the teachers in this group made changes in the management of the learning environment during the year in which the observations took place. But the most interesting feature to emerge concerned the manner in which these changes were made. These were three types of style changers and these will now be described.

Style 4a: infrequent changers

The first sub-group (Table 6.2) were the *infrequent changers* and accounted for 10.3 per cent of the whole sample. In some cases the reasons for bringing about these alterations were very different. For example, Miss S, who taught thirty-four nine-year-olds in a box type classroom began by putting the children in mixed ability groups with the exception of four 'good' girls who were allowed to sit behind her desk and five 'bad' boys who were seated immediately in front. Most of the attention was given to individuals and she encouraged pupils to think for themselves by 'getting them to plan their own timetables and get on with their own tasks'. Such class work as there was mostly centred on a daily discussion of the school TV broadcast. As the term proceeded however Miss S was increasingly forced to give attention to the 'bad five' and she told our observer that eventually the difference in the levels of attention between various groups became so marked that she decided to switch her strategy and increase the amount of formal class work with all children working on the same task. There took place, therefore, a definite and deliberate change of style with her class as a response to pupil behaviour.

A similar situation is found in the case of Mr H who also made a change but, in this case, in a reverse direction. Mr H, who also taught nine-year-old pupils, began by using a very formal class structure with the children seated at eight tables and streamed according to their mathematical ability. Quite often the class were called to attention and asked to help solve a problem which had arisen from an individual pupil's work. About half-way through the year, when Mr H was satisfied that the children had acquired 'correct learning habits', this formal structure was relaxed and the seating arrangements changed so that children were no longer based in ability groups. After one term's work, according to Mr H, 'the range within groups is now quite wide' so that there were now as many problems in organizing the work of the streamed groups as for those of mixed ability. Coupled with this change in group organization there was a gradual increase in the amount of responsibility that pupils were expected to take in planning their own work and eventually quotas were set for individual pupils for each week. The amount of individual attention given to pupils gradually increased.

The observers' descriptive accounts indicate that, in the case of both these teachers, teaching tactics changed as the pattern of organization changed. Mr H *increased* the amount of problem solving while Miss S, who began by encouraging children to 'think for themselves', was so taken up with class control that she found, as she said to our observer, 'there is only time to teach basics'. For this task she used books and work cards because 'children are then bound by the book's rules rather than mine or theirs'. Thus in terms of our teaching model the mis-match between the pupils' actual behaviour and that desired by Miss S forced her to re-think her aims and modify her strategy and tactics accordingly. In contrast Mr H, who shared Miss S's aims of promoting independent learning, had thought out his strategy carefully. Once the pupils' behaviour matched what he desired, namely good working habits, he modified both strategy and tactics in order to pursue his aim of allowing his pupils to take more responsibility for their own learning.

Style 4b: rotating changers

The second sub-group of teachers, comprising 15.5 per cent of the sample, all have groups of children working at tables where each pupil's activity relates to the same specific curricular area as other members of the group. Nevertheless, unlike the *group instructors*, the individual tasks are often so varied that there is little opportunity for the teacher to talk with the group as a whole. The main feature of these teachers' classrooms is that pupil groups rotated from one curricular 'activity' area to the next so that at certain points during the day the whole class was on the move. We may thus describe them as *rotating changers*. Mr C was typical of this style. In his classroom the tables were grouped together to give working areas for mathematics, English, general studies and art and craft. At the beginning of each week the pupils were set a quota of work in each of these activity areas. At regular intervals throughout the day Mr C would call out 'all change now', at which point pupils working in the English base area would move to, say, mathematics. The order of rotation was pre-arranged and written up on the blackboard. While in other classrooms the arrangements were not so formalized, most teachers in this group operated with a system of specific curricular areas; the pupils then went to each area in rotation.

In one team teaching situation in an open plan area the same principle applied but with a slight modification to reduce the amount of movement. Groups changed curricular areas at different times. As with Mr C, all pupils on a given table worked on the same curricular area. At some tables pupils were doing mathematics, at some topics and so on. When the time came for a change all pupils doing mathematics went to collect the relevant books and materials for the new curricular area, but returned to the same base. Thus the composition of a group at any table remained the same but the activity changed while in Mr C's case the composition of the group at a table changed but the activity remained constant.

Style 4c: habitual changers

The third sub-group (4c) contained nearly half of the style changers (24.2 per cent of the total sample). They were the *habitual changers*. These teachers made regular changes between class and individualized instruction. In many cases these seemed to be unplanned and appeared to be a reaction to pupils who behaved in an undesired way. Thus Miss P, according to the observer's account, tended to move swiftly from individual work to class activities as soon as the general level of 'busyness' dropped and the volume of noise noticeably increased.

Interaction patterns of style changers

So far the discussion of the three sub-groups of *style changers* has been mainly in terms of their use of different organizational strategies. In Table 6.2, however, the variation in their use of the interaction categories is shown. As might be expected, having originated from the mixed style, each sub-group shares some common features, in turn, with the *individual monitors*, the *class enquirers* and the *group instructors*.

The *infrequent changers* like the *group instructors* (Style 3) were interacting during more than 80 per cent of all recorded observations, indeed they reached the highest level of interaction of all styles (86 per cent). Where they show similarities with other styles it is usually due to the relatively high frequency with which they used a given category. Thus they resembled Style 3 teachers in the amount of feedback they gave while supervising tasks (S5) and were similar to Style 1 teachers in telling pupils what to do (S3) and in marking silently. However, in their use of the higher level cognitive interactions (Q2 + Q3 + S2) they were closest to the *class enquirers* (Style 2). The *infrequent changers* were less direct in that they did even more asking and slightly less telling than the class enquirers. This along with the high use of statements providing routine information and directions (S6), suggests a well-run classroom where the level of cognitive activity was above average. All this is in keeping with the observer's description of Mr H's classroom, reported earlier.

The *rotating changers* had the highest level of questioning concerning task supervision (Q4) more often praised work or effort (S4) and had more frequently to exercise critical control (S8). Only the *infrequent changers* made more routine statements. Some of these features appear, from the observers' accounts, to take place when directions were given for the groups to rotate around the different activity tables. The accounts commented on the general air of disturbance which resulted from this mass movement of pupils and, no doubt, this occasioned the need for firm control.

The *habitual changers* showed a similarity with other styles in terms of the infrequent use of certain conversation categories. Like Style 1 teachers they made relatively little use of higher level cognitive questions (Q2 + Q3), neither did they give much routine information (S1) nor provide feedback (S7). They did, however, have the highest level of small talk (S9). Like Style 2 teachers they showed pupils what to do by demonstrating or writing on the blackboard while along with the *group instructors* they were above average in pausing during conversation to encourage pupils by making smiling or nodding gestures and

Table 6.2 Cluster characteristics of the sub-groups within style 4

			Infrequent changers	*Rotating changers*	*Habitual changers*
Questions	Q1	recalling facts	3.8	3.2	3.6
	Q2	solution (closed)	4.1	2.5	1.7
	Q3	solution (open)	1.4	0.4	0.4
	All task questions		9.3	6.1	5.7
	Q4	task supervision	4.1	6.5	3.4
	Q5	routine	2.4	2.0	1.8
	All other questions		6.5	8.5	5.2
Statements	S1	of facts	6.5	4.9	6.5
	S2	of ideas	3.2	2.5	2.4
	All task statements		9.7	7.4	8.9
Task supervision	S3	telling	13.3	12.0	10.9
	S4	praising	0.9	1.4	1.0
	S5	feedback	12.1	7.2	6.8
Routine	S6	information	8.0	7.5	5.8
	S7	feedback	3.1	1.9	1.5
	S8	critical control	2.7	3.4	2.1
	S7	small talk	0.9	1.0	1.9
	All other statements		41.0	34.4	30.0
Other interaction	Gesturing		1.5	0.6	2.8
	Showing		2.1	2.3	3.0
	Marking		10.3	7.4	10.2
	Waiting		1.9	1.7	2.2
	Story		0.4	1.4	0.4
	Reading		2.9	5.5	3.0
	All other interactions		19.1	18.9	21.6
Audience	Individual		63.0	53.9	53.3
	Group		6.4	6.5	6.0
	Class		16.3	14.8	12.1
	Total interaction		85.7	75.2	71.4
	N =		6	9	14
	% of sample		10.3	15.5	24.2

waiting while children raised their hands or showed that they were ready to begin work. Part of the reason why they were below average on so many of the conversation interaction categories may be due to the rapidity of change from one activity to the next, usually involving change in organization. These changes were described by the observers in their accounts. Although these teachers would appear to be *flexible* in that they used *different sets of teaching tactics*, they may never have operated one style of teaching for long enough to allow many of the conversation interaction categories to dominate their profile.

The general features of the six teaching styles (with the *style changers* broken down into their three sub-groups) is shown in Figure 6.2. For each category the range between its highest and lowest use has been divided into four equal parts, using the data in Tables 6.1 and 6.2. Those styles where the use of a particular category was within the bottom quartile of the range are described as making 'relatively low use' of it. A value within the top quartile is described as 'relatively high use', while values falling between these two extremes are described as 'average'. Some caution must be exercised when interpreting the figure since what is now lost, from the more detailed presentation in the two tables, is an indication of how wide or narrow the range is as well as information about the relative use of each individual category by each style.

Nevertheless, the figure shows the main features of each style in a comparatively simple and effective way. The *individual monitors* can be seen to have given little feedback other than by silent marking and to have devoted the largest proportion of their questions to asking pupils for information. The difference between the higher cognitive activities of the *class enquirers* and the *infrequent changers* can also be seen. The latter carried on instruction mainly through the use of questions reserving their use of statements for routine matters. The *group instructors* emphasized telling (a didactic approach) and provided feedback on work during the course of conversation with pupils. Unlike the *rotating changers* they appeared to need only average amounts of routine activity to keep their groups functioning smoothly and did not appear to have so many problems of control. Finally the relatively low use of the conversation categories by the *habitual changers*, coupled with the use of several of the non verbal categories can be seen. This group of teachers, accounting for nearly a quarter of the total sample, had the lowest level of interaction of all the styles and like the *individual monitors* asked relatively fewer questions and made fewer statements. It remains to be seen in Chapter 8 just what effect this comparatively low level of conversation had upon their pupils' behaviour.

129

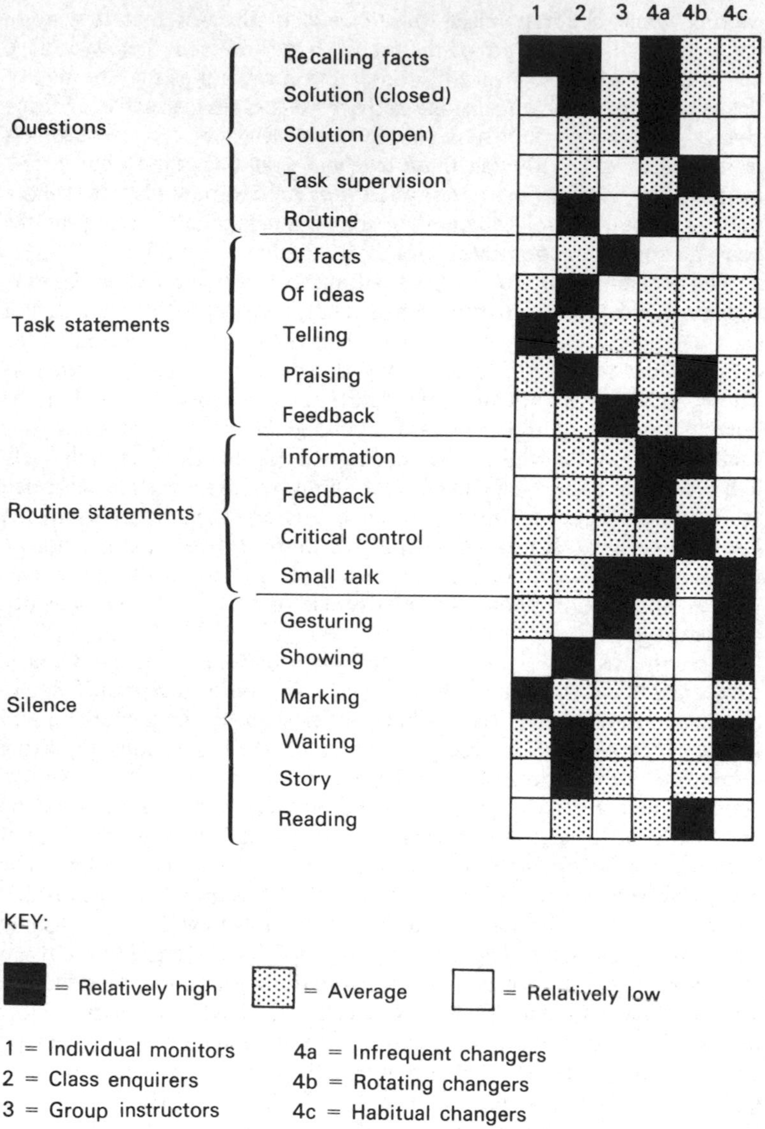

Teaching styles in junior school classrooms

	1	2	3	4a	4b	4c
Questions — Recalling facts	■	□	□	□	▦	▦
Solution (closed)	□	□	▦	□	▦	□
Solution (open)	□	▦	▦	□	■	□
Task supervision	□	▦	■	▦	■	□
Routine	■	□	□	□	▦	▦
Task statements — Of facts	□	□	■	□	□	□
Of ideas	▦	□	□	▦	▦	▦
Telling	■	▦	▦	■	□	□
Praising	▦	■	□	▦	□	▦
Feedback	□	▦	■	□	□	□
Routine statements — Information	□	▦	▦	□	□	□
Feedback	□	▦	▦	□	▦	□
Critical control	▦	▦	□	■	□	□
Small talk	▦	▦	■	□	▦	□
Silence — Gesturing	▦	▦	■	□	□	□
Showing	□	□	□	□	■	□
Marking	■	▦	▦	▦	□	▦
Waiting	□	□	▦	■	■	□
Story	□	■	▦	□	▦	□
Reading	□	□	▦	▦	■	□

KEY:

■ = Relatively high ▦ = Average □ = Relatively low

1 = Individual monitors 4a = Infrequent changers
2 = Class enquirers 4b = Rotating changers
3 = Group instructors 4c = Habitual changers

Figure 6.2 Relative frequency of use of the Teacher Record observation categories by each teaching style

130

Further information on teaching styles

Some additional information about the teachers using each teaching style is given in Table 6.3. Most of the *individual monitors* tended to be under thirty and were also predominately female. In contrast, most of the *class enquirers* were over thirty and tended to be male. The *group instructors*, like the monitors had a majority of females but were similar to the enquirers in that most of them were over thirty. The *style changers* came nearest to achieving a balance between younger and older teachers although over two-thirds were female.

Table 6.3 Age and sex distribution (percentages) of teachers using each style

Teacher characteristics		Individual monitors	Class enquirers	Group instructors	Style changers
Age	20–9	69	11	14	41
	30–9	23	33	43	28
	40–9	0	45	29	24
	50+	8	11	14	7
Sex	Male	15	67	43	31
	Female	85	33	57	69
N =		13	9	7	29

The contrast between the *individual monitors* with over two-thirds of the teachers under thirty, the *group instructors* with a majority in their thirties and the *class enquirers* with half the teachers over forty has a possible explanation in that it may represent 'cycles of fashion' in the training of these teachers while in college. Other studies have also shown that age and sex differences are reflected in the choice of teaching method (Barker Lunn, 1970; Gray, 1978), and in overall aims (Ashton *et al.*, 1975). None of these studies, however, has demonstrated that a teacher's age is a factor affecting pupil performance. With the ORACLE sample, this must remain an open question until the process-product data are examined in the second volume of the series.

In Table 6.4 the average class size, together with the percentage of open plan and vertically grouped classes is shown for each of the four main styles. Class size shows little variation across all four styles whereas, as might perhaps have been expected, most of the open plan classrooms were taught either by *individual monitors* (Style 1) or *style changers* (Style 4). In every style at least a small percentage of teachers had vertically grouped classes so that it would appear that vertical grouping does not necessitate use of any one special style. Clearly then, this aspect of school policy does not significantly restrict a teacher's choice of tactics nor her freedom to use a particular combination of individual, group and class teaching.

Table 6.4 Average class size and distribution of open plan and vertically grouped classes (percentages) across teaching style

Type of class	Individual monitors	Class enquirers	Group instructors	Style changers
Open plan	39	0	0	35
Box	61	100	100	65
Vertical groups	8	11	14	41
Single age	92	89	86	59
Average class size	29.0	28.9	30.9	30.4
N =	13	9	7	29

This concludes our description of the teaching styles that were used in the fifty-eight classrooms during the first year's observation in the ORACLE study. The next stage is to examine how the behaviour of the pupils in these classes varied and its relation to the style of teaching used. Before doing this, however, we turn briefly to consider the links between these teaching styles and the organizational strategies used by the teachers, with special reference to the prescriptions set out by the Plowden Committee which were discussed in Chapter 3.

CHAPTER 7

Teaching style, organizational and curricular strategy

It was made clear at the beginning of this book that one aim of the ORACLE research was to illuminate aspects of classroom practice for the benefit of teachers and those concerned with their training. Nevertheless it was felt that, in the aftermath of the 'great debate' it would be difficult to ignore issues raised by the continuing argument over the merits of 'progressive' and 'traditional' teaching, in so far as the results of this study have a bearing on them.

But there is another reason for commenting on these issues. This arises from the experience of those concerned with the publication of the Lancaster studies (Bennett, 1976). Although the researchers were careful to emphasize that their findings should be treated with caution the report was seized on in certain quarters to support the case for the return to those values and practices associated with traditional didactic teaching.

To avoid a similar occurrence and to prevent any possible misinterpretation of the ORACLE findings it is necessary to comment on the relationship between the teaching styles, described in the previous chapter, and the organizational and curricular strategies used by the ORACLE teachers, since the latter are two important areas in the continuing debate. In this short section relevant statements from the Plowden Report will be examined and the views of the supporters of traditional teaching discussed in the earlier part of the book will also be considered.

Plowden and discovery methods

In a now famous paragraph in the conclusion of their Report, the Plowden Committee stated that *'finding out had proved to be better for children than being told'* (para. 1233). This has been taken as an endorsement of the 'discovery method' a term which the committee admit has 'the disadvantage of comprehensiveness' so that 'it can be loosely interpreted and misunderstood' (para. 549).

Studies conducted under carefully controlled conditions have sought to test the truth of the above assertion by setting a series of problems to two equivalent groups. One group was told the rules for solving the problems (the didactically taught group) while the other was left to discover the rules for themselves. The research has generally shown that the subjects, usually college students, obtained the correct solution more often when they were given the rules rather than when they were left to find them out for themselves.

A second set of studies, however, showed that once the students had either been told or had found out one rule, the discovery group tended to do better at finding new rules for fresh situations (Anthony, 1979). This suggests that, when talking about discovery methods, it is useful to distinguish between two different processes; first, learning the method by which rules can be discovered and second, using these methods to discover new rules for solving unfamiliar problems. Taba's 'productive thinking' strategies are concerned with the first part of this process. The pupil in the example given earlier (p. 112) had discovered a method for solving problems in the four rules of arithmetic, but it was so specific it had little general application.

The level of reasoning required to solve problems which require pupils to develop and test hypotheses involves thinking at what Piaget calls the 'formal' reasoning level. A typical task designed to test whether an individual can engage in this level of reasoning consists of a pendulum made of string with a weight attached to its end. The subject is provided with several different lengths of string and a set of weights and asked to find out whether the length of the string, the weight, or the point at which the pendulum is released determines the period of its swing.

To provide evidence of formal reasoning the subject should be able to appreciate that two of the variables must be kept constant at any one time while the third is varied. In this way he should be able to work out that the time for the pendulum to complete one swing depends only on its length. The 'bright' child is said to enter the 'formal' stage between the age of eleven and twelve (Lovell, 1968), although as a recent study suggests, over half of fourteen-year-old pupils in the top 40 per cent of the ability range cannot appreciate that in order to determine whether the swing depends on the length of string it is necessary to hold other factors constant (Shayer *et al.*, 1976). What was not tested, however, was whether pupils, if they had first been taught some general techniques for solving problems of this kind, could have arrived at the correct solution. Neither has there been much study on the effect of different teaching styles in helping pupils to learn these techniques.

Some earlier research, carried out at a comprehensive school, has shown that one reason why pupils were unable to solve the pendulum problem is that they were unable to time the swing sufficiently accurately to obtain consistent results (Mealings, 1963). In theory this should be irrelevant in determining whether the pupils were capable of thinking in formal terms, since they could still have varied the length, weight and distance of swing *in turn* and then reached the conclusion that all three variables affected periodicity. In practice, however, once more than one solution was possible, the problem proved too complicated and the pupils gave up the attempt to find an answer.

It would seem that primary teachers are aware of these difficulties and thus tend to concentrate on the first part of the process where pupils learn how to discover. Thus the emphasis is placed on learning the methods and techniques by which discoveries can be made. Plowden endorses this approach. When considering primary school science the Committee state of learning by discovery that 'in a number of ways it resembles the best modern university practice. Initial curiosity, often stimulated by the environment the teacher provides, leads to questions and to a consideration of what questions it is sensible to ask and *how* to find out the answers' (our italics) (para. 669).

In project work, for example, the researchers in the Ford Teaching Project found that teachers tended to encourage pupils to explore ways of collecting and organizing information (Elliott, 1976a). An important element in persuading pupils to acquire these skills was for the teacher to refrain from imposing her ideas too quickly on the class. Pupils saw this intervention as a 'takeover' and gave up thinking because they felt their own ideas to be undervalued. In terms of the observation categories on the Teacher Record one would expect teachers having these objectives to ask fewer factual questions (Q1) but instead to allow alternative solutions to problems (Q3). Only gradually would the teacher close down the discussion by posing questions requiring specific answers (Q2) and injecting her own ideas into the discussion (S2).

It is not possible, with an observation system like the Teacher

Record, to identify the precise pattern of interaction, but it can be said that those teachers who use a relatively greater proportion of these higher level cognitive questions and statements (Q2 + Q3 + S2) are more likely to engage their pupils in these discovery processes than those who make more use of those categories relating to the supply of information (Q1 + S1). The descriptive accounts of the observers support this. In the case of *infrequent changers* (4a), who use the higher level cognitive categories most frequently, there are descriptions of lessons where, for instance, pupils are encouraged to explore different methods of measuring objects of various size or shape or different ways of representing data on how the class came to school that morning. In the latter case it was clear that the teacher eventually wanted the pupils to recognize that a block graph was the best way of showing the number of pupils who came by bus, the number brought by car, the number who walked to school and so on. But pupils were first allowed to suggest and try out their own ideas. Only during the final class discussion, when the results of all their efforts were inspected together, were firm conclusions drawn.

The Plowden Committee support the idea that the use of these high level cognitive interactions is an essential part of the 'discovery learning' process. They argue that the teacher 'will miss the whole point if he tells the children the answers or indicates too readily or completely how the answers may be found' (para. 669). At the same time stress is continually laid on the value of group work, with allowances for individual contributions, when organizing and promoting these enquiries because 'children are less shy in risking a hypothesis in a group' (para. 758), while not forgetting that 'there should be opportunity for each child's individuality to show itself' (para. 759). Class discussion should be introduced towards the end when the individual pupil's contributions are complete so that 'the pieces of the jig-saw can be fitted together − or seen not to fit' (para. 760). In so far as the use of the higher level cognitive categories on the Teacher Record can therefore be taken to indicate the promotion of 'enquiry' or 'discovery' approaches, it is possible to examine whether teachers in the ORACLE sample matched the appropriate individual or grouping organizational strategy with a set of tactics, designed to promote 'discovery learning'.

Higher level cognitive interactions and organizational strategy

It was noted in Chapter 5 that the use of the higher level cognitive categories (Q2 + Q3 + S2) was not a major component of teaching in

Table 7.1 Teaching style, audience and higher cognitive level interaction (Teacher Record) (as a percentage of all conversation interactions)

Audience	Types of interaction	All teachers	Teaching style			
			Individual monitors	Class enquirers	Group instructors	Style changers
Individual	Higher level	6.9	4.9	9.2	4.1	7.8
	Other	93.1	95.1	90.8	95.9	92.2
Groups	Higher level	8.9	10.5	7.1	7.4	9.3
	Other	91.1	89.5	92.9	92.6	90.7
Class	Higher level	16.8	16.7	15.2	19.5	12.4
	Other	83.2	83.3	84.8	80.5	87.6
All interactions	Higher level	9.3	6.5	13.9	6.1	9.9
	Other	90.7	93.5	86.1	93.9	90.1

the typical junior school classroom. However there was considerable variation in the frequency of use of these three interaction categories across the teaching styles. This variation is examined in Table 7.1. It can be seen that for all teachers only 9.3 per cent of all interaction involving questions or statements belonged to this higher cognitive level. The *class enquirers* had the highest level, 13.9 per cent and the *group instructors* the lowest. For this style the figure was only 6.1 per cent, for the *individual monitors* 6.5 and for the *style changers* 9.9.

The figure for the *style changers* arises chiefly from the use of these higher level categories by the *infrequent changers*, who asked more open questions (Q3) than any other style (Table 6.2, p. 128). The fact that both they and the *class enquirers* make greater use of class teaching suggests that the use of these tactics may be linked to this specific type of organization. If this relationship can be shown to hold across all styles, then these findings appear to run counter to Plowden's recommendations that 'discovery' is best done when teaching is organized on a group basis with opportunities for individual contributions.

Table 7.1 also shows the proportion of higher cognitive level interactions (Q2 + Q3 + S2) as a percentage of all interactions involving conversation (Q1 to S9) for each audience category across each of the four main styles. Although the total amount of higher cognitive level interaction varied across the styles, in every case the highest figure was recorded with a class rather than a group or individual audience. Thus for the *group instructors*, who engaged less frequently in this kind of activity, only 4.1 per cent of all conversation with individual pupils consisted of higher level cognitive exchanges. When these same teachers were talking to the whole class, then 19.5 per cent of all observations involving questions or statements were of higher cognitive levels.

The fact that the same trend is shown across all four styles suggests that all the teachers found class activities particularly helpful in promoting more open ended discussion. If such discussion is indicative of a 'discovery' rather than a 'didactic' approach to teaching then it appears that the ORACLE teachers do not operate within the Plowden prescription.

Teaching style and formal-informal strategies

The second issue arising from the links between class teaching and certain teaching styles is the extent of the similarity between the ORACLE teachers and those in former studies such as those by Barker Lunn (1970) and Bennett (1976). Some of their teachers also engaged in greater amounts of class teaching than others.

It was pointed out at the start of this chapter that, in spite of Bennett's cautions, supporters of traditional teaching have taken his results to mean that the criteria used to describe the most formal teachers were those responsible for the success of the pupils taught by these methods. Bennett's most extreme formal group (type 12) were,

> an extreme group in a number of respects. None favour an integrated approach. Subjects are taught separately by class teaching and individual work. None allow pupils choice of seating, and every teacher curbs movement and talk. These teachers are above average on assessment and procedures (weekly testing) and extrinsic motivation (awarding stars and grades) predominates. (Bennett, 1976, p. 47)

If similarities do exist between Bennett's most formal group and those on the ORACLE project, then the *class enquirers* (Style 2), who did most class teaching should also exhibit these formal characteristics, while the *individual monitors* (Style 1) should have more in common with his informal group (type 1). The Bennett typology was based upon nineteen variables. The five which described variations in the use of class, group or individual teaching were excluded from the comparison made below since its purpose was to see if the two samples of teachers had anything in common other than similar use of these aspects of organizational strategy. Data about the remaining fourteen variables was collected for ORACLE teachers in a variety of ways. The observers completed the teaching questionnaire, giving such information as whether there were weekly tests in mathematics and spelling, whether pupils were given a choice where to sit, whether the class were expected to work in silence and so on. From the observer records, the session and daily summary sheets (S1 and S2), it was possible to estimate the percentage of single subject and integrated subject teaching.

The results were then analysed in exactly the same way as in Bennett's original study. For example, the data on single subject teaching was dichotomized to differentiate between teachers who were above and below the mean of this variable. The same procedure was used for integrated subject teaching. As with the Lancaster teachers, because aesthetic subjects were given so little time, some of the ORACLE sample were 'above average' on both 'single' and 'integrated' subject teaching.

The data is presented in Table 7.2. For comparison the figures for Bennett's formal and informal types are included. In general the differences between the *individual monitors* and the *class enquirers* were less marked than those between the two groups of teachers in the Lancaster study. Only on two of the variables, concerning *choice of seats* and *free movement*, were the differences among the ORACLE teachers almost as extreme as in the case of Bennett's two groups. In contrast to his informal teachers, 75 per cent of the *individual monitors* insisted on quiet. Of *individual monitors* 41 and 50 per cent gave weekly tests in arithmetic and spelling respectively compared to only 9 and 23 per cent of Bennett's informal teachers. Far fewer *class enquirers* gave homework, awarded marks or stars, and smacked pupils than did the formal teachers. Further, on three of the key items, held by supporters of traditional methods to be essential components of 'good' teaching, the differences were completely eliminated or actually reversed. *Class enquirers* were equally likely to use the same balance of integrated and single subject teaching as the *individual monitors* and an equally large percentage were opposed to seating by ability within the class. The *individual monitors* were more likely to discipline pupils by sending them out of the classroom. This latter finding conflicts with Barker Lunn's claim that teachers who favoured less 'traditional' methods were likely to be more permissive (Barker Lunn, 1970, p. 55).

Table 7.2 Percentages of teachers in each teaching style who were above average on 'formal-informal' characteristics

	Individual monitors	Class enquirers	Bennett informal	Bennett formal
Choice of seats	67	22	63	0
Seating by ability	25	22	14	50
Free movement	92	11	51	0
Quiet	75	89	31	100
Out of school visits	8	0	51	42
Homework	8	0	9	56
Marks	0	11	3	97
Stars	17	44	9	75
Arithmetic tests	41	78	9	81
Spelling tests	50	100	23	92
Children smacked	33	44	34	58
Sent from room	33	11	11	11
Single subjects	66	67	20	92
Integrated subjects	41	44	97	0

One further important finding from the Barker Lunn study was that the teachers using the traditional approach (designated as type 2), were less interested in the slow child. In the ORACLE study the two teachers who were most typical of the *class enquirers*, in that their use of the categories of the Teacher Record was closest to the means for the cluster, both told observers that they used class teaching to gain more time for dealing with the slow learners. In each case the observers commented that both classes were 'pleasant places to be in' where the teachers were observed to 'interact for lengthy periods with individual children who were experiencing difficulties with the work'.

Thus none of the ORACLE teaching styles can be identified with the extremes of Bennett's formal-informal dichotomy. In so far as any relationship does exist, the teachers in the present study would be found within the so-called 'mixed' types. This leads to an alternative suggestion as to why the formal group, who emphasized class teaching, were more successful in the Lancaster Study. As was certainly the case with the ORACLE class teachers, they may have engaged in more higher level cognitive interactions with their pupils than did the 'informal' group. Since the Lancaster study ignored teaching variables of this kind when collecting data it is impossible to test out this hypothesis directly. Evidence on the effect of such interactions on pupil perform-ance in the ORACLE project forms part of the analysis in the second volume of this series.

Nor is there evidence that teachers in the ORACLE junior school classrooms used the approach advocated by Plowden. All teachers, when they engaged in higher level cognitive exchanges with pupils, tended to do so in a class rather than an individualized setting. The balance struck between using an integrated or single subject curriculum strategy was approximately the same for both *class enquirers* and *individual monitors*, the two styles having the most and least amounts of individualized instruction respectively. Rather than concurring with the critics that the Plowden approach has failed we would argue that it has still to be tried at this stage of schooling. The reasons for this will be suggested in the concluding chapter.

Having established the lack of congruence between teaching styles used by the ORACLE sample and those aspects of curricular and organizational strategy reflecting either a 'traditional' or a 'progres-sive' approach, we may now turn to the discussion of some relevant issues concerning particular aspects of classroom practice. In the next chapter the question as to which teaching style appears to promote certain types of pupil behaviour will be considered. In almost every instance it will be shown that each style can claim to offer advantages and disadvantages to different pupils. Unlike the conclusion drawn by critics of present day primary teaching, the evidence presented here suggests that no one style enjoys an obvious over-all advantage.

CHAPTER 8

Teaching styles
and
pupil behaviour

Having, now, removed some possible misconceptions about the ORACLE findings and discussed their relevance to important issues raised both by Plowden and its critics, we return to our main theme, and begin to consider the links between teaching style and pupil behaviour. In Chapters 4 and 5 observation data from the Teacher and Pupil Records was used to provide information about the teacher and pupils in a typical classroom. But just as groups of teachers differed from this portrait of the typical teacher in their use of certain categories on the Teacher Record, so too groups of pupils show similar variations from the typical pupil in respect of the Pupil Record data. The use of certain categories by those groups of teachers defined their teaching style. In a similar manner each group of pupils may be identified as a 'pupil type'. Each type (or group) can be defined by the relative use they make of the different categories on the Pupil Record.

The clustering procedure which was described in Chapter 6 was again used to identify these types. This time there were 489 pupils instead of only fifty-eight teachers. In each class eight target pupils were originally selected (two high, two low and four medium achievers) but some substitute pupils were also included in the analysis providing a term's data had been collected for them (see Appendix 2B). The data for each pupil consisted of the total number of observations in each of the fifty-five sub-divisions of the main categories on the Pupil Record. These totals were converted to a percentage of the total number of observations recorded for that individual. Analysis again yielded four stable clusters whose characteristics are now described.

142

Description of pupil types

There is a special problem in presenting the data used to describe the characteristics of each of the four pupil types. Whereas in the analysis of the teaching style based on the Teacher Record there were only twenty categories, on the Pupil Record there are fifty-five. Thus a table giving the average frequency of use of each category for each of the four pupil types would contain 220 values. Referring continually to such a cumbersome table while following the descriptions of each style given in the text would be both difficult and time consuming. The table giving these 220 values is therefore placed in Appendix 5 to which the reader is referred for this detailed information, and, instead a diagrammatic representation, similar to that presented at the end of Chapter 6, is provided in Figure 8.1.

In order to construct Figure 8.1 the range between the highest and lowest use of each category by the pupil types was again divided into four parts. A 'relatively low use' of the category indicates values in the bottom quartile of this range. Those making average use are in the two middle quartiles, while 'relatively high use' indicates that the value for the pupil type is in the top quartile of the range. It should be noted that, as with the Teacher Record, this arrangement gives no information about the relative frequency of use of different categories nor does it indicate the breadth of the range across the types. For such information it is necessary to refer to Appendix 5. Of the fifty-five categories sixteen are omitted from Figure 8.1, where none of the values for any pupil type exceeded one per cent of recorded observations. It may be helpful in following the descriptions of the clusters to look back briefly at the full description of the Pupil Record categories given in Table 1.1 (p. 12).

Type 1 pupils: attention seekers

These pupils, amounting to 19.5 per cent of the sample, either co-operate on task or routine work during 66.6 per cent of the time they are observed. However, the major characteristic of this group relates to their use of the *pupil-adult* categories. They either seek or are the focus of most of the teacher's contacts with individuals (INIT or STAR). Most of these interactions are concerned with routine or task work. These pupils sustain average amounts of interaction with other pupils but tend to respond rather than to initiate such discussions (COOP). The main distinguishing features of the activity categories concern the movement of these pupils and the demands they make on the teacher. This type of pupil is more likely to be observed either waiting for the

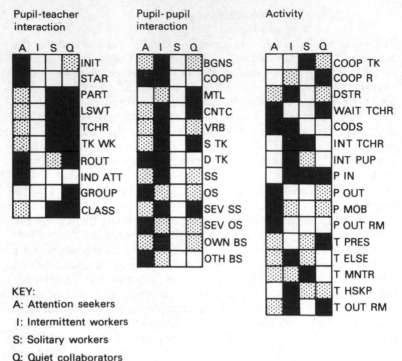

KEY:
A: Attention seekers
I: Intermittent workers
S: Solitary workers
Q: Quiet collaborators

= Relatively high ▨ = Average ☐ = Relatively low

Figure 8.1 Relative frequency of use of the Pupil Record observation categories by each pupil type

teacher (WAIT TCHR) or out of his base area (POUT), moving around the classroom (P MOB) or leaving the room (P OUT RM) than were any of the members of the remaining groups. The portrait which emerges, therefore, is of pupils who, although working on their tasks for considerable periods, frequently leave their place of work, either to queue at the teacher's desk, or to wait while she talks to another pupil on a different table. The emphasis on these attempts to initiate contact with the teacher suggests that such pupils should be called *attention seekers*.

Type 2 pupils: intermittent workers

35.7 per cent of pupils are in this group. In terms of pupil-teacher interaction this group of pupils appears to be the exact opposite of the *attention seekers*. They have the lowest levels of such interaction of all four clusters. They have, however, the highest levels of contacts with other pupils. When engaging in these exchanges, few of which extended into the next twenty-five-second time unit, they either initiate the conversation or respond to the other pupils' overtures (BGNS or COOP). Such conversations are generally with a single pupil or several pupils of their own sex (SS or SEV SS), and take place in their own base area (OWN BS). Examining the activity categories it appears that, although these pupils are working for 64.4 per cent of the time (COOP TK or COOP R), they are also involved in some form of distraction (DSTR) during one-fifth of the observation periods. They seem to go out of their way to avoid contact with the teacher (T ELSE) although they watch what she and other pupils are doing (INT TCHR and INT PUP) while remaining in their place (P IN). The fact that the relatively high level of distraction is associated with low amounts of teacher contact suggests that these pupils are adept at carrying on their private exchanges with other pupils without drawing attention to themselves. This type of pupil appears to flit from one brief conversation to another while in between getting on with their tasks. They seem best described as the *intermittent workers*.

Type 3 pupils: solitary workers

This group of pupils (32.5 per cent of sample) is perhaps the most interesting of the four types. They receive very little individual attention from the teacher (IND ATT). They make contact with the teacher either as a member of her audience when she is talking with the whole class (PART) or when listening and watching while some other pupil receives her attention (LSWT). They show great reluctance to interact with other pupils. When they do so, as with all other pupil types, such interactions are rarely continued into the next twenty-five-second time unit. Nevertheless, in spite of the relatively small amount of individual teacher attention or contact, and their passive role during class discussion where they prefer to remain a part of the audience, this group of pupils co-operate on their set tasks for a higher proportion of the time than any of the other types (77.1 per cent on COOP TK or COOP R). They remain relatively static (P IN), seated in their base.

145

Wragg describes how a pupil, his own daughter, completed the same work-card three times rather than 'bother' the teacher or 'waste time' waiting in a queue (Wragg, 1979). These pupils appear to take a similar view and to be single-minded in their approach. Although they are best described as *solitary workers*, they may also be thought of as 'undeflected workers', a term taken from McClelland who, commenting on the behaviour of some science students, described them as 'human cannon balls' since they remained 'undeflected by the vagaries of the teaching' (McClelland, 1963).

Type 4 pupils: quiet collaborators

The main feature of this type of pupil, who constitute 12.3 per cent of the sample, is that they usually interact with the teacher not so much as individuals as when they are part of a group or class audience (GROUP or CLASS). Such interactions are usually about task work (TK WK).

This appears to be an example where, as suggested in Chapter 6, a teaching strategy influences pupil behaviour directly. The relatively high level of group attention must be the result of a teacher's decision to adopt an organizational strategy based upon grouping. It is therefore somewhat surprising to find that pupils of this type initiate and respond to fewer contacts with other pupils (BGNS or COOP) than do the *intermittent workers* (type 2). They have only average levels of verbal contact (VRB) but relatively higher levels through sharing materials (MTL) or by gesture or physical contact (CNTC). As would be expected of pupils who are part of either spontaneous or organized groups, they work on similar tasks (S TK). In common with the findings for a 'typical' junior classroom, presented in Chapter 5, most of the pupil-pupil interactions are with members of the same sex (SEV SS).

These pupils have the second highest level of work interaction (72.6 per cent on COOP TK or COOP R) with relatively more routine activity than the other types. They also wait for the teacher (WAIT TCHR) and are fairly static (P IN). Although the teacher is more often present (T PRES) with this type of pupil than with those of other clusters, most of this attention takes place in a group or class setting.

The fact that these pupils engage in relatively little interaction among themselves may be due to the tactics used by teachers who set up such groups. The *group instructors* (Style 3 teachers) used a telling rather than an asking approach when talking with pupils. Most of their interaction involved the transmission of information rather than of ideas. The Ford Teaching Project researchers found that this approach tended to stultify pupil discussion. It seemed, from questioning pupils, that these children resented the teacher's interventions which they took as indication that she rejected their ideas (Elliott, 1976a). Certainly the interaction pattern here would appear to portray groups of pupils who rely heavily on the teacher's support and are prepared to wait for her to come rather than search for solutions to their problems among themselves. Although working in groups they can best be described as *quiet collaborators*.

Distribution of pupil types across teaching styles

The question of whether teaching style is related to pupil behaviour is of major importance, with obvious implications at classroom level. However, before examining what the data has to say on this issue a note of caution should be introduced. The relationship suggested in the previous chapter between teaching tactics and pupil behaviour was seen as a two-way interactive process; tactics may influence behaviour and behaviour may affect tactics. The presence of a high or low proportion of any pupil type in a class may be the result of using a particular style of teaching but it is also possible that the teacher adopts the style as a response to certain pupil behaviours. More evidence about the relative importance of the teaching style should emerge when data from subsequent years in the ORACLE programme is analysed. Some pupils will then have been observed for a further two years. During this time certain pupil types will be taught by teachers using a different style from that experienced in the first year. Some teachers will have fresh classes with very different proportions of pupil types. It will be possible to see how far the teachers and pupils change their behaviour in the new situation. At this stage, however, only tentative conclusions can be drawn about these relationships.

The data given in Table 8.1 is, for convenience, represented in pie-chart form in Figure 8.2. For this analysis the largest of the teaching style clusters, the *style changers* (Style 4), has been broken down into its sub-categories, of *infrequent changers*, *rotating changers* and *habitual changers*. The comparison between teaching style and pupil types therefore concerns six different groups of teachers, the *individual monitors*, the *class enquirers*, and the *group instructors* in addition to the three styles already listed.

It has already been shown that, in the typical classroom, approximately a third of the pupils were *intermittent workers*, and a further third *solitary workers*. The remaining third were divided in a ratio approximately of three to two between the *attention seekers* and the *quiet collaborators* respectively.

147

Table 8.1 Distribution of pupil types across teaching styles

Pupil types	All classes	Individual monitors 1	Class enquirers 2	Group instructors 3	Infrequent changers 4a	Rotating changers 4b	Habitual changers 4c
1 Attention seekers	19.5	19.0	18.4	5.4	27.5	21.7	22.8
2 Intermittent workers	35.7	47.6	9.2	32.1	35.3	44.9	38.6
3 Solitary workers	32.5	31.4	64.5	25.0	33.3	23.2	21.2
4 Quiet collaborators	12.3	1.9	7.9	37.5	3.9	10.1	17.5
	100.0	100.0	100.0	100.0	100.0	100.0	100.0
N =	471[a]	105	76	56	51	69	114

a Although data was collected on 489 pupils, some of these could not be matched with a particular teaching style because of teacher changes during the year.

148

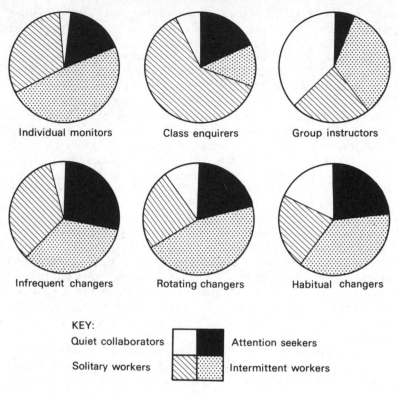

Figure 8.2   Distribution of pupil types across teaching styles

The most striking feature of Figure 8.2 concerns the proportions of *intermittent workers* and *solitary workers* who were taught by different teaching styles. Nearly 50 per cent of the pupils taught by *individual monitors*, for example, were in the group who worked intermittently, while at the other extreme the *class enquirers* contained only 9 per cent of this type of pupil. It appears that teachers who made use of class-directed activities succeeded in cutting down the amount of distraction, a feature of the intermittent worker type. This resulted in a large proportion of the class adopting a non-participating role since this was the main characteristic of the *solitary workers*. Sixty-five per cent of pupils taught by teachers using this style had very little individual contact with their teachers (see p. 145). A high proportion of their time was spent listening to the teacher talk to the whole class. Among such a high proportion of the class not all pupils may have understood equally well and some may have needed more individual assistance from the teacher.

The distribution of pupil types for *group instructors* and *infrequent changers* also gives rise to some interesting comparisons. It would seem that in using the former style, which increased the level of group interaction, these teachers were able to share their time more evenly among the pupils. The proportion of *quiet collaborators* to *attention seekers* among their pupils is in a ratio of seven to one while almost the exact reverse is true for the *infrequent changers*.

This latter group of teachers, because they had the highest level of interaction of all, were able to compensate for the lack of group activity by giving more attention to individual pupils. The proportion of *attention seekers* (who respond to as well as initiate individual contact with teachers) was highest for this style. The *group instructors*, however, had considerably fewer *solitary workers*, presumably because when they were with a group they drew their pupils into the conversation. The proportion of *intermittent workers* for both these styles was close to the figure of 35.7 per cent for the whole sample. No doubt this was because, when the group instructors were interacting with a group and the permanent changers with individuals, it provided opportunities for some of the other pupils to talk among themselves about other things than work.

The remaining two styles, the *rotating changers* and *habitual changers*, show interesting variations. Compared with the averages for all classes given in Table 8.1 they have higher proportions of *intermittent workers* but fewer *solitary* ones. The *rotating changers* for example, have 9.2 per cent more of the former but 9.3 per cent less *solitary workers*. The *habitual changers* have 11.3 per cent fewer *solitary workers* and increased proportions of other pupil types, particularly *quiet collaborators*. The main characteristic of both these styles as described in Chapter 6 was the regular transition from one type of organizational or curricular strategy to another. The observer accounts describe how these transitions had an unsettling effect on some pupils. It would seem from the data presented here that a proportion of pupils who might have been *solitary workers* if taught by one of the other styles, have become *intermittent workers* and *quiet collaborators* as a result of exposure to these styles of teaching.

One observer's account illustrates the situation vividly. He describes Mr D, a rotating changer, whose instructions to groups for changing from one activity to another followed no set pattern but appeared at times to depend solely on the whim of the teacher. The observer comments,

150

The effect of these sudden and unplanned changes on the pupils'
concentration was very marked. A group would be sent to the mathematics
table. Some minutes would lapse while they collected the necessary work-
cards, found their exercise books, sharpened their pencils, engaged in
conversation and then finally settled down to work. Sometimes after
as little as ten minutes the teacher would look up and say suddenly,
'Right. I think it's time for a change. Maths group to art and craft.' Once
more a period of upheaval would ensue before the group again began
to settle down to work. The effect was even more marked when pupils
were engaged in creative writing where they often become deeply
interested in their work only to be switched to another activity at the
peak of their commitment.

Thus some of the potentially 'solitary' workers may find their concentration broken and be deflected into the 'intermittent workers'
category.

While this account perhaps over-emphasizes the unplanned nature
of these changes within the *rotating changers'* style, when the move
from one activity to the next was more carefully controlled it still
resulted, according to some descriptive accounts, in a period of confusion and unrest followed by a further period of time before the class
settled down once more to their work. The *habitual changers* may
experience similar problems in that their rapid alteration in the classroom organization could also disturb pupils' concentration and disrupt
their work.

The *infrequent changers* reduced these problems by having fewer
switches from one type of organization to another. The *group instructors*,
in contrast to the *rotating changers*, tended to have all the groups
working on the same activity with a set timetable. It would appear
from the observers' accounts, that the transfer of pupils between four
or five different activity tables aggravates the problems of control in
that it increases the general feeling of disorder. This it would seem
encourages increased amounts of distraction and time wasting. With so
many different activities going on it becomes difficult for the teacher to
supervise the changeovers and to quell the inevitable disagreements
which result when one pupil is 'finishing off' work while another is
trying to 'persuade' him to vacate his place at the table.

Some comments on the distribution of pupil types
across teaching styles

Some important issues have emerged from this study which invite
comment. The first concerns the differences in the proportions of

intermittent workers across teaching styles. These pupils, on average, spend 20 per cent of their time in class looking out of the window, gossiping to a friend, playing aimlessly with their rubbers or watching other pupils play or fight. All these activities would be coded as distraction (DSTR). Most teachers, while not expecting children to work continuously, would probably agree that 20 per cent is too high a level and should, if possible, be reduced.

For two of the styles, *individual monitors* and *rotating changers*, the proportion of these pupils was between 40 and 50 per cent. Only the *class enquirers* reduced this figure to negligible proportions. But this raises a second issue. Sixty-five per cent of their pupils, the *solitary workers*, rarely contributed to any kind of conversation either with a teacher or with other pupils. Given that there is now an increasing emphasis on the development of communication skills in pupils some teachers would also be unhappy to have such a high proportion of silent although single-minded workers in their class (though some might be only too pleased!).

One way of reducing the proportion of these *solitary workers* appeared to be the adoption of a grouping strategy where pupils worked at the same or a very similar task. This brings up a third issue. It appears that, while the use of this strategy did encourage some of these silent, passive pupils to become involved, it was still most often as listeners rather than active conversationalists. Once the teacher gave his attention to another group these *quiet collaborators* became remarkably like the *solitary workers*, in that they rarely discussed their work within the group. It would seem from these results that the *group instructors*, although telling a group of children what to do, nevertheless expected them to work as individuals. If the aim of this organizational strategy was to promote discussion among pupils it appears to have failed in its purpose.

Finally there is the issue as to the composition of *attention seekers* in each style. These pupils either received or requested more individual contact with the teacher than did children belonging to other 'types'. Although for the whole class it was shown in Chapter 4 that the 'typical' teacher distributed her attention equally between high, medium and low achieving pupils, this may not be true for each style in respect of children who enjoyed these extra contacts. Other studies have suggested that it is the brighter pupils who receive greater amount of teacher attention (Garner and Bing, 1973).

If no one group of pupils is favoured in this way in a given, specific class, then the distribution of achievement among *attention seekers* in that class should be the same as for the sample as a whole. For each style, therefore, 25 per cent of the *attention seekers* should be high achievers, since two of the eight target pupils came from the top quartile when pupils were ranked according to their pre-test scores. In the same way there should also be 50 per cent and 25 per cent who were medium and low achievers respectively. In Table 8.2 the composition of the *attention seekers* in terms of initial achievement is examined for each style. The data for the *group instructors* are omitted since these teachers had very few pupils of this type.

Table 8.2 Percentage distribution of high, medium and low achieving attention seekers in each teaching style

Teacher style	High	Initial achievement Medium	Low	N
Individual monitors	30.0	40.0	30.0	20
Class enquirers	21.4	57.2	21.4	14
Group instructors	–	–	–	3
Infrequent changers	21.4	50.1	28.5	14
Rotating changers	20.0	40.0	40.0 [a]	15
Habitual changers	23.1	42.3	34.6[a]	26

a $p < 0.05$.

In only two cases, that of the *rotating changers* and the *habitual changers* did the proportions differ significantly from the expected values. For both these styles it was the low achieving group who were over represented and in no style was the percentage of high achieving *attention seekers* significantly different from the proportion in the whole sample. Thus no group of the ORACLE teachers appeared to give extra attention to bright children at the expense of others. It should be remembered, however, that the *rotating changers* and *habitual changers* engaged in relatively low amounts of individual interaction as compared to some of the other styles. Low achieving pupils who were not *attention seekers* but were taught by styles other than these may still have enjoyed more teacher contact because there was more of it to share out.

Conclusion

This completes our discussion of the first year process data. It can be seen from the discussion that each style has both strengths and weaknesses. Our classroom visitor of Chapter 4 has now become more discerning and should be able to perceive this.

However, our visitor has yet to complete a full evaluation of the events he has observed during his time in the classroom. He would be pleased to note the absence of any sizeable amount of disruption and the generally high level of interactions concerned with work. He may feel, however, that the relatively large number of pupils engaged in 'distracted activity', when taught by certain styles of teaching, is enough to cast doubts on the suitability of these particular approaches. Yet even our *intermittent workers* would be engaged on their tasks for over two-thirds of the time when the visitor was present. Although the *class enquirers* do succeed in preventing almost all time wasting activity, many of their pupils would be seen working throughout the day with relatively little individual assistance from their teacher. The visitor cannot be sure whether this isolation may not be too high a price to pay for the increased amounts of time that pupils taught by this style spend on their tasks.

Such judgments can be assisted by obtaining information about changes in pupil performance during the year. Usually this is assessed, as in this study, by product measures; that is, by giving pupils both a pre-test and a post-test on the basic skills at the beginning and end of the school year. Such tests are, however, of limited value in that they are designed to examine a specific range of skills. During the year the pupils in the ORACLE study, therefore, completed a series of alternative assessments, with the object of measuring their performance in such related skills as drawing graphs and making maps. Teachers have also been asked to assess their pupils' capacity in relation to certain more general aims which research has shown teachers value highly (Jasman, 1979). Only after a full analysis of all these measures has been carried out and comparisons made between pupils taught by different styles, will it be possible to come to conclusions about the effectiveness of the different approaches described here. The relationships between the processes and products of teaching are the main theme of the second volume in the series.

CHAPTER 9

Conclusions and implications of the ORACLE study

Main conclusions of the ORACLE study

The evidence presented in this volume, based on close and detailed observation of primary classrooms, is important for a number of reasons.

First, the weight of evidence on the *curriculum* shows very clearly that, in spite of widespread claims in the mass media, by industrialists, and by Black Paper propagandists, the general pattern of the traditional curriculum quite certainly still prevails, and has not changed in any fundamental way, let alone vanished. Such claims appear to have been founded on mythology. It may, perhaps be argued that the traditional curriculum was in fact largely abandoned in the late 1960s and early 1970s and has now shifted back; but this view cannot be supported by evidence from research studies. By the 'traditional curriculum' we mean a central focus on skills relating to literacy (language) and numeracy (mathematics).

It is worth noting that the HMI survey (1978), utilizing different methods from the ORACLE study (questionnaires, inspection visits, etc.), and a nation-wide sample, reached very much the same conclusions in this respect, and, indeed, suggested that the concentration on 'basic skills' is exaggerated; a judgment based on their conclusion that, where the curriculum was broadened, pupils did better. Bassey's survey (1978) of 900 Nottinghamshire teachers also produced evidence which again brought out the central focus of Nottinghamshire teachers on skills relating to literacy and numeracy.

Second, the weight of the massive amount of data collected on pupil behaviour in the classroom in the ORACLE study lends no support whatever to the claim that anarchy and confusion prevail in primary school classrooms. This myth, which, according to Adam Hopkins in *The School Debate* (1978), originated in Black Paper 1 was apparently based on an article by Timothy Raison, MP. It received prestigious support in *The Times* leader of October 1976 on the 'wild men of the classroom' (based largely on the Tyndale affair), though we are not aware of any systematically gathered evidence or research giving it credence. As earlier noted in this book, the only *systematic* surveys of junior school classroom organization over this period were those carried through by Moran (1971) and Bealing (1972) and these, far from bringing out anarchistic or libertarian approaches and attitudes, concluded generally that teacher control remained tight within the 'integrated day' and 'informal' classroom structures by now widely adopted. There is no need to repeat evidence presented earlier but the over-all pattern of activities in the 'typical' junior classroom in the ORACLE study, particularly the high level of involvement of pupils in their tasks, is a clear indication of close teacher control and, within present constraints, of effective forms of classroom management. It is worth noting that here, also, the HMI survey specifically stresses the good order found in junior school classrooms (p. 108).

We make these points to clear the air for a serious discussion about the nature of primary school teaching, free from the mythologies that have bedevilled this issue and soured the atmosphere in which primary teachers have worked over the last few years. While mythologies of this kind held sway and were given credence not only in the mass media but even in the educational press, serious analysis and discussion of the real issues at stake was impossible or at least greatly handicapped. The ORACLE evidence presented in this volume, supported by related studies and surveys, provides a mass of factual data on the basis of which such analysis and interpretation becomes possible.

There can be no doubt that big changes have taken place within primary schools over the last fifteen to twenty years. In place of the traditional arrangements of the past, very many schools have adopted flexible forms of classroom organization. But while we find that, in general, good order and effective classroom management prevail in this new situation, one thing that does seem clear is that 'progressive' teaching, if by this is meant teaching having the characteristics defined by the Plowden Report, hardly exists in practice. Indeed in one important respect we find the contrary. It is certainly the case that individualization, both of work and of attention, is utilized very widely; in particular, as we have noted, by the teachers grouped together as Style

1 in our sample, but also, if in varying degrees, by the teachers using the other styles. Individualization, both of work and of attention, was certainly given overriding importance in the Plowden prescripts and to this extent this aspect of 'progressivism' is widely implemented. But central to the Plowden thesis was the questing, exploratory character of the individual child's actual activity; the stress on discovery methods, on finding out for oneself; while the teacher was seen as stimulating this activity by probing, questioning, guiding – leading the child from behind. It is here that classroom practice, according to our data, does not match the prescripts. Individualized teaching (or interaction) is not 'progressively' oriented, in this sense; it is overwhelmingly factual and managerial. Such probing and questioning as does take place is to be found largely in the whole class teaching situation, one generally to be avoided, according to Plowden, in favour of individualization; and, paradoxically, the teaching situation popularly held to be best adapted to didactic teaching (telling).

In our view, based both on analysis of the ORACLE data and on the experience of much classroom observation, a main reason for this apparent contradiction is that, with classes averaging thirty in size, a high degree of individualization both of work and attention imposes a management problem on the teacher of a relatively new type. True, the grouping structure frequently used, as suggested in Chapter 3, eases this problem, but where children are working individually within this structure the teacher is confronted with very complex problems – the Plowden Report itself described the demands now made on the teachers as 'frighteningly high' (para. 875). In this situation the teacher's interactions with *individual* pupils are in fact, as our data shows, primarily of a task supervision or 'routine' type (see pp. 92-4, Table 5.6); that is, they are centrally concerned to keep the pupil working or involved on his task, as they must be in the circumstances. In this situation, wider pedagogical considerations are inevitably ignored or left out of account in the interest of keeping the class *as a whole* busily engaged on the tasks in hand. This has, in fact, been a major preoccupation of class teachers from the inception of this approach.

The fact is that the teacher does not have time to devote her mind to, or to engage in, the kind of interaction with individual pupils which Plowden prescribed. This kind of probing, questioning relationship with *individual* pupils is characteristic of university teaching, a point specifically made in Plowden (para. 669). It is particularly characteristic of the one-to-one university tutorial, when twenty-nine other students are not also present requiring the same, simultaneous relationship. Even at that level teaching of this kind is generally recognized as an art requiring a high degree of skill. A teacher with a classroom populated by young children is in a different situation altogether and cannot easily afford either the time or the mental energy to engage in such discussions with individual children. On the contrary she must always be conscious of the other twenty-nine pupils who, in this case, *are* present, and who, given the system of individualization, are also, if in varying degrees, demanding her attention.

Our conclusion, then, is that, given contemporary class sizes, the Plowden 'progressive' ideology, based essentially on individualization, is impractical; and, we would claim, our data bear this out beyond question. Far from utilizing probing, higher order type questions and statements with individuals, teachers *in practice* utilize this approach largely in the whole class teaching situation, the technique specifically discouraged by Plowden. But it is precisely in this situation, of course, that teachers *can* concentrate on such teaching tactics, as we have seen our Style 2 teachers (*class enquirers*) do — but not only these. All teachers of whatever style, as we showed in Chapter 7, use higher order questioning more in the whole class situation than when interacting with individuals (Table 7.1, p. 137). In this situation the teacher does not have to concentrate her mind and her activity, on the management of thirty individualized tasks, but on one only, the subject matter under discussion, on which she aims to focus the attention of the class as a whole.

This brings the technique of grouping, and of group work, into the discussion. The Plowden Committee, as we pointed out in Chapter 3, recommended the use of grouping in the primary classroom largely for two sets of reasons; first, because they recognized the impracticability of total individualization of *all* work (which, on theoretical grounds, they preferred), and second, for a number of socializing and pedagogical reasons as, for instance, the gains from explaining, from participating in the cut and thrust of the debate, from formulating hypotheses, from learning to get along together, and so on. Indeed it appears from a close reading of the report (and especially the curriculum Chapter 17) that the Plowden view generally is that the grouping structure gives scope for individualization; that, if children are brought together in groups they will there develop and pursue their own interests and activities. Individualization realizes itself through group structures.

However, as was suggested earlier, no consistent rationale for the organization of group work was elaborated in the report, nor indeed was any clear guidance given to teachers as to how such work might be organized (or managed in practice). The Bullock Report, published eight years later, and focusing specifically on language (where the nature of small group interaction is clearly important), does give rather more specific guidance; but even here there is little of direct relevance to the primary school classroom in terms of the actual *organization* of group work.

On this whole, confused question, there is so much that might be said that it is difficult to know where to begin. The ORACLE observations bring out two aspects of grouping in primary classrooms beyond any doubt. First, that seating in groups is in fact the mark of the typical classroom today and, second, that while in most classrooms the pupils are organized in one or more seated groups for the various activities undertaken, with few exceptions they then work largely alone, as *individuals*. The setting is socialized in this sense but the work is individualized; and this, as we have seen, is a main principle of classroom organization as articulated by Plowden and implemented in practice by most teachers in the ORACLE sample.

It is here, however, that we have a striking finding indicating that current practice is far out of line with the Plowden prescripts. That is that those teachers (in our sample) who maximize the use of grouping, the *group instructors* (Style 3) appear also to be primarily didactic in their approach, emphasizing 'telling' and task supervision more than any of the other three main styles (Table 6.1, p. 121). Further this particular group of teachers has the *lowest* proportion of higher cognitive level interactions with individual pupils of any style (Table 7.1, p. 137), while even in the group situation the proportion of higher level interactions is low (*ibid.*); indeed of all the four main styles it is the *group instructors* who maximize the proportion of higher level interactions in the *whole class situation* (*ibid.*). It is worth noting also that it is teachers using this style, which maximizes group work, who have by far the highest proportion of 'quiet collaborators' among their pupils (Table 8.1, p. 148). In other words, it would appear that these teachers are not feeding stimulating ideas and questions to their pupils and that they are not stimulating high levels of pupil-pupil interaction on the tasks in hand. Basically, their interaction with their grouped pupils largely takes the form of giving them facts and instructions.

But an analysis of the other three main styles indicate that neither do these teachers use grouping in the manner prescribed by Plowden, a conclusion supported by observers' accounts as set out earlier (see Chapter 4, pp. 68-76). There is no clear evidence that co-operative group work of the investigating, problem solving, discovery kind which Plowden held that all children should experience, features more than sparsely in our primary schools.

It seems evident that the system of grouping which, as we saw

159

earlier (Chapter 3), developed autonomously in primary schools in relation to the move towards unstreaming, though based on earlier experience and practice, represents so far primarily an organizational, rather than a pedagogical, adaptation of classroom practice to the new situation, and was not developed deliberately with specific pedagogical objectives as its primary concern. Until very recently, there has been no serious research, nor indeed, educational literature of an impressionistic, subjective kind, where the problems involved in setting up and monitoring small group interaction in the classroom are identified and investigated, though relevant studies have been made both in the secondary school (Barnes, 1976; Barnes and Todd, 1977), in the infant school (Tough, 1976; 1977) and at the level of higher education (Abercrombie, 1970; Rudduck, 1978). It is ironic that it is specifically in the junior school, where grouping is both most fully implemented in terms of organization and officially prescribed (Plowden), that relevant research is almost entirely lacking (but see Worthington, 1974). In particular no serious attention appears to have been given, even in relation to the teaching of science and mathematics, to the key issue as to how the teacher, responsible for the work of a whole class (perhaps split into four, five or more groups), is to ensure that *each* group, engaged on co-operative tasks involving discussion and the use of materials and apparatus, is effectively and meaningfully occupied.

To think out, provide materials for, and set up a series of group tasks having the characteristics just described in the different subject areas which comprise a modern curriculum would in itself clearly be a major undertaking, even if use is made of relevant curriculum development projects. To monitor the subsequent group activities; to be ready and able to intervene in the work of each group when this is educationally necessary or desirable; this also would clearly be a major undertaking for the teacher requiring, as a first condition, a high degree of involvement by the pupils in their tasks and so a high level of responsible behaviour. For the pupils to gain from such work also certainly requires the development of a number of social as well as cognitive, skills; a degree of tolerance and mutual understanding, the ability to articulate a point of view, to engage in discussion, reasoning, probing and questioning. Such skills are not in themselves innate, they have to be learnt and so taught.

Total individualization on the one hand, or whole class teaching on the other, allows all these problems to be evaded, as does using group work in a didactic manner, the pupils' work being basically individualized. It is our conclusion, from the experience of a full year's classroom observation, that the whole issue of the purpose and organization of group work in the primary school classroom requires a great deal more attention than it has had to date.

Some implications of the ORACLE study

In conclusion, it may be helpful if we bring out some of the implications of the ORACLE study of classroom process which may have relevance for primary school teachers and for those engaged in teacher education. The analysis which we have made, not only of the 'typical' classroom but more particularly of the characteristics of the six teaching styles, will, we hope, prove of value to teachers in reflecting on their own approach. This analysis was undertaken in pursuit of our own research objectives which are developed in the second volume, where differences in style are related to pupil learning across the main curricular areas. Such analysis will make it possible to identify the degree of effectiveness of different styles. Nevertheless, the analysis conducted so far has a value in its own right as bringing out and clarifying how teachers do in fact differ in their approaches. The characteristics by which the styles differ have been defined and set out in Chapter 6 and it can be seen that each involves different practices which are related on the one hand to differences in what we have termed 'strategies' which are themselves related to aims, and on the other, to differences in pupil behaviour.

While teachers may take satisfaction at the relatively high levels of work activity which were maintained in the classes studied there must be some concern about the isolation of many children while engaged on this work. Most pupils return home after a day in school having had very little conversation on matters relating to work either with their teacher individually, or with their fellow pupils. If they do interact with the teacher they probably will be 'talked at' not 'talked with' and conversation between pupils will, in many cases, have nothing to do with work as such. While grouping, by increasing contact with the teacher, would seem to provide a partial answer to this situation, it is disturbing to find that, as used by the ORACLE teachers, it does not increase the amount of pupil-pupil interaction to any significant extent.

Some teachers may also be concerned at the low level of problem solving activity and may perhaps feel that the emphasis placed on the traditional curriculum and the transmission of factual information is in need of examination. When pupils are told to 'find out', they are more often than not expected to use books and work-cards to extract information. Miss S, one of the *infrequent changers*, probably spoke for many teachers when she told the observer that there was 'only time to teach basics' (see p. 125). She seemed to imply that she chose to use work-cards because they provided pupils with rules and ideas which she herself was too busy to present to the pupils. Nor could she take time off from monitoring work to interact with individual pupils to discuss and check ideas of their own.

The use of work-cards as substitutes for teacher contact has obvious dangers. Many of the observers' descriptive accounts emphasized that the work the pupils were doing often appeared repetitive and that many children seemed to be bored. There is a strong link between those teaching styles having the lowest levels of interaction and the highest proportions of *intermittent workers* among the pupils who engaged in the greatest number of distractions. This finding tends to confirm the observers' impressions that pupils sometimes 'fool around' because they find their work uninteresting.

It is possible to see how the use of work-cards contributes to this boredom. The work-cards are graded in difficulty rather like items on an attainment test. Many of the tests used in schools are developed for 'norm reference' purposes, that is to assess a pupil's performance relative to some other group (the class or a cross section of the total population). For this purpose pupils must be carefully graded and this is often done by seeing if they can solve increasingly complex problems relating to a particular skill or topic rather than trying to see if they can tackle completely different ones. For example, a series of problems on the four rules of arithmetic will be made increasingly difficult by adding more numbers, increasing the number of digits and so on. When mistakes are made they are as likely to be the result of a pupil's boredom as a failure to understand and be able to apply the principles of addition or subtraction. In some cases, moreover, the observers' accounts indicate that such pupils have their books marked silently and then return to their place to work through the same problems yet again until they have completed a correct set of answers. Then the pupil will be back for a new work-card with more difficult examples of the same thing. It is not surprising if, under these circumstances, some pupils prefer to talk to their neighbour about other things rather than getting on with their work.

Such difficulties can only be avoided through very careful monitoring. It has to be recognized, however, that with present class sizes, such a policy must of necessity be selective. It would be impossible to give all pupils the same degree of attention or to check up on every single piece of work. Several approaches seem worth consideration. The first is to adopt the technique used by the Ford Teaching Project where teachers tape-recorded part of their own lesson. According to one of the teachers, the first time this was done the effect was quite traumatic. He told the researchers that,

'The playback of a class discussion was a shattering blow! I had no idea how much discussion was dominated by me, how rarely I allowed children to finish their comments, what leading questions I asked, and how much I gave away what I considered to be the "right" answers.' (Elliott, 1976b)

The use of this technique, particularly with small groups, might pay large dividends in giving a teacher clues about where her intervention may have prevented discussion or stifled pupils' ideas. It might also help the curriculum strategy by identifying topics which were particularly useful for promoting higher level cognitive interactions within the group.

The second approach involves the use of checklists, for monitoring individual children's progress, similar to those developed by Harlen (1977a) and by the ORACLE project (Jasman, 1979). It is important that teachers should not think that the checklists have to be used in their complete form or not at all. The time available for such activity clearly prevents this. But the use of one or two features of the checklist when associated with particular topics can be most useful in bringing to a teacher's attention pupils who are either under-achieving or who have genuine difficulties. In the ORACLE project it has been found valuable to provide teachers with what have been termed 'structured' exercises (or work-sheets), each relating to a different aspect of the skill. These can be used in conjunction with the checklist. They enable teachers to check their own judgments against a more objective measure of pupil performance, and then to concentrate on those pupils who are poor on both measures or where there appears to be some discrepancy between the two assessments.

The third possibility is the use of other teachers as consultants who could make helpful comments. This would seem a particularly fruitful approach in the team situation, yet it is our observers' collective experience that 'team teaching' usually consists of a teacher working almost exclusively with the same group of pupils in one area of the base with very little contact between team members. While we would not advocate that teachers should spend time learning to use observation systems like those in the ORACLE research, the major categories could act as a focus for discussions between team members about each others lessons.

Much of the above discussion also has implications for those responsible for training teachers. It would appear from the evidence presented in Chapter 6 that 'cycles of fashion' may operate. In the ORACLE sample, the younger the teacher the more likely she was to use an individualized rather than a class organizational strategy. She was also less likely to engage her pupils in problem solving, enquiry activities. It would seem, however, that many of the younger teachers have absorbed the rhetoric of Plowden but lack an awareness of its implications, in terms of teaching tactics. Yet, in spite of this 'fashion' towards individualization it seems from the relationship between each style and the different 'types' of pupil behaviour, discussed in Chapter 7, that no one approach can claim complete superiority.

Sharp and Green (1975) report the comments of some teachers about the 'irony in a situation where an educational ideology (progressivism), which stresses the importance of child centredness and the child finding out on its own should be imposed, often in a very authoritarian way, upon trainee teachers'. College tutors who advocate the Plowden approach will be more likely to send their students to practice in schools where they know the head is supportive of this view. Thus the student, while subjected to the rhetoric, may have little opportunity to discuss the implications of putting the theory into practice. If he does have doubts he may feel intimidated by the weight of expert opinion lined up against him, particularly when the same experts are responsible for assessing his teaching practice.

We would hope that the findings presented here will make possible a fuller discussion about the theory and practice of different teaching approaches. It might be wiser to begin by acknowledging that no one method enjoys total superiority over the rest, that some proportion of class teaching, at least in present circumstances, appears to be desirable and that setting up and maintaining group interaction requires careful monitoring. We echo the view of the Chairman of the Schools Council Examination Committee, a headmaster who, in a recent contribution on what schools looked for from teacher training, argued that studies of classroom process and of the relationship between different styles of teaching and pupil learning should be a central component of training (Jennings, 1978). Greater emphasis on discussion of studies such as ORACLE, allied to the use of such techniques as micro-teaching to practice aspects of teacher-pupil interaction, can only be of benefit in helping new teachers to understand the complexities of classroom life.

The use of techniques such as systematic observation also has another value in teacher training. In a previous study concerned with science teaching (Eggleston *et al.*, 1975) the forty observers were all method tutors in university departments and colleges of education. Many testified to the fact that training in the use of systematic observation had greatly improved their capacity to diagnose problems during teaching practice and to give appropriate remedial help to their students. These tutors did not use the Science Teaching Observation Schedule (STOS) to assess students but as a means of focusing their own attention on behaviours deemed desirable which were picked out by the categories of the observation schedule. In the same manner, the use of both the Teacher and Pupil Record categories by those responsible for training teachers at the primary and middle school stage could have a similar beneficial effect.

Thus the research methods used and the information collected in the ORACLE study may be of benefit both to teachers and to teacher educators. For too long both primary teaching and the teachers have been subjected to criticism and exhortation based upon beliefs which were largely unsupported by evidence. Researchers have for the most part been uninterested in detailed study of the classroom process or have been content to observe a few teachers for very short periods. Both groups tend to end up by categorizing teachers and their methods in the grossest of terms. It is, therefore, to be hoped that this first large scale systematic survey of the primary classroom process, with its precise descriptions of teacher and pupil behaviour, will be of practical help to all who work in primary schools. At the same time it should make a modest contribution to the debate on primary education which, as a result of the findings presented here, should now be carried out in a more conciliatory and informed manner with less conviction on either side that they hold a monopoly of the truth.

APPENDIX I

Training observers in the use of systematic observation techniques
Anne Jasman

At the School of Education, University of Leicester, two major research studies have made extensive use of systematic observation for collecting data about classrooms. This has allowed considerable experience to be gained in training procedures. In the ORACLE programme, ten observers were trained in the use of the Teacher Record and the Pupil Record, utilizing the extensive training manuals prepared for each instrument by Deanne Boydell,[1] while in a Schools Council project on secondary science teaching, forty observers were trained in the use of the Science Teaching Observation Schedule (STOS) (Eggleston *et al.*, 1975).

ORACLE training programme

All observers were trained teachers with experience of primary class-rooms. This eased their entry into schools, since the teachers and observers had a common understanding of the routines and day-to-day problems of organizing and teaching in a primary school. However, this presented a training problem. All observers come with their own interpretations of classroom events. The training must be structured so that observers describe events in the same terms otherwise they will continue to view these idiosyncratically and find difficulty in accepting the framework which use of the instruments requires, as explicated within the two relevant observation manuals.

It has been found that a period of intensive training focusing on a few categories at a time and involving the sequence outlined below, proved effective in overcoming this problem.

166

Appendix 1

Training procedure

1   Teaching: The category definitions from the manuals were read and illustrated with written and videotaped examples of classroom behaviours. This enabled observers to become familiar with the content of the manuals and relate what they had read to video-taped examples of relevant teacher and pupil behaviours.

2   Testing: Observers were given written examples and shown video-taped extracts both of which they then coded independently.

3   Feedback: Discussion of these coding decisions then took place. Where disagreements occurred these were considered and, during discussion, differences in interpretation or misunderstandings of definitions became apparent, and were clarified. These sessions were crucial for the correct interpretation of the category system and in helping observers overcome their preconceptions.

4   Practice: Pairs of observers then undertook practice sessions in schools. This early experience in a classroom setting greatly reassured the observers since they found coding 'live' events easier than coding from videotaped or written examples.

5   Retesting: Agreement trials, using videotaped extracts from class-room events, were held on each observation schedule at the end of the training period. This ensured that observers viewing the same event were coding it in the same way.

Training for the Pupil Record took place first since it was generally thought the easier of the two observation instruments. After an explana-tion of the general observation and coding procedures — for example, the twenty-five-second time-sampling technique and the ordering of the pupils and teachers for sequential observation — the various cate-gory definitions were divided into sections and studied in turn. The *target's activity* and *location* and the *teachers' activity* and *location* (categories 8, 9, 10) were discussed followed first by *pupil-pupil* inter-action (categories 5, 6, 7 abc) and then *pupil-adult* interaction (cate-gories 1, 2, 3, 4).

This rearrangement of the order presented in the manual facilitated training since it reflected the sequence of coding when used in the classroom.

The Teacher Record posed particular problems for training. It is a category system where decisions are made at three levels. The first decision is whether conversation or silence[2] occurs at the time of the signal. If silence occurs then one of the eight *silent interaction* or one of the four *no interaction* categories is coded. If conversation occurs the observer has to decide whether the utterance is a question or a statement and then whether it is concerned with *Task, Task supervision* or *routine*, before deciding on the minor category to be coded. This is summarized in the accompanying flow chart (Figure 1A1).

167

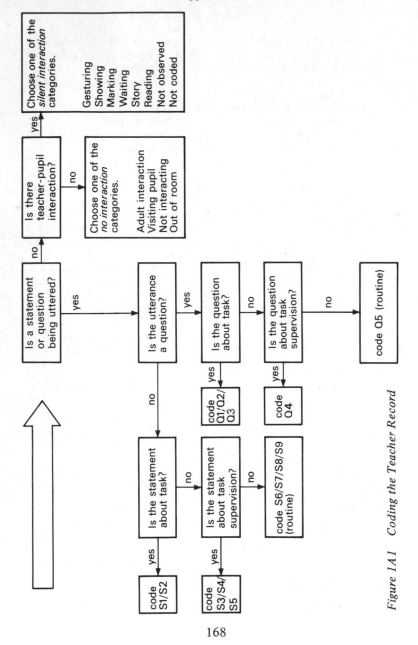

Figure 1A1 Coding the Teacher Record

Appendix 1

Problems in training

Observer preconceptions

Observers with previous experience of the classroom may find it difficult to adjust to the systematic nature of the recording and may doubt
their ability to code in a reliable manner. In the initial stages of training
observers need to receive confirmation of their ability to tick the 'right'
box, so that they are able to agree with each other. It helps to build up
this confidence if easy examples are provided at this early stage. If this
does not happen then uncertainty is created about the validity and
reliability of the observation schedules in use. First, an observer may
justify failure by refusing to accept that the observation system focuses
on relevant aspects of classroom events. Second, an observer, on finding
that this view is not shared by successful observers, may lose all confidence in her ability to operate the schedule successfully.

Once confidence has been gained, the underlying assumptions of
the observation system may be examined more closely. The observers,
being confident of the reliability of their coding, now discuss problems
of validity more openly.

A 'training' situation is unfamiliar for teachers and the importance
of creating a relaxed, informal work atmosphere within the group
should not be underestimated. The use of training techniques as described here initially runs contrary to the questioning, discussion,
consensus approach which observers may previously have experienced
as teachers. It is essential at the outset to explain the rationale for
training and discuss the limitations and advantages of an approach
based on 'low inference' systematic observation, or observers may feel
that they are reduced to 'automatons'.

Use of videotape

Videotape provides an excellent method of presenting illustrative
examples of various categories on the observation schedules, as events
can be replayed and definitions discussed until the coding is agreed.
During training emphasis is placed on coding the more difficult categories. These may be used relatively infrequently in the classroom and
thus videotaped extracts tend to present a more complicated picture
of classroom events than exists in 'real life'. It is important for observers
to experience the classroom situation as soon as possible in order to
realize that the coding of live events is much easier than coding from
videotape. Videotaped extracts present another disadvantage in that
the camera cannot capture all the information which may be necessary
in order to make the appropriate coding decision. An observer in the
classroom will often use peripheral information to interpret the behaviour of the pupil under observation. This kind of additional information must sometimes be made available orally when using videotape
before coding decisions can be made. Another difficulty when using

the pre-recorded time signal is to persuade observers to code at the same point of the signal. A difference of a second can result in a change of behaviour so that observers code different events; and unless attention is given to this point, reliability checks can yield disappointing results.

Practical considerations for working as an observer in a school context

In addition to training in the use of the schedules, observers must also be given help in using the instrument in the classroom. For example, the observer must identify target pupils without the teacher's help; know what to do when a target is absent or not in his usual place; be able to cope with interruptions and questions about the research, and know when to begin the observation session, what to observe and how to end.

Specific guidance was given on each of these points and this is summarized in a booklet 'Survival kit for observers'. It was vital for the success of the ORACLE programme that those undertaking observation should maintain their position within the schools, since in some cases contact extended over three years and it was essential that the same pupils should be observed regularly over this entire period. Observers were instructed to answer all questions openly and to recognize that judgments or evaluations would threaten some teachers. So far as possible they should aim at being a 'fly on the wall'. It was surprising and encouraging to find, that, in general, they were readily accepted into the schools and quickly developed easy relationships with the teachers.

It is to the credit of both teachers and observers that at no time during three years of research in schools did the situation become untenable in any school in the research programme. In some cases close working relationships were established which greatly facilitated communication between the schools and the research team. The importance of establishing and maintaining good working relationships of this kind for a longitudinal study of the ORACLE type cannot be over-estimated.

Use of systematic observation techniques

The use of these systematic observation techniques in a wide range of classrooms has yielded a wealth of data on the nature of classroom events. The systematic observation schedules used in this project require training and the expenditure of considerable time and application by trainee observers. It is possible, though difficult, to learn these procedures directly from the manuals, although probably few practising teachers would feel that this was a useful exercise. Nevertheless, the categories and their definitions can provide a framework for examining aspects of classroom activity. Other techniques are available for observing and monitoring a teacher's own practice and the behaviour of individual children; for example, the Ford Teaching project materials (Elliott, 1978) and techniques described in *Progress in Learning Science* (Harlen *et al.*, 1977a, 1977b, 1977c) and Communication Skills in Early Childhood project (Tough, 1976; 1977). Class teachers are ideally placed to observe and monitor the behaviour of individual children and to evaluate their own classroom practice. The Pupil and Teacher Records and the other techniques just mentioned provide ideas and guidance which can be helpful for this purpose.

APPENDIX 2

Data presentation, analysis and statistical methods
Paul Croll

2A Systematic observation and data reliability

Most of the data reported in this volume are derived from systematic observations in classrooms by trained observers using the two schedules, the Teacher Record and the Pupil Record.

All observers' impressions of classrooms are personal and, in the end, subjective. Systematic observation methods, however, involve the development of unambiguous criteria for assigning events into categories so that different observers are basing their responses on a common observation system. In a successful systematic observation system the categories on the schedule and the criteria for determining their use should be sufficiently unambiguous and explicit to ensure that any observers using it will arrive at identical descriptions of a particular occurrence. Fundamental to systematic observation is high inter-observer reliability — implying that different observers make identical recordings at particular points in time. High inter-observer reliability does not mean that a schedule gives a fully objective description of the pupils or classrooms being studied since, like any description, it inevitably involves selection from the infinity of observations which could be made. However in establishing high levels of reliability the investigator ensures that his own criteria for selection and categorization are shared by the other observers and this removes one aspect of the subjectivity inherent in an individual's perception of events. Unlike descriptions which are not based on reliable schedules the basis for the response is fully explicit. Consequently anyone reading the description knows exactly how it was arrived at. The reader may disagree with the definitions and criteria employed, but he knows exactly what they are, and he knows that the results are unaffected by the personal idiosyncrasies

172

of the observer. It is in this limited but crucial sense that systematic techniques may be called objective. An element of subjectivity arises in the choice of variables to be studied — the categories of the system and the criteria for attributing occurrences to them. This very specific selectivity is sometimes thought to be a weakness in that it reflects one aspect of classroom life. But this in fact is true of all observational techniques, since all such descriptions involve selection. There is no such thing as a 'total view' of a pupil or a classroom. Like any data-gathering technique, systematic observation abstracts from the totality of the social world those aspects thought to be relevant *for particular investigatory purposes*. The choice of variables to be studied may be made in the expectation that they will be related to learning outcomes or to systematic differences between pupils or classes.

Inter-observer agreement on the schedules used in the ORACLE programme was first measured with groups of observers coding the same videotaped events. However the reliabilities reported here were calculated from live observations in real classrooms using pairs of observers coding the same pupils and teachers simultaneously. From this it is possible to calculate the degree of inter-observer agreement by comparing the paired codings at each individual signal. Reliabilities have been calculated for each variable, which here means each set of exclusive categories. The twenty-six interaction categories on the Teacher Record form a single variable as only one of them may be ticked at each signal and the three audience categories form a second variable for the same reason. The Pupil Record contains twelve variables as there are twelve sets of categories and a code could be made in each of them at a particular signal. This means that reliabilities have not been calculated for individual categories such as SUST or RIS in the Pupil Record. Where a category occurs relatively infrequently (such as RIS) it would take an impossibly large number of reliability trials to generate sufficient data to establish a unique category reliability, while where a category does occur frequently it contributes substantially to the reliability of the variables as a whole (Scott, 1955).

Variables which are not always coded such as the pupil-adult and pupil-pupil interaction categories in the Pupil Record can be treated in one of two ways for the purpose of calculating reliability. They can be treated as though they were always coded, regarding a blank as an implicit 'no interaction' coding. Alternatively two separate reliabilities can be calculated: observer agreement on whether or not interaction is taking place, and agreement on the category of interaction when it is agreed to be taking place. This second procedure has been adopted here and, as well as reliabilities for each of the pupil-adult variables, over-all reliabilities for the presence of pupil-adult and pupil-pupil interaction have also been calculated.

Two values are reported for each reliability. The first is the percentage of occasions on which the paired observers agreed, the second is

173

the Scott coefficient of reliability (Scott, 1955). This corrects the percentage agreement to allow for the fact that, even if the observers were interpreting the schedule quite differently, with a limited number of categories they would sometimes arrive at the same coding by chance. The Scott coefficient (which takes values between one and zero) therefore gives lower values than the equivalent percentage agreement and is a more rigorous test of reliability. The Pupil Record reliability figures are based on 300 joint observations by four pairs of observers and the Teacher Record on 200 joint observations, by five pairs of observers.

In general the reliability levels for the Pupil Record are satisfactorily high, only the first pupil-pupil interaction variable is less than 0.8. Of the remainder, most are above 0.9 (Table 2A1). The reliability of the Teacher Record is not quite so satisfactory since the main variable just fails to reach 0.8 although the audience variable is over 0.9 (Table 2A2).

Table 2A1 Reliability: Pupil Record

Variable		Percentage Agreement	Scott coefficient
Pupil-adult interaction	1	98.4	0.93
	2	100.0	1.00
	3	94.3	0.83
	4	100.0	1.00
Pupil-pupil interaction	5	82.7	0.75
	6	100.0	1.00
	7a	100.0	1.00
	7b	93.3	0.86
	7c	97.4	0.92
Activity	8	91.7	0.87
	9	98.7	0.94
	10	95.7	0.91
Presence of pupil-adult interaction		98.7	0.96
Presence of pupil-pupil interaction		95.0	0.84

Table 2A2 Reliability: Teacher Record

	Percentage Agreement	Scott coefficient
Interaction category	81.0	0.79
Audience	95.5	0.93

The measure of reliability employed here is concerned purely with the extent of agreement between observers. Another approach to reliability is concerned with the extent to which the measures discriminate between the pupils or teachers studied, a highly reliable measure being one that successfully discriminates (Medley and Mitzel, 1963). Satisfactory reliability levels of this kind have already been established for the two instruments (Boydell, 1974b; 1975).

2B   Presentation of the data

The data derived from the observation schedules described in Chapter 1 and in Appendix 2A are the source of most of the tables presented in Chapter 4 and in subsequent chapters. The observations were made of one teacher and eight pupils in each of fifty-eight classrooms (or classroom areas in the case of open plan settings). Because children who left during the first year of observation were replaced, the data are based on 489 pupils rather than the 464 who were originally selected. All the children included have been observed for at least one full term. Each teacher was observed at forty-five points in time and each pupil at ten points in time in each of eighteen one-hour teaching sessions, or at equivalent numbers of times in a larger number of shorter sessions where the teaching day was so organized. The eighteen teaching sessions, or their equivalents, were divided evenly between the three terms of the school year. Thus the information from the Teacher Record is based on 47,000 observations of fifty-eight teachers and data from the Pupil Record on 84,000 observations of 489 pupils.

Where tables are based on data derived from the observation instruments, as the great majority are, the figures are percentages of observations, not percentages of individuals. For this reason, where the figures refer to the whole sample, as in Tables 4.1, 4.2 and 4.3, Ns are not given for the tables because of the risk of confusing individuals and observations. In such tables, where no N is given, the figures are based on the total number of pupils or teachers, but the percentages are percentages of the observations made of the individuals not of the individuals themselves. However, where information is given separately for groups within the sample, as occurs in Tables 4.4 and 4.5, the number of individuals within that group are given. But, as before, the figures are percentages of observations, not of the Ns at the foot of the columns. In tables not based on the observation instruments such as Table 4.6, normal conventions have been followed and the figures are percentages of the N given.

The figures in the tables are occasionally referred to in the text as percentages of time. Strictly speaking they should be considered as percentages of observations; classroom activities were not timed in the sense that we can say that a particular number of minutes or seconds were devoted to a specific activity or interaction. However the observations carefully sample many thousands of instances in time (135,000) in all, and the results can be safely regarded as reflecting the relative amounts of time spent on the different categories of activities and interactions.

The only occasions when tests of statistical significance are used are when groups of pupils (such as boys and girls or high, medium and low achievers) are being compared. The pupils are a random sample of all the pupils in the classes in the study and the tests refer to the confidence with which we can assert that differences found between such groups in the sample reflect differences in the population of pupils from which the sample is drawn. No equivalent sampling procedure could be followed with the teachers and tests of significance are therefore not used when groups of teachers are being compared.

Significance tests are not used in Chapter 8 when data are presented for groups of pupils derived from the cluster analysis. This is partly because of the essentially exploratory nature of this chapter but is also enforced by the nature of the clustering technique used. The criterion for optimizing clusters is to minimize the within-group variance of the variables used in the analysis (see Appendix 2C). But the within-group variance is a key element in computing the F ratio used to obtain significance levels. Therefore to compute the statistical significance of differences between variables used in the cluster analysis would be a circular procedure, as the groups have been derived in such a way as to minimize the within-group variance and consequently to maximize the F ratio.

2C   Cluster analysis

Cluster analysis is a technique (or more properly a family of techniques) for sorting individuals or objects into groups on the basis of the similarity of members of a given group and their relative distinctness from members of other groups. It differs from the more generally used correlational approach to data, which uses techniques such as cross-tabulation, regression and factor analysis, in that while these techniques look for relationships between variables, cluster analysis looks for similarities and differences between people.

Cluster analysis starts with a collection of individuals (in our case teachers or pupils) who have scores upon a set of variables. It looks for similarities between individuals in terms of their scores on the variables, and on the basis of these similarities attempts to divide the original set of individuals into a number of distinct groups. In general the aim is to find groups which are relatively homogeneous internally with respect to the variables, while differing from the other groups. The resulting groups or clusters can then be subjected to further analysis both by making comparisons between the groups and by looking at correlations between variables within them.

There are a variety of different methods used in cluster analysis (Everitt, 1974). The hierarchical methods commonly used in biology and other natural sciences involve constructing a matrix of similarities between objects and then progressively joining the objects and groups which are most similar. A more common method in social and educational research is known as relocation or optimization. Here, individuals are assigned to groups in such a way as to minimize or optimize some criterion. In the most commonly used of these methods, which is the one adopted here, this involves minimizing the variation within each group, while having high between group variations. Relocation methods have the advantage of not assuming a hierarchy which is rarely realistic in social research (in contrast to biology where objects may be divided into species, sub-species, etc.) and allows initial poor allocations to be corrected later in the analysis.

There are however a number of problems with this technique. It is impracticable to consider every possible way of partitioning the data. Consequently individuals are placed into a set number of groups, usually at random, and then relocated between them in accordance with the criterion being optimized. This means that the final solution will be influenced by the initial allocation. The analysis also has to decide on a fixed number of groups into which individuals are to be allocated, although this is rarely known with any confidence in advance. In practice a series of linked analyses are conducted, first allocating the individuals within a relatively large number of groups and then merging the two most similar groups and reallocating. This process is repeated so that optimum allocations are provided for a variety of numbers of groups and a decision is then made as to which is the most satisfactory.

Another problem which should be mentioned is the choice of the criterion to be optimized. To minimize the within-group sum of squares which is the approach adopted here has the advantage of being relatively simple and has a meaning which can easily be grasped intuitively. It has the disadvantage however that it only uses part of the available information, ignoring any variation in the inter-relationship between the variables used. (Technically the criterion minimizes the trace of the variance-covariance matrix. It therefore uses only the variance elements of the matrix and ignores the covariance elements.) However it was felt that the relative simplicity of this method and its ease of interpretation outweighed this limitation.

The analysis was conducted using a relocation procedure contained in the *Clustan* system of computer programs (Wishart, 1969). This involves an initial random allocation of the teachers or pupils to groups and a relocation in order to minimize the variation within groups. This was then repeated for progressively smaller numbers of groups and the final solution adopted when a further reduction of the number of groups resulted in a disproportionate increase in within group compared with between group variation.

This is the same procedure as was used by Bennett in the Lancaster study discussed in Chapter 6 (Bennett, 1976). However in the Lancaster study all the variables were input as dichotomies while in the present study they were all input as scores. Dichotomizing simplifies the clustering process, but if the variables are not true dichotomies, as the ORACLE variables and some of the Lancaster variables were not, it is a rather unsatisfactory procedure. The reason for this is that if the variables are distributed in anything approximating to a normal curve, a large number of the individuals on one side of the dichotomy will have scores closer to many people on the other side than to those with whom they have been grouped, with consequent effects on the clustering. Another commonly used procedure, that of standardizing the variables, was not employed for similar reasons; standardization tends to dilute the true differences between groups (Fleurs and Zubin, 1969).

It was suggested earlier that cluster analysis is in some sense the opposite of conventional correlational analysis. However it should be thought of as a complementary rather than an alternative approach to data analysis since it may often be appropriate to look at relationships between variables within clusters rather than for the sample as a whole. Just as an arithmetic mean is a poor summary of a bimodal distribution, correlations between variables may be misleading if the form of the relationship or the values of the variables differ for different groups in the population. In the hypothetical example in Figure 2C1 the over-all relationship would appear as a positive correlation between the two variables, while within the two groups the relationship is actually negative. In this example the effect can easily be seen in a scattergram, but if more than two variables are involved it can be very difficult to detect.

Clustering can, therefore, lead to a better description of the data by isolating distinct and relatively homogeneous groups for which averages and correlations can then be presented. Similarly clustering may make clearer the relationship between variables used in the cluster analysis and other external variables. The groups created from cluster analysis can then be used for comparisons in quasi-experimental designs for studying the effects of different naturally occurring treatments, as, in this study, between one teaching style and another.

It is sometimes mistakenly thought that multi-variate techniques such as cluster analysis and factor analysis are purely inductive methods which will 'make sense' of a mass of data in an 'untouched by human hand' fashion. In fact the choice of variables implies, as we have seen in the ORACLE research, a theory about the data being studied although not necessarily one that is precisely formulated. Consequently the usefulness of the groupings arrived at will be dependent on the precision and relevance of the variables selected for analysis. Moreover, the type of analysis chosen also implies assumptions about the nature of the variables and the kinds of groupings likely to be found.

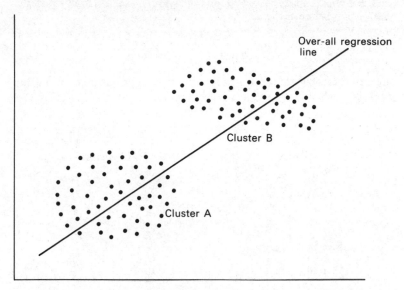

Figure 2C1   Correlations and clusters: a hypothetical example

The importance of the choice of variables in cluster analysis is matched by the importance of the choice of objects (individuals) to be clustered. This is both because of conventional sampling errors – the risk that with small samples apparent relationships may be the result of chance fluctuation – and because of the risk that 'real' groupings in the population may not be well represented in the sample. In consequence, if the sample is small the analysis must concentrate on relatively large general groupings.

This difficulty is related to the fact that cluster analysis is not a statistical technique in the true sense. There are no known distributions which particular findings can be related to, or criteria for accepting or rejecting hypotheses. The present study partly deals with this problem by building a strong element of replication into the research design. The analysis of data from the second and third years of the research, to be reported in subsequent volumes, will show how stable the groupings are when applied to different individuals, and to the same individuals at different points in time.

Despite these difficulties with cluster analysis (and they are difficulties shared with other multi-variate techniques) it provides a valuable technique both for summarizing data and for separating out different groups in a sample or population which can be used as the basis for comparisons. In the present study it provides a method of distinguishing teacher styles and types of pupil behaviour, and for looking at the relationship between them.

2D   Times of observation

The percentage of total observations made at different times in the day are shown below.

Table 2D1 Times of observation

Time period	Percentage of observations
9.00 − 9.30	2.6
9.30 − 10.00	10.9
10.00 − 10.30	10.5
10.30 − 11.00	3.8
11.00 − 11.30	17.0
11.30 − 12.00	11.0
12.00 − 12.30	0.1
12.30 − 1.00	2.3
1.00 − 1.30	14.6
1.30 − 2.00	10.6
2.00 − 2.30	6.6
2.30 − 3.00	6.2
3.00 − 3.30	3.8
Morning (9.00 − 12.00)	55.8
Afternoon (12.00 − 3.30)	44.2

The discrepancies between the numbers of observations made at different times reflect the selectivity in the choice of activities to be observed and the similarity of timetabling practices in different schools and classrooms.

Excluded from observation were administrative breaks such as lunch and play-times, collection of dinner money; and curriculum areas such as physical education, drama and singing. The small proportions of observations made between 9.00 and 9.30, 10.30 and 11.00, and between 12.00 and 1.30 reflect administrative breaks, and these also influence the figures for 9.30 − 10.30 and 11.30 − 12.00 as breaks, assemblies and lunch-breaks sometimes intrude into these periods. The lower level of observations in the afternoon is largely due to the changing balance of curricular activities during the day. The afternoons are more likely than the mornings to involve 'non-observed' activities such as physical education, music and drama, and these tend to occur more frequently as the afternoon wears on.

APPENDIX 3

The Pupil Record and Teacher Record, aggregated results

Table 3A1 The Teacher Record, percentage of total observations

Questions			*Silence*	
Task			Silent interaction	
Q1 recalling facts	3.5		Gesturing	1.9
Q2 offering ideas, solutions (closed)	2.2		Showing	2.6
Q3 offering ideas, solutions (open)	0.6		Marking	10.1
			Waiting	1.9
Task supervision			Story	0.9
Q4 referring to task supervision	3.9		Reading	3.4
			Not observed	1.0
Routine			Not coded	0.5
Q5 referring to routine matter	1.8			
			No interaction	
Statements			Adult interaction	1.7
Task			Visiting pupil	0.4
S1 of facts	6.9		Not interacting	17.1
S2 of ideas, problems	2.5		Out of room	1.3
Task supervision			*Audience*	
S3 telling child what to do	12.6		Individual	55.8
S4 praising work or effort	1.0		Group	7.5
S5 feedback on work or effort	9.6		Class	15.1
Routine				
S6 providing information, directions	6.5			
S7 providing feedback	2.0			
S8 of critical control	2.3			
S9 of small talk	1.3			

Table 3A2 The Pupil Record, percentage of total observations

	Pupil-adult			Pupil-pupil			Activity	
1	INIT	1.2	5	BGNS	5.4	8	COOP TK	58.1
	STAR	1.6		COOP	6.2		COOP R	11.9
	PART	11.0		TRIES	0.2		DSTR	15.9
	LSWT	2.3		IGN	0.3		DSTR OBS	0.3
2	TCHR	15.9		SUST	6.3		DSRP	0.1
	OBSR	0.002	6	MTL	0.9		HPLY	0.2
	OTHER	0.16		CNTC	1.4		WAIT TCH	4.3
3	TK WK	13.2		VRB	16.2		CODS	1.9
	ROUT	2.4	7a	S TK	14.1		INT TCHR	1.7
	POS	0.03		D TK	4.3		INT PUP	3.4
	NEG	0.3	7b	SS	13.1		WOA	0.4
	IGN	0.1		OS	2.2		RIS	0.8
4	IND ATT	2.2		SEV SS	2.1		NOT OBS	0.5
	GROUP	1.5		SEV OS	1.1		NOT LIST	0.02
	CLASS	11.8	7c	OWN BS	14.8	9	P IN	86.1
	OTHER	0.5		OTH BS	3.6		P OUT	9.9
							P MOB	2.7
							P OUT RM	0.6
						10	T PRES	22.2
							T ELSE	67.2
							T MNTR	3.2
							T HSKP	4.1
							T OUT RM	2.7

Base: Alone 5.1: 2SS 15.3: 2OS 2.0: SSS 30.8: SOS 43.5.

APPENDIX 4

The primary curriculum and the Bullock Report
John Willcocks

As part of the survey carried out by the Bullock Committee during its enquiry into 'the teaching in the schools of reading and the other uses of English', 1,253 teachers each estimated the amount of time spent on particular activities in English by a particular nine-year-old child during a specific week. The child was in every case the one whose name came alphabetically first on the class list, the reasonable assumption being that, in this way, the selection would be random for sex, temperament, ability and so on. The results are presented in Tables 48 to 59 of the Bullock Report in such a way that class time (when the whole class was engaged in the same activity) is separated from optional time (when individual children were given some freedom in what they chose to do); and the ranges of estimated time spent are presented with no mean values.

A comparison of these data with those from the ORACLE study requires the computation of mean total (i.e. class plus optional) times from the Bullock tables; and these are set out in Table 4A1.

The relevant figures from the ORACLE study appear in Table 4.10 (p. 77) but there the values are expressed as percentages of observations rather than as minutes per week. The activities observed in the ORACLE study accounted for about eighteen hours of the children's school week (a figure which agrees closely with the estimate, in the recent Nottinghamshire primary schools research project (Bassey, 1978), of time spent on mathematics, language, thematic studies and art and craft). For the purposes of comparison with the Bullock data, the Pupil Record figures from Table 4.10 have been converted to percentages of eighteen hours, and these are set out in Table 4A2.

Some comparisons between the two sets of data can now be made, although the matter is not entirely straightforward since the Bullock and ORACLE subject categories do not always exactly coincide. We have already compared the figures for oral English (p. 80). To compare the amount of time spent on reading in the two studies it is necessary to add together the figures from Tables 54 and 55 of the Bullock Report; and for writing, the figures from Bullock Tables 52, 56, 57, 58 and 59 must be summed and compared with the summed total of the ORACLE categories of writing and creative writing. (The Bullock category of poetry and verse poses a special problem, since it presumably involves reading as well as oral and written work in unknown proportions. It has been omitted from this comparison.)

Table 4A1 Mean total estimated times (i.e. class time plus optional time) spent by nine-year-old children in the Bullock survey on various curricular activities

Bullock Table	Activity	Minutes per week
48	Poetry and verse	24.4
49	Listening to stories or TV	53.3
50	Oral English	61.8
51	Improvised drama	18.4
52	Writing	79.3
53	Topics	85.7
54	Story reading	59.8
55	Reading practice	43.7
56	Comprehension and vocabulary	57.9
57	Language usage	28.4
58	Spelling	24.4
59	Handwriting	20.7

Table 4A2 Curricular areas (Pupil Record) expressed as percentages of observations and as minutes per week

Activity	Percentages of observations	Minutes per week
Number	14.0	151.2
Practical maths	4.3	46.4
Abstract maths	10.2	110.2
Reading	4.4	47.5
Writing	21.2	229.0
Spoken English	2.0	21.6
Creative writing	8.5	91.8
Art and craft	10.9	117.7
General studies	24.4	263.5
Total	99.9	1078.9

Appendix 4

Table 4A3   Mean number of minutes spent by pupils on reading, writing and oral English during one week

	ORACLE observation data	Bullock teachers' estimates
Reading	47.5	103.5
Writing	320.8	210.7
Oral English	21.6	61.8
Total	389.9	376.0
	(6 hrs 30 mins)	(6 hrs 16 mins)

It will be seen from Table 4A3 that the over-all time spent on these three areas was very similar in the two studies, but that the ORACLE children seem to have spent considerably more time in writing and considerably less in reading and talking than the Bullock children.

These discrepancies may reflect real differences between the two samples in the amount of time spent on these subjects. The Bullock survey involved a random sample of schools in England (excluding some categories of middle schools) whereas the ORACLE sample was made up of those primary schools which fed pupils into six previously selected transfer schools. It has been argued in Chapter 1 that the characteristics of the ORACLE sample schools were broadly representative of the type of catchment areas in which they were situated. Nevertheless there remains the possibility of a different balance of time allocation in these areas such as that suggested in Table 4A3.

However, there are probably other factors involved. The discrepancy may be in part attributable to differences of definition and interpretation. For example, the ORACLE observations were coded as spoken English only if the sole purpose of the lesson was the development of oral communication skills. On very many occasions, even though a teacher was taking the opportunity to foster spoken English skills during an individual conversation or class discussion about the task in hand, the observations were coded according to the avowed curricular content of the lesson and not as spoken English. The aim, in short, was to discover the proportion of time in which oral English was not only the way in which the lesson was conducted, but also its curricular content; and the ORACLE finding that in general teachers set aside very little time specifically for this purpose by no means implies that they do not interest themselves in the fostering of oral communication skills throughout the whole of the curricular range. In the Bullock survey, on the other hand, the interpretation of the term oral English was left to the individual teacher; and it is acknowledged in the Bullock Report that this might account for 'the wide spread of times spent'. 3.4 per cent of the teachers said that no time at all, neither class time nor optional time, was devoted to oral English, while at the other end of the scale, 0.4 per cent of the teachers stated that it accounted for more than five hours a week.

A further possible source of discrepancy arises from the different methods of data collection in the two studies. The ORACLE figures come from observed activities, whereas the Bullock figures come from teachers' estimates. The ORACLE approach raises the question of how adequately the activities observed reflect the 'real' curriculum (cf. Table 4.12, p. 81); and in fact the discrepancies between the Bullock figures and the ORACLE 'real' curriculum figures are in each of these three curricular areas somewhat smaller than those found with the Pupil Record.

The Bullock approach raises problems of a different kind. In the survey teachers were asked 'to estimate the amount of time spent on particular activities in English' during one week by a particular child chosen essentially at random. Whether a teacher could accurately remember in detail even how she herself allocated her time during a week is not known; whether she could make a valid estimate on behalf of someone else — who may in some cases have been deliberately keeping well out of her way — must be considered at best doubtful. This being so, it is pertinent to ask why the teachers in the Bullock survey may have had a consistent tendency to over-estimate the amount of reading and oral work, and under-estimate the amount of writing done by the children in their classes.

We have seen from Table 4.10 (p. 77) that ORACLE teachers devoted more time to spoken English and reading than the average child spent on these subjects, and less time to children doing written work than the average child spent on writing. It may be that teachers generally tend to be more aware of the spoken English and reading that goes on in the classroom than of the writing because of their own greater involvement in these activities. Consequently it would not be surprising if some of them over-estimated the time spent by their pupils on spoken English and reading while under-estimating the time spent on written work.

It should not be overlooked that estimates of the over-all time spent by their pupils on English during a week, by teachers included in the Bullock survey and by those taking part in the Nottinghamshire primary schools research project, were remarkably close to the findings of the ORACLE observers. Even if it is not always easy to judge how children allocate their time within a particular subject such as language, teachers seem to be both consistent and accurate in their estimates of time spent on the broader curricular areas. The evidence from these three studies clearly indicates that English, including its more formal aspects, still plays a large and important part in the curriculum; and suggests that when teachers are mistaken in their judgments of the amounts of time spent by pupils on its various aspects, they may tend to err in the direction of under-estimating the more traditional formal activities such as writing, whilst over-estimating the amount of time spent on less structured activities involving oral English. It is interesting in this context that although the Nottinghamshire teachers generally gave very full responses to the survey questions, 32 per cent gave no answer when asked whether they had any deliberate procedures for promoting spoken language other than everyday class discussion and conversation. It seems in general that, although oral English looms large in teachers' minds, and although it is in constant use as a medium of instruction and communication, as a subject entity in its own right it accounts for a very small proportion of a junior school child's time in the classroom.

APPENDIX 5

Characteristics of the four pupil clusters

Table 5A1 *Characteristics of the four pupil clusters*

		Pupil-adult interaction			
		Attention seekers	Intermittent workers	Solitary workers	Quiet collaborators
1	INIT	2.3	0.7	1.1	1.4
	STAR	4.1	0.9	0.9	1.5
	PART	9.6	6.8	14.6	16.3
	LSWT	2.2	1.1	3.3	3.5
2	TCHR	17.9	9.3	19.6	22.5
	OBSR	0.006	0.003	0.0	0.0
	OTHER	0.4	0.1	0.1	0.3
3	TK WK	14.3	7.3	17.1	18.6
	ROUTINE	3.0	1.8	2.4	3.4
	POS	0.1	0.01	0.01	0.02
	NEG	0.6	0.2	0.2	0.5
	IGN	0.3	0.1	0.1	0.1
4	IND ATT	5.5	1.3	1.4	2.0
	GROUP	1.1	0.7	0.7	7.1
	CLASS	11.3	6.9	16.9	13.5
	OTHER	0.4	0.4	0.7	0.2
		Pupil-pupil interaction			
5	BGNS	5.3	7.0	3.7	5.4
	COOP	6.7	7.6	4.9	5.0
	TRIES	0.2	0.3	0.2	0.2
	IGN	0.2	0.3	0.3	0.4
	SUST	6.6	8.2	3.3	8.1

		Pupil-pupil interaction			
		Attention seekers	*Intermittent workers*	*Solitary workers*	*Quiet collaborators*
6	MTL	0.6	1.1	0.5	1.4
	CNTC	1.1	2.0	0.7	1.8
	VRB	17.3	20.2	11.1	15.6
7a	S TK	13.5	17.5	9.5	16.7
	D TK	5.4	5.7	2.8	2.4
7b	SS	12.9	16.7	8.9	13.1
	OS	2.7	2.4	1.6	2.2
	SEV SS	1.8	3.0	1.2	2.6
	SEV OS	1.6	1.1	0.7	1.0
7c	OWN BS	13.7	19.4	9.9	16.3
	OTH BS	5.4	3.9	2.4	2.7

Activities

8	COOP TK	54.8	52.4	65.7	59.1
	COOP R	11.8	12.0	11.4	13.5
	DSTR	16.7	20.5	10.8	14.5
	DSTR OBS	0.5	0.3	0.2	0.2
	DSRP	0.09	0.05	0.03	0.07
	HPLY	0.4	0.2	0.1	0.2
	WAIT TCHR	6.4	3.8	3.3	5.5
	CODS	2.1	2.4	1.5	1.4
	INT TCHR	1.6	1.8	1.9	1.4
	INT PUP	2.8	4.3	3.3	2.3
	WOA	0.4	0.4	0.3	0.3
	RIS	0.9	0.8	0.7	0.5
9	P IN	78.4	87.0	89.6	85.8
	P OUT	16.0	9.0	7.3	10.2
	P MOB	3.4	2.9	2.0	2.7
	P OUT RM	1.2	0.6	0.4	0.5
10	T PRES	24.2	15.1	24.8	32.9
	T ELSE	67.7	71.7	64.9	58.5
	T MNTR	2.6	3.3	3.9	1.6
	T HSKP	1.7	5.9	4.3	2.5
	T OUT RM	2.8	3.4	1.4	3.8
	N =	96	174	156	60

Notes

1 Researching the primary classroom

1 Systematic observation is only one of the various observational methods which can be used to study classroom process. Sociologists, in particular, prefer to use a different technique, called *participant* observation, where the researcher attempts to describe just what it is like to take part in school either as a teacher or a pupil. The data is gathered by means of case studies, interviews and anecdotal accounts of classroom events (Delamont, 1976).

Critics of this approach (McIntyre and MacLeod, 1978) argue that, unlike systematic observation, it can only generate and not test hypotheses about teaching. Recent studies of primary classrooms using participant techniques appear to aim either at raising teacher consciousness by providing highly readable accounts of events such as the labelling of pupils (Nash, 1973) or at demonstrating links between the social system within the school and the wider societal context (Sharp and Green, 1975).

Some of the studies in Stubbs and Delamont (1976) appear to regard the classroom as yet another source of data which can be used to validate sociological theory. Hence the frustrations of many teachers who find the language of these particular accounts difficult to understand and their relevance to practice obscure.

3 Primary school teaching: theory and practice

1 Their validity has, of course, been questioned; see especially R.S. Peters, ed., *Perspectives on Plowden* (1969).

2 A typical book of this kind is that by D. Salmon, Principal of Swansea Training College, *The Art of Teaching* (1898). Under the heading 'Everything should be regulated' in a chapter entitled 'Order, Attention, Discipline', Salmon writes:

> The whole routine of the school should be regulated literally by clock-work. Lessons should always begin and cease precisely at the minute set down, and the time-table should be observed in the smallest particular. All general motions should be regulated by word of command. There should be a settled plan for assembling, standing, sitting, changing places and tasks, giving out and collecting books, pencils and etc. Nothing should be haphazard, nothing left to the caprice of the children.

4 Teachers and pupils in the junior school classroom (1)

1 The discrepancy between the Teacher Record and Pupil Record figures for whole class interaction (15.1 per cent and 12.0 per cent respectively) probably arises from coding problems in the different situations. When the teacher is being directly observed, accurate coding as to whom she is addressing presents few difficulties. When pupils are under observation, coding of the *teacher's* audience when she is interacting is less easy. It seems likely that, in the latter situation, concentrating on a pupil, observers may have missed occasions when the teacher was, in fact, interacting with the *whole class*. Such interaction, it must be remembered includes forms of silent interaction, particularly difficult to pick up when observing *pupils*.

2 The standardized tests were administered and sampling completed at the beginning of the year in which the observational data were obtained. It should be remembered that, for reasons given in Chapter 1, the teachers whose classes were observed did not have access to this information.

3 Further data shows that the greater amount of individual attention given to low achievers is the result of the teacher seeking out these pupils rather than the weaker pupils actively attracting the teacher's attention. The amount of interactions initiated by pupils is the same for all three groups; it is in the teacher initiated interaction that they differ. The data also show that 'disruptive' pupils receive slightly more individual attention than others ($r = 0.1$, significant at $p < 0.05$).

4 We find in addition that the size of class does not affect the *number* of task interactions (correlation of 0.003) although it does appear to affect the quality (see p. 90); another finding is that in the larger classes there is less time for small talk (correlation of -0.35).

5 Further analysis shows that the 'typical' pupil is working in his base (whatever kind of group that may be) for 86 per cent of his time.

For 10 per cent he is out of his base, probably usually on 'routine', for 3 per cent of time he is 'mobile', and for 0.6 per cent he is out of the room (Pupil Record).

6 A general breakdown of this curricular area may, however, be made from our data (observers' records, S1). These show that the 24.3 per cent (on average) of curriculum time devoted to general subjects, as given by the Pupil Record (Table 4.10), may be split into two main categories, (i) time spent by the pupil on topic and project work (14.8 per cent of curriculum time), and (ii) time spent on single subject work (9.5 per cent of curriculum time).

A further breakdown can be made within each of these two categories, to indicate the time spent in each case on (i) religious education, (ii) history, geography and social studies, (iii) science and nature study. In the case of topic and project work, these amount to 0.9 per cent, 9.5 per cent and 4.4 per cent of curriculum time respectively. In the case of single subject work they amount to 3.1 per cent, 4.3 per cent and 2.1 per cent respectively.

A few points should be made about these data: (i) the category 'history, geography, social studies' is very general and imprecise, but, given the 'integrated' nature of much project and topic work, it proved impossible, in many cases, to distinguish between main subject areas; (ii) some religious education is given in morning assembly; this was not observed and is, therefore, not included; (iii) some science, for instance, calculating volume, may have been coded as practical mathematics; (iv) our data show that the amount of teaching-learning in the fields of science and religious education varies very greatly between schools.

7 It is worth noting that 'writing' was only coded when formal written English work was being done: comprehension exercises, grammar, punctuation, SRA, spelling, etc. Writing as part of a topic or project was coded under 'general studies'. Creative writing was also coded separately.

8 Under this heading, observers coded all activities concerned with oral and aural communication skills, e.g. drama, discussions, debates, story telling (by the pupils), listening to a story. The 1931 Hadow Report specifically stressed the importance of 'systematic training in oral expression' (p. 140).

Appendix 1   Training observers in the use of systematic observation techniques

1 Manuals are available for the Teacher Record and Pupil Record from The Secretary, University of Leicester School of Education, 21 University Road, Leicester.

2 It is acknowledged that the terms *silence* and *silent interaction* are

not always entirely appropriate (for example, the teacher's telling of a story is inconsistent with her being silent). However, the more accurate label 'interaction other than by question or statement' proved too cumbersome for everyday use. Similarly it is recognized that with the term *no interaction* strict accuracy is sacrificed for the sake of brevity. The complete description would have been: 'no interaction with class member(s)'.

Bibliography

Abercrombie, M.L.J. (1970), *Aims and Techniques of Group Teaching*, Society for Research into Higher Education, SRHE working party on teaching methods, Publication 2.

Anthony, W.S. (1979), 'Progressive Learning Theories: The Evidence', in Bernbaum, G. (ed.), *Schooling in Decline*, Macmillan, London.

Ashton, P., Kneen, P., Davies, F. and Holley, B.J. (1975), *The Aims of Primary Education: A Study of Teachers' Opinions*, Schools Council Research Studies, Macmillan Education, London.

Barker Lunn, J.C. (1970), *Streaming in the Primary School*, NFER, Slough.

Barnes, D. (1976), *From Communication to Curriculum*, Penguin, Harmondsworth.

Barnes, D. and Todd, F. (1977), *Communication and Learning in Small Groups*, Routledge & Kegan Paul, London.

Barr, A.S. (1935), 'The Validity of Certain Instruments Employed in the Measurement of Teaching Ability', in Walter, H. (ed.), *The Measurement of Teaching Efficiency*, Macmillan, New York, pp. 73-141.

Bassey, M. (1978), *Nine Hundred Primary School Teachers*, NFER, Slough.

Bealing, D. (1972), 'The Organisation of Junior School Classrooms', *Educational Research*, 14, pp. 231-5.

Bennett, N. (1976), *Teaching Styles and Pupil Progress*, Open Books, London.

Bennett, N. (1978), 'Recent Research on Teaching: A Dream, a Belief, and a Model', *British Journal of Educational Psychology*, 48, pp. 127-47.

Bennett, N. and Jordan, J. (1975), 'A Typology of Teaching Styles in

Primary Schools', *British Journal of Educational Psychology*, 45, pp. 20-8.

Board of Education, (1905), *Reports on Children under Five Years of Age in Public Elementary Schools, by Women Inspectors*, HMSO, Cd 2726.

Bowen, H.C. (1903), *Froebel and Education by Self Activity*, Heinemann, London.

Boydell, D. (1974a), 'Open Space and Follow-through: Some Recent Developments in American Elementary Education', *Education 3-13*, vol. 2, 1, pp. 44-9.

Boydell, D. (1974b), 'Teacher-Pupil Contact in Junior Classrooms', *British Journal of Educational Psychology*, vol. 44, pp. 313-18.

Boydell, D. (1975), 'Pupil Behaviour in Junior Classrooms', *British Journal of Educational Psychology*, 45, pp. 122-9.

Bullock Report (1975), *A Language for Life*, HMSO, London.

Burke, E. and Lewis, D.G. (1975), 'Standards of Reading: A Critical Review of Some Recent Studies', *Educational Research*, 17, pp. 163-74.

Callaghan, J. (1976), 'Towards a National Debate – The Prime Minister's Ruskin Speech', *Education*, 22 October, pp. 332-3.

Coleman, J. (1966), *Equality of Educational Opportunity*, US Department of Health, Education and Welfare Office in Education, Washington.

Cox, C.B. and Dyson, A.E. (eds.) (1969a), 'Fight for Education: A Black Paper', *Critical Quarterly Society*.

Cox, C.B. and Dyson, A.E. (eds.) (1969b), 'Black Paper Two: The Crisis in Education', *Critical Quarterly Society*.

Delamont, S. (1976), *Interaction in the Classroom*, Methuen, London.

Department of Education and Science (1966), Statistics of Education, *Schools*, vol. 1.

Department of Education and Science (1977), *Education in Schools: A Consultative Document* (The Green Paper), HMSO, Cmnd 6869.

Department of Education and Science (1978), 'School Building Surveys 1975 and 1976', *Statistical Bulletin*, Issue 5/78, October 78.

Devlin, T. and Warnock, M. (1977), *What Must We Teach*, Maurice Temple Smith, London.

Dunkin, M.J. and Biddle, B.J. (1974), *The Study of Teaching*, Holt, Rinehart & Winston, New York.

Eggleston, J.F., Galton, M.J. and Jones, M.E. (1975), *A Science Teaching Observation Schedule*, Schools Council Research Studies, Macmillan Education, London.

Eggleston, J.F., Galton, M.J., and Jones, M.E. (1976), *Processes and Products of Science Teaching*, Schools Council Research Studies, Macmillan Education, London.

Elliott, J. (1976a), *Developing Hypotheses about Classrooms from Teachers' Practical Constructs – An Account of the Work of the*

Ford Teaching Project, North Dakota Study Group on Evaluation, University of North Dakota.

Elliott, J. (1976b), 'Preparing Teachers for Classroom Accountability,' *Education for Teaching*, 100, pp. 49-71.

Elliott, J. (1978), 'Classroom Accountability and the Self-Monitoring Teacher', in Harlen, W. (ed.), *Evaluation and the Teacher's Role*, Schools Council Research Studies, Macmillan Education, London.

Everitt, B. (1974), *Cluster Analysis: An SSRC Review of Current Research*, Heinemann Educational Books, London.

Fleiss, J. and Zubin, J. (1969), 'On the Methods and Theory of Clustering', *Multivariate Behavioural Research 4*, pp. 235-50.

Freeland, G.F. (1957), 'Purpose and Method in the Unstreamed Junior School', Simon, B. (ed.), *New Trends in English Education: A symposium*, MacGibbon & Kee, London, pp. 19-33.

Galton, M.J. (1978), *British Mirrors: A Collection of Classroom Observation Systems*, School of Education, University of Leicester.

Garner, J. and Bing, M. (1973), 'Inequalities of Teacher-Pupil Contacts', *British Journal of Educational Psychology*, 43, no. 5, pp. 234-43.

Gray, J. (1978), 'Reading Progress in English Infant Schools, Some Problems Emerging from a Study of Teacher Effectiveness', Paper presented to the *Symposium on Recent Research in Primary Education at the Annual Conference of the British Educational Research Association*, Leeds, September 1978.

Gray, J. and Satterly, D. (1976), *Two Statistical Problems in Classroom Research*, School of Education, University of Bristol.

Gruber, K.H. (1977), 'Backwards to Europe', *Times Educational Supplement*, 24.6.77, no. 3238, pp. 18-19.

Hadow Report (1926), *Education of the Adolescent*, Report of the Consultative Committee, HMSO, London.

Hadow Report (1931), *Report of the Consultative Committee on the Primary School*, HMSO, London.

Hamilton, D. and Delamont, S. (1974), 'Classroom Research: A Cautionary Tale', *Research in Education*, no. 11, pp. 1-15.

Harlen, W., Darwin, A. and Murphy, M. (1977a), *Match and Mismatch: Raising Questions, Leader's Guide*, Oliver & Boyd, Edinburgh.

Harlen, W., Darwin, A. and Murphy, M. (1977b), *Match and Mismatch: Raising Questions*, Oliver & Boyd, Edinburgh.

Harlen, W., Darwin, A. and Murphy, M. (1977c), *Match and Mismatch: Finding Answers*, Oliver & Boyd, Edinburgh.

Harnischfeger, A. and Wiley, D. (1975), 'Teaching/Learning Processes in Elementary Schools: A Synoptic View', *Studies of Education Processes*, no. 9, University of Chicago.

HMI Survey (1978), Department of Education and Science, *Primary Education in England: A Survey by HM Inspectors of Schools*, HMSO, London.

Hopkins, A. (1978), *The School Debate*, Penguin, Harmondsworth.

Bibliography

Isaacs, S. (1930), *Intellectual Growth in Young Children*, Routledge & Kegan Paul, London.

Isaacs, S. (1932), *The Children we Teach: Seven to Eleven Years*, University of London Press.

Isaacs, S. (1933), *Social Development in Young Children: A Study of Beginnings*, Routledge & Kegan Paul, London.

Jackson, B. (1964), *Streaming: An Education System in Miniature*, Routledge & Kegan Paul, London.

Jackson, P. (1968), *Life in Classrooms*, Holt Rinehart, New York.

Jasman, A. (1979), 'Developing Teacher-Based Assessment for Primary Schools', in *British Journal of Educational Research*, vol. 5, no. 1.

Jencks, C. (1972), *Inequality: A Reassessment of the Effects of Family and Schooling in America*, Basic Books Inc., New York.

Jennings, A.H. (1978), 'What does the Teaching Profession want from the Universities?', *Proceedings of a One-Day Conference, The Universities and Teacher Education*, pp. 26-31, The Committee of Vice Chancellors and Principals and The Universities Council for the Education of Teachers.

Kimmins, C.W. and Rennie, B. (1932), *The Triumph of the Dalton Plan*, Nicholson & Watson, London.

Lovell, K. (1968), *An Introduction to Human Development*, Macmillan, London.

McClelland, D.C. (1963), 'On the Psychodynamics of Creative Physical Scientists' in *Contemporary Approach to Creative Thinking*, Gruber, M.E. *et al.* (eds.), Atherton, New York.

McIntyre, D. and MacLeod, G. (1978), 'The Characteristics and Uses of Systematic Classroom Observation', in McAleese, R. and Hamilton, D. (eds.), *Understanding Classroom Life*, NFER, Slough.

Mealings, R.J. (1963), Problem-Solving and Science Teaching, *Educational Review*, vol. 15, pp. 194-207.

Medley, D.M. and Mitzel, H.E. (1963), 'Measuring Classroom Behaviour by Systematic Observation', in Gage, N.L. (ed.), *Handbook of Research on Teaching*, American Educational Research Association, Rand McNally, Chicago.

Medley, D.M., Quirk, T.J., Schluck, C.G., Ames, N.P. (1973), 'The Personal Record of School Experience' (PROSE), in Boyer, E.G., Simon, A. and Karafin, G. (eds.), *Measures of Maturation: An Anthology of Early Childhood Observation Instruments*, vol. II, Research for Better Schools, Philadelphia.

Moran, P.R. (1971), 'The Integrated Day', *Educational Research*, 14, Part 1, November 1971, pp. 65-9.

Nash, R. (1973), *Classrooms Observed*, Routledge & Kegan Paul, London.

Newsom Report (1963), *Half our Future*, Report of the Central Advisory Council for Education (England), HMSO, London.

Nuthall, G. (1968), 'Studies of Teaching: Types of Research on

Teaching', *New Zealand Journal of Educational Studies* 3, pp. 125-47.

Nuthall, G. and Snook, I. (1973), 'Contemporary Models of Teaching', in Travers, R.M.W. (ed.), *Second Handbook of Research on Teaching*, Rand McNally, Chicago.

Olson, W.C. (1929), 'The Measurement of Habits in Normal Children', *Institute of Child Welfare*, Monograph 3.

Peters, R.S. (ed.) (1969) *Perspectives on Plowden*, Routledge & Kegan Paul, London.

Plowden Report, (1967), *Children and Their Primary Schools* (2 vols), Report of the Central Advisory Council for Education in England, HMSO, London.

Resnick, L. (1972), 'Teacher Behaviour in the Informal Classroom', *Journal of Curriculum Studies*, 4, pp. 99-109.

Robbins Report (1963), *Higher Education*, Report of the Committee on Higher Education, HMSO, London.

Rosenshine, B. (1970), 'Evaluation of Classroom Instruction', *Review of Educational Research*, 40, pp. 279-300.

Rosenshine, B. and Furst, N. (1973), 'The Use of Direct Observation to Study Teaching', in Travers, R.M.W. (ed.), *Second Handbook of Research on Teaching*, Rand McNally, Chicago.

Ross, A.M. (1960), *The Education of Childhood*, Harrap, London.

Rudduck, J. (1978), *Learning Through Small Group Discussion*, Society for Research in Higher Education, University of Surrey.

Scott, W.A. (1955), 'Reliability of Content Analysis: The Case of Nominal Coding', *Public Opinion Quarterly*, 19, pp. 321-5.

Selleck, R.J.W. (1972), *English Primary Education and the Progressives 1914-1939*, Routledge & Kegan Paul, London.

Sharp, R. and Green, A. (1975), *Education and Social Control: A Study in Progressive Primary Education*, Routledge & Kegan Paul, London.

Shayer, M., Küchemann, D.E. and Wylan, H. (1976), 'The Distribution of Piagetian Stages of Thinking in British Middle and Secondary School Children', *British Journal of Educational Psychology*, vol. 46, pp. 164-73.

Silberman, C.E. (1970), *Crisis in the Classroom*, Vintage Books, New York.

Simon, A. and Boyer, E.G. (eds.), (1970), *Mirrors for Behaviour: An Anthology of Classroom Observation Instruments*, Research for Better Schools, Philadelphia.

Simon, B. (1974), *The Politics of Education Reform, 1920-1940*, Lawrence & Wishart, London.

Sokal, R.R. and Sneath, P.H. (1963), *Principles of Numerical Taxonomy*, W.H. Freeman, San Francisco.

Start, K.B. and Wells, B.K. (1972), *The Trend of Reading Standards*, NFER, Slough.

Strasser, B. (1967), 'A Conceptual Model of Instruction', *Journal of Teacher Education*, 18, no. 1, pp. 63-74.

Stubbs, M. and Delamont, S. (eds.) (1976), *Explorations in Classroom Observation*, John Wiley, London.

Taba, H. and Elzey, F.F. (1964), 'Teaching Strategies and Thought Processes', *Teacher College Record*, 65, pp. 524-34.

Taylor, P.H., Reid, W.A., Holley, B.J. and Exon, G. (1974), *Purpose, Power and Constraint in the Primary School Curriculum*, Macmillan, London.

Tough, J. (1976), *Listening to Children Talking: A Guide to the Appraisal of Children's Use of Language*, Schools Council Communication Skills in Early Childhood project, Ward Lock Education in association with Drake Educational Association, London.

Tough, J. (1977), *Talking and Learning: A Guide to Fostering Communication Skills in Nursery and Infant Schools*, Schools Council Communication Skills in Early Childhood project, Ward Lock Education in association with Drake Educational Association, London.

Weber, L., (1971), *The English Infant School and Informal Education*, Prentice-Hall, Englewood Cliffs, N.J.

Whitbread, N. (1972), *The Evolution of the Nursery-Infant School: A History of Infant and Nursery Education in Britain, 1800-1970*, Routledge & Kegan Paul, London.

Wilkinson, M. (1977), *Lessons from Europe: A Comparison of British and Western European Schooling*, Centre for Policy Studies.

Wishart, D. (1969), *Clustan 1A: User Manual*, University of St Andrews Computing Laboratories, Fife, Scotland.

Withall, J. (1949), 'The Development of a Technique for the Measurement of Social Emotional Climate in Classrooms', *Journal of Experimental Education*, vol. 17, pp. 347-61.

Worthington, F. (1974), 'A Theoretical and Empirical Study of Small-Group Work in Schools', unpublished PhD thesis, University of Leicester.

Wragg, E.C. (1976), 'The Lancaster Study: Its Implications for Teacher Training', *British Journal of Teacher Education*, 2, no. 3, pp. 281-90.

Wragg, E.C. (1978), 'A Suitable Case for Imitation', *The Times Educational Supplement*, 15 September, p. 18.

Wragg, E.C. (1979), 'Superteach and the Dinosaurs', *Education Guardian*, 9 January, p. 9.

Index

200